A Strange

The Diary and Scrapbooks of Cordelia Leigh

1914-1919

Commentary by Sheila Woolf & Chris Holland

2012

John
Best Wishes
from
Sheila Woolf

Warwickshire Great War
Publications

Cover Design by James Cooper

Published by:
Warwickshire Great War Publications
Plott Bungalow, Plott Lane, Stretton on Dunsmore, Nr Rugby CV23 9HR, UK
Tel: +44 (0)2476 542493
Email: poors_plot@tiscali.co.uk

ISBN: 978-0-9574216-0-8

A CIP catalogue record for this book is available from the British Library

Printed and bound by:
Warwick Printing, Caswell Rd, Leamington Spa, Warwickshire, CV31 1QD

Contents

Stoneleigh Abbey, Kenilworth, Warwickshire, the Leigh ancestral home.

Foreword

Cordelia Leigh was an unconventional and intriguing woman. This volume provides a fascinating combination of sources: her Great War diary brought together with scrapbooks, including letters she received from the front. These are combined with an illuminating commentary in a volume that provides a new perspective on the 1914-18 war and a detailed picture of a remarkable woman.

Philip Errington, August 2012

Dr. Philip W. Errington is Director of Printed Books and Manuscripts at Sotheby's and author of *John Masefield's Great War*.

Preface: The Diary and the Scrapbooks of Cordelia Leigh

When Cordelia Leigh began her 'Diary of the War', in August 1914, she used an ordinary, small notebook of a type that would have been commonly available. By the end of the war, she had added another two notebooks of similar size and type. She expressed the hope that her "short record of this time of war" might "possibly be of interest to members of my family at some future time" and her diary was subsequently typed up and bound in a leather volume, which would have gone into the library at Stoneleigh Abbey. It is not known who did the typing but the occasional handwritten correction to the text suggests that Cordelia took a personal interest in the process. Cordelia's stated intention in 1914 was to keep "a private record of a few personal experiences". However, as the Great War progressed, her own contributions to the diary became less frequent and she relied increasingly on the testimony of others – both family members and close friends. From a modern perspective, this is a pity, although it no doubt reflects the way in which events that were 'extra-ordinary' in 1914 and 1915 became increasingly 'ordinary' as the war progressed. Nonetheless, the inclusion of accounts by others certainly widens the scope of the events described: for example, Emily Ward's description of her experiences in Ireland during the Easter Rebellion in 1916, or Mabel Leigh's letter in 1917 describing crossing the Atlantic on the same ship as General Pershing.

During the Great War, Cordelia Leigh also kept scrapbooks of items that were of interest. Many of these are letters written to her by village men who had enlisted in the forces. By the end of the war, she had filled two scrapbooks, one volume somewhat larger than the other. Although the order is generally chronological, the scrapbooks are not organised in a particularly systematic manner, with some items simply fitted in where there was space available. Regrettably, no dates accompanied the inclusion of an item, which creates a problem with some of the letters. Nor are there any captions; in many cases, these were clearly not needed but in others it leaves one wondering as to the nature of Cordelia's interest. For example, was the front cover of "The Suffragette", for July 9th 1915, included simply as something of general interest, or out of satisfaction that a radical group was now patriotically behind the war effort, or was there perhaps just a hint of fellow-feeling for outspoken women of clear convictions? Despite these limitations, the scrapbooks provide a valuable adjunct to the diary and offer further insights into the impact of the war and the personality of Cordelia Leigh.

The three handwritten notebooks and the bound volume that constitute Cordelia Leigh's 'Diary of the War' were handed to the Shakespeare Birthplace Trust in the belief that they were of general interest and should be publicly accessible.[1] The scrapbooks have been retained at Stoneleigh Abbey.

The text of Cordelia Leigh's diary has been included in its entirety. A very occasional lapse in spelling has been corrected and, for the sake of appearances, some consolidation of the letters from her friends and relatives has been carried out. Explanatory notes have been added and these are to be found at the end of the relevant diary entry, rather than included as footnotes or end-of-chapter notes. Items from the scrapbooks have been used to illustrate the diaries but a separate chapter has also been devoted to the scrapbooks, allowing a more systematic appraisal of their contents.

Cordelia Leigh was not a major public figure. Indeed, at the start of her wartime diary, she described herself as "a private individual living at Stoneleigh Abbey, in the Midlands". Nonetheless, she was a member of an influential and well-connected family and she was actively involved, both in peace and war, in helping the Leigh family fulfil their social responsibilities. Many of these responsibilities related to those who lived on the Stoneleigh estate and Cordelia had a particularly close knowledge of that community through her work with local children. Despite her generally unassuming manner, she was, in fact, remarkably well-qualified to keep a diary of her wartime experiences, with its insights into both the upper echelons of British society as well as local villagers. Through her, we can also enter into that "strange time", when so many pre-war certainties were challenged and "all one's thoughts and interests were changed, former interests forgotten, thoughts concentrated on the one great matter which filled all minds".

Sheila Woolf and Chris Holland, August 2012

[1] Shakespeare Birthplace Trust, DR 671/510

Acknowledgements

First, and most obviously, we would like to thank Mr Tony Bird, OBE, Chairman of The Founding Trustees of Stoneleigh Abbey Ltd, for his support of the project, for permission to publish the War Diary and for permission to research Cordelia's work via papers held at Stoneleigh Abbey. Paula Cornwell, Curator/Manager of Stoneleigh Abbey, has supported the venture and has helped provide access to the scrapbooks and other relevant material held at the Abbey. We would also like to thank the staff at the Shakespeare Birthplace Trust, in Stratford-upon-Avon, first under John Benson and now Amy Hurst, for their help, as well as the staff at the Warwickshire County Record Office and at the Coventry History Centre. Philip Errington kindly read our work and provided us with a Foreword. Chris Baker's 'Long, Long Trail' website is always an invaluable source for the period.

We are most grateful to James Cooper, who used his considerable skills to design our cover – and did so at short notice – and to David Woolf, who kindly undertook the arduous task of formatting text and generally made-good the limitations of his less computer-literate sister and her colleague. Peter Huxford has proof-read the text, offered helpful comments about the structure of the book and has been an enthusiastic supporter of the project throughout. Mr Will Blagburn kindly photographed Cordelia's scrapbooks. In addition, we would like to thank Mrs Sheila Skinner for information concerning Cordelia's Young Naturalists' Club and for lending a copy of "A Sunday in Keswick"; Miss Celia King for allowing access to Joseph Charles King's "Khaki Bible"; Mr Stephen Harvey, Churchwarden of the Church of the Assumption of Our Lady, Ashow, for information about Cordelia's burial in the churchyard; and Ms Rebecca Dyson of The Kingsley School, Leamington Spa, for permitting access to the Governors' Minutes of the School. Others who have kindly assisted, in a variety of ways, in the publication are David Farmer and Diane Holland.

Nearly all the pictures used in the publication are taken from Cordelia's scrapbooks and are reproduced with the kind permission of the Stoneleigh Abbey Preservation Trust. As acknowledged above, they were photographed by Mr Will Blagburn.
The exceptions are:

- the two photographs of the younger Cordelia Leigh and one of the frontispiece to Cordelia's book "The Adventures of a Boy Called Thomas", which are held at Stoneleigh Abbey and used with the Stoneleigh Abbey Preservation Trust's permission;
- the photograph of Cordelia Leigh, which accompanied her obituary, is reproduced by kind permission of the Leamington Courier;
- the photograph of "four friends" is reproduced by kind permission of Mr Dennis Craddock;
- the photograph of Ernest Thorley's cross is reproduced by kind permission of Mrs Shirley Ball;
- photographs of Charles King's Bible and Stoneleigh Abbey were taken by Sheila Woolf;
- photographs of the War Diary were taken by Chris Holland by kind permission of the Shakespeare Birthplace Trust;
- the photograph of the 'Name Tree' at Stoneleigh Abbey is contained within an album of photographs held at the Shakespeare Birthplace Trust (DR 962/37) and is reproduced by kind permission of the Trust.

~

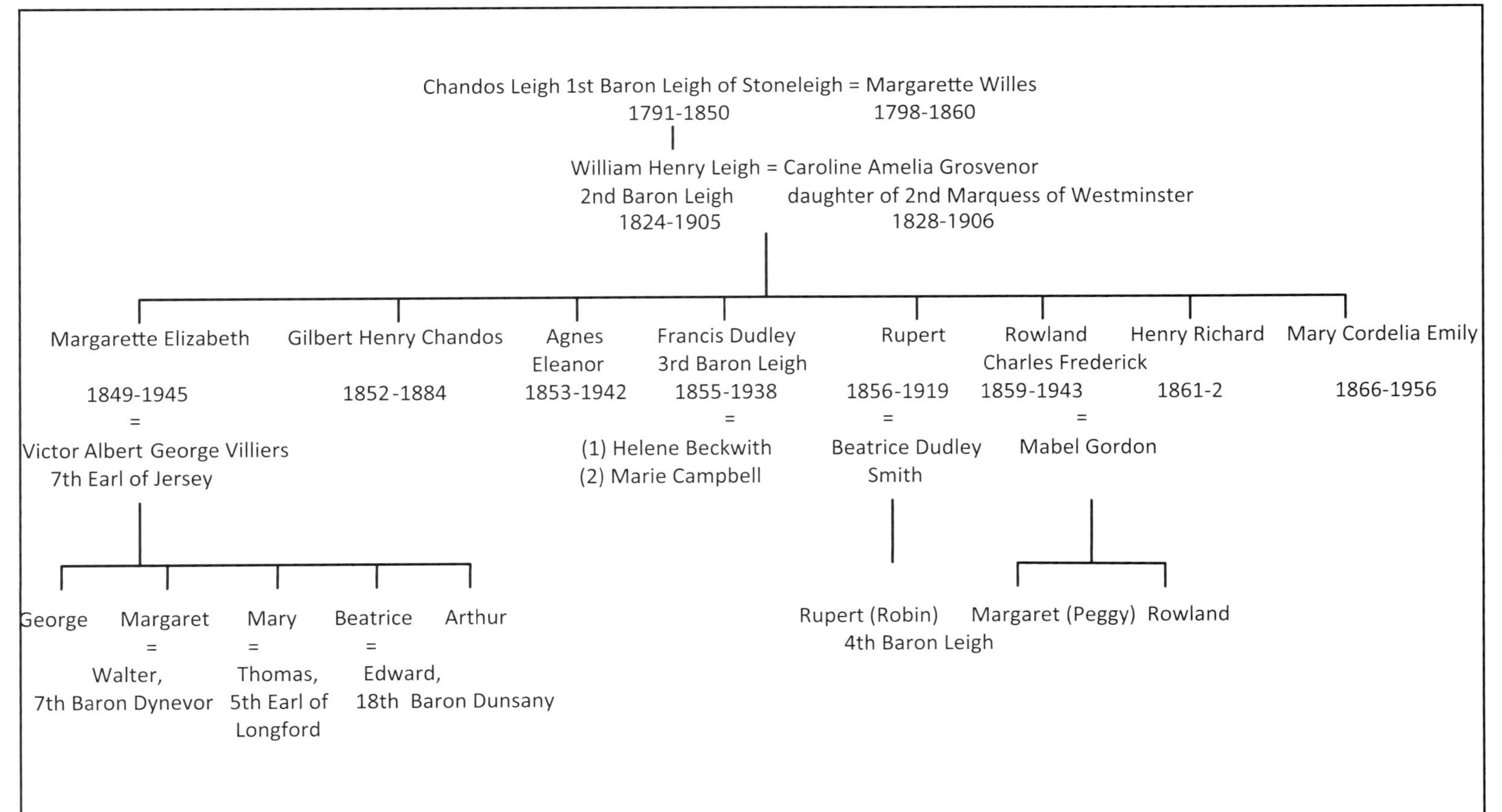

Leigh Family Tree showing Cordelia's immediate family.

Chapter 1: Introduction

By late July 1914, when a European war was becoming increasingly likely, Cordelia Leigh would have seen clearly what part she might play "for King and Country". Although the opening page of her War Diary states that in that "strange time" before the declaration of war "all one's thoughts and interests were changed, former interests forgotten", it was in fact those former interests which were to lead her to engage her local community in the war effort. In her late forties at the outbreak of war, she had spent most of her life in the education of others and in assisting her family in caring for the welfare of those who lived and worked on the Stoneleigh Estate in Warwickshire.

Mary Cordelia Emily Leigh was born in 1866 at Stoneleigh Abbey near Kenilworth, the youngest child of eight of William Henry, 2nd Baron Leigh and his wife Caroline Grosvenor, a daughter of the 2nd Marquess of Westminster. She was thus descended from particularly well-connected families, her many aunts on both her parents' sides of the family having married into some of the most influential dynasties of Victorian times. Cordelia (known as Cords to her family) was able to draw on these connections in her own "war effort".

Cordelia had grown up realising that generations of her forebears had played the role of monarchs of their own little kingdom: from the early days of their acquisition of the Abbey in 1561 by Sir Thomas Leigh, one-time Lord Mayor of London and Master of the Mercers' Guild, right through to her own immediate family, there had been an impulse to provide for the poor and needy. In 1575 Sir Thomas' wife, Dame Alice, had founded almshouses in Stoneleigh village for ten poor people, and almost three hundred years later, Cordelia's grandmother Margarette had continued the tradition by establishing another almshouse, specifically for widows.[1] In the eighteenth century a school was built in the village by the family, and through the generations they maintained a keen interest in it, until its closure in 1976. Indeed for a short period in the late eighteenth century there had even been a workhouse in Stoneleigh, entirely provided for and overseen by the Leighs.[2] The growing hamlet of Westwood, on the estate, was provided with its own church by Cordelia's grandfather, the 1st Lord Leigh, and when she was only six years old Cordelia was given a taste of the family's responsibilities when she was sent in a pony cart with her nurse to lay the foundation stone of a new school there, stating "I declare this stone well and truly laid"![3]

Cordelia Leigh as a young girl. Undated c. 1880.

In the latter half of the nineteenth century the Leigh family had entered upon its golden years. Cordelia's father was one of the wealthiest land-owners in the county and, in his capacity as Lord Lieutenant of Warwickshire, he had the honour of entertaining Queen Victoria and the Prince Consort for three nights at Stoneleigh Abbey in the summer of 1858. A great philanthropist, his reputation as a benevolent, paternalistic head of his vast estate remains to this day: he would frequently forgive tenant farmers their arrears in times of agricultural depression; he kept detailed surveys of the state of each building on the estate, down to the meanest hovel, with recommendations for repairs; he also considered the employment of each

Golden Wedding of Lord and Lady Leigh, August 1898. Cordelia's father, Lord Leigh, is seated centre. To his left is Margarette, Lady Jersey; the Earl of Jersey stands behind Lord Leigh. To the Earl's left are Cordelia and then her sister Agnes. The gentleman in the bowler hat, far right, is Edward Chandos Leigh. Lady Leigh is not pictured!

family's children as they grew up, finding places for them all and moving families from one house to another as their numbers grew or reduced in size.[4] Each Sunday after church in Stoneleigh village he would visit the old people in the almshouses, and in 1895 Charles Booth, in his report on the condition of the aged poor, stated that the parishes of Stoneleigh, Ashow and Westwood were among the parishes where the old were kept on at light work or pensioned off. William Henry and his wife took a keen interest in the education of local children, and encouraged their own children to become involved in this, too. Soon after succeeding to the barony he opened Reading Rooms in Stoneleigh and Westwood, to extend the knowledge of the adult population. A strong supporter of Gladstone, his philanthropy extended to the nearby city of Coventry, where, for example, in the 1860s he raised over £40,000 by public appeal to assist distressed ribbon weavers, and had set up Leigh Mills to provide employment. His interests included prison welfare and the rehabilitation of prisoners on their release; he presided over the Coventry Emigration Committee as one means of providing for their futures.[5] He was particularly exercised by the need to place the young in education and employment, and established the County Reformatory for Boys at Weston under Wetherley, where various trades were taught – Cordelia noted in her reminiscences how her father then found work for them, or took trouble to place them in the army or navy.[6] He is reported to have referred to Kenilworth as the "capital of my kingdom" and he understood the responsibility which went with being its ruler.

The family were not only interested in the physical welfare of their estate workers, but very much in their spiritual well-being. From the beginning of the nineteenth century, when the estate had passed to the Reverend Thomas Leigh of Adlestrop in Gloucestershire – a cousin, incidentally, of Jane Austen's mother – documents reveal a clear sense of pastoral leadership. Perhaps this reached its apogee in 1864 when Cordelia's uncle, her father's youngest brother, James Wentworth Leigh, became the vicar of Stoneleigh. He took his pastoral responsibilities seriously, keeping, as his brother did, detailed notebooks concerning villagers, often commenting on their characters and relationships with neighbours![7] An eccentric, larger-than-life man himself, he was succeeded by clergy well into the twentieth century who formed close connections with their congregations and with the Leigh family.

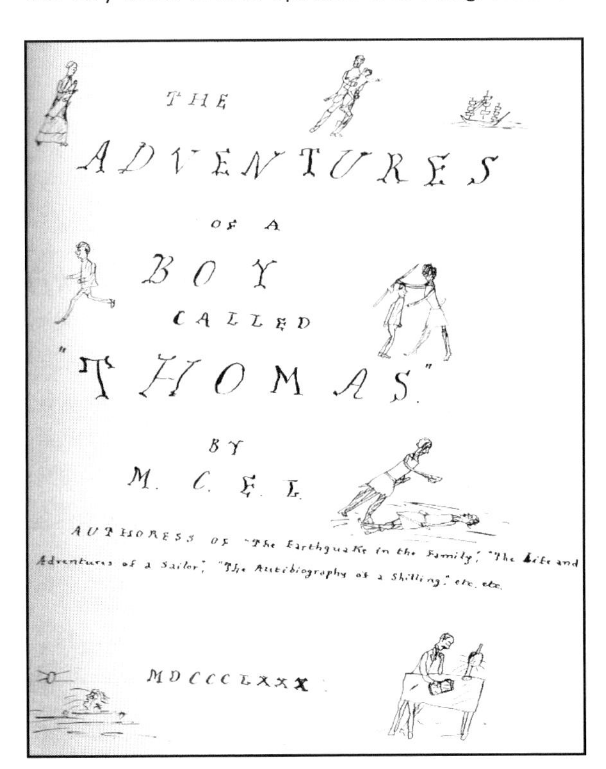
THE ADVENTURES OF A BOY CALLED "THOMAS"

BY M. C. E. L.

AUTHORESS OF "The Earthquake in the Family," "The Life and Adventures of a Sailor," "The Autobiography of a Shilling," etc. etc.

MDCCCLXXX

The title page of Cordelia's first known book, written when she was fourteen and dedicated to her brother, Francis Dudley.

The Leighs of Stoneleigh, then, lived a privileged life through their landed wealth and family connections, dividing their time between a variety of residences both in London and "the country", but at the same time, like so many philanthropic dynasties, keeping close ties with those who depended on them for shelter, employment, education and spiritual guidance. This dichotomy is intriguingly revealed through the pages of Cordelia's War Diary and her scrapbooks of letters and newspaper articles from the war years.

Lord Leigh's attitude to the upbringing of his children was relaxed; his one stipulation was that the whole family attend prayers each day. Although Cordelia's four brothers went away to school and university, she and her two sisters were educated privately at home. A flavour of her childhood is given in her diary of reminiscences, compiled in her old age.[8] She recalls Mrs Wallace, the Abbey housekeeper, a fearsome Scotswoman, who described Lord Leigh as "the handsomest man in England", being asked to open the traditional Servants' Ball on his birthday by dancing with Lord Leigh himself, whilst Lady Leigh danced with the butler. Her nurse, another strict Scot, refused to allow play on Sundays, except with toy soldiers who could be lined up and marched into an improvised model church. The children, the eldest of whom was seventeen years older than Cordelia, were keen writers and performers, and kept little books in which they each wrote stories and poems; their speciality was writing and performing plays, some of which achieved large audiences in the grand Saloon at the Abbey. Creativity was greatly encouraged: the family had a literary tradition, their grandfather, Chandos, having been a poet of some repute and a close friend of Lord Byron. Cordelia herself would go on to be a prolific published writer.[9]

"An enemy to worldly pleasures", according to one of her great-nieces, Cordelia's principal interest from an early age seems to have been education. When her eldest sister, whom Cordelia had called "Head Girl", announced she was to marry, Cordelia, aged six, declared that if only her other sister, Agnes, were to marry or die, then she, Cordelia, would fulfil the role of one who "heard the boys their lessons,"[10] – an ambitious goal, since the youngest of them was six years older than Cordelia herself! Regarded by her family as a hopeless case when it came to dancing and socialising – "chronically uninterested in social life"[11] – she was described as a wallflower at balls and had no interest at all in clothes, or, indeed, potential suitors; she declared in her reminiscences that in her childhood reading, "I was always sorry when some nice animals, such as the Beast in Beauty and the Beast turned into magnificent princes – the animals seemed so much more attractive than the dull human beings!"[12] So it was that Cordelia remained single throughout her life and devoted herself to helping others.

Cordelia Leigh at work as a naturalist. Undated c. 1890.

During her explorations of the extensive Estate belonging to the Abbey, Cordelia acquired a love of nature which never left her; by her twenties a combination of this interest in nature and her firm Christian faith led her towards a vocation in educating the young. She and her sister Agnes followed in their mother's footsteps by becoming regular visitors at the schools in the neighbouring villages of Stoneleigh and Ashow to hear the children read or to give Bible lessons; although it would not have been appropriate for a daughter of the house to become a full-time teacher, she evidently enjoyed the contact with children and considered it important to inculcate in them a love of their natural surroundings and a firm religious knowledge. The Stoneleigh School Logbooks note the frequent occasions on which Cordelia took classes, principally on nature study, and she donated flower bulbs for the school garden as well as hundreds of books for the school library. For many years she held regular Bible Study classes for young men from the two villages, who walked to Stoneleigh Abbey on a Sunday afternoon. This continued well into her old age (she died, aged 89, in 1956) and she is still remembered by many today as their Sunday School teacher.

In 1889 Cordelia began a Young Naturalists' Club, which encouraged children to observe the world around them. She was the editor of their magazine, recording first sightings of various seasonal wild flowers and answering their questions about natural phenomena ("why does a red sky in the morning mean bad weather and red sky at night mean good weather the next day?"). The motto of the Club was *Through Nature up to Nature's God*, and Cordelia seized the opportunity to acquaint the children with Bible stories. They went on frequent rambles, and as part of their subscription, gave money towards helping children from inner-city London take holidays in the countryside.[13] The London Children's Country Holiday Fund still exists today and its ethos and practice still remains as it was in the nineteenth century.

The Stoneleigh School Logbook records in 1906 that this scheme had been formulated by the editor of *The Countryside* "for linking together for mutual benefit pairs of Metropolitan and Rural schools" and that Cordelia was its secretary. Stoneleigh was to be paired with Gloucester Road School in Peckham[14]; Cordelia became acquainted with the London children in this way, and not only did she stand godmother to several, but corresponded with and supported them in adulthood.

At the outbreak of the First World War, Cordelia's experiences with the schools and her contact with young people via these various organisations were to stand her in good stead as she sought how to help the war effort. Her family, too, played their part. Perhaps the most public figure of her siblings, her eldest sister Margaret, Countess of Jersey, threw her weight as a London society hostess into rallying the influential and the moneyed to the cause. As the heir to Child's Bank and the Governor of New South Wales between 1890 and 1893, Margaret's husband Victor Albert Child-Villiers, the 7th Earl of Jersey, had a wealth of connections, and she drew on these to the full: among their friends and visitors to Osterley Park, their London home, was Lord Kitchener.[15] She served on several committees and since 1901 had been President of the Victoria League, an organisation with the original object of drawing British citizens throughout the world more closely together. In particular Margaret assisted Lady Lugard in her work with Belgian refugees; in this capacity, she helped Cordelia settle Belgian families in Stoneleigh. Her letters reveal aspects of the war which differ greatly from Cordelia's own experiences: her son-in-law, Thomas Pakenham, 5th Earl of Longford, was killed at the Dardanelles and her younger son Arthur was twice wounded and awarded the DSO; Margaret herself was made a DBE after the war.

Francis Dudley Leigh ('Duddy' to the family, and usually referred to as 'D' in Cordelia's diary) had succeeded to the barony following the death of his father in 1905, his eldest brother Gilbert having been killed in a tragic accident in America in 1884. 'Duddy' was a keen supporter of the growing Scouts movement and encouraged a hearty patriotism in the young. When his beloved wife Helene died in 1909 it was evident that he needed something to occupy his mind, and with the outbreak of the war he had found it: he and Agnes, Cordelia's older sister, who had been drafted in to act as his consort on social occasions, were keen to motor to France themselves – he to help evacuate casualties in his car, and Agnes to assist in letter-writing for the soldiers, since she was not qualified as a nurse. Cordelia's diary includes information on his travels, and in her scrapbooks she pasted his long letters to her from France and Belgium, together with newspaper articles concerning his recruiting activities later in the war. Agnes, too, features in the diary with a long description of the Armistice celebrations. Although Cordelia's other two brothers, Rupert and Rowland, were too old to enlist, each worked for the war effort in his own way, Rupert in the London Censor's Office and Rowland in Stoneleigh supervising the manufacture of soldiers' crutches and other medical aids, with which to supply local hospitals and the Red Cross.

Apart from her close family ties, Cordelia drew considerable support from her long-time friend Alice Skipwith. Alice's father had been Rector of Hamstall Ridware in Staffordshire, one of the Leigh family estates, and the Skipwith family were regular visitors to Stoneleigh. Alice and Cordelia shared a strong Christian faith, and when Alice inherited a property in Leamington upon her father's death in 1911, the two women shared the house until Alice's death in 1954. Cordelia's diaries reveal that they often travelled together. Few other close friends, however, are mentioned in the diary, Cordelia seeming to be happy to correspond principally with members of her extended family and the young men she had determined to help.

[1] William Henry, Lord Leigh's notebooks, Shakespeare Birthplace Trust, Stratford (SBT) DR18/31/739-746

[2] Norma Hampson "The Poet and the Paternalist" in *Stoneleigh Abbey, the House, Its Owners, Its Lands*, edited by Robert Bearman (2010) ISBN 0904-201-05-8

[3] Diaries and commonplace books SBT DR962/15

[4] Letter from Margarette [widow of Chandos] Leigh, re endowment and construction of almshouses SBT DR18/17/58/764

[5] Documents re establishment of workhouse at Stoneley SBT DR 18/3/69 1-17

[6] Diaries and commonplace books SBT DR962/15

[7] Stoneleigh Parish 1864, notebook kept by Rev. James Wentworth Leigh, Warwick Record Office DRO 318/80

[8] Diaries and commonplace books SBT DR 962/15

[9] See Appendix for list of books

[10] *Margaret, Countess of Jersey*, Violet Powell. Heinemann 1978

[11] *Ibid.*

[12] Diaries and commonplace books, SBT DR962/15

[13] The Stoneleigh & Ashow Naturalists' Record, October 1893. Privately printed and edited by M.C.E. Leigh

[14] An account of Gloucester Road, Peckham school journey to Stoneleigh, 1910. Warwick Record Office CR/689/43

[15] *Margaret, Countess of Jersey*, Violet Powell. Heinemann 1978

12. Aug. 1914.
My intention, if I have the
time, is to write a short record
of this time of war as it
appears to a private individual living at Stoneleigh Abbey,
in the Midlands – thinking
it may possibly be of interest
to members of my family
at some future time. If I
have ~~the~~ to use the personal
pronoun a great deal, I hope
it may be forgiven, as of
course this is not meant to
be a historical account, such
as appears in the newspapers,
but only a private record
of a few personal experiences.
On July 25th my friend
Alice Skipwith (living at

The first page of Cordelia's Diary.

Chapter 2: 1914

Introduction

At the outbreak of war Cordelia Leigh occupied her time in educational work. She worked as an adviser in Sunday School teaching, and continued to give lessons in Nature Study and the Bible at the local schools in Stoneleigh and Ashow. As stated, her parents had died less than a decade earlier, and her brother, Francis Dudley, Lord Leigh, now widowed for five years, was often accompanied by his other unmarried sister, Agnes, on official occasions. Cordelia was particularly involved in the work of the London Country Holidays Fund and, it appears, in giving what support she could to the families on her brother's estate. Her Sunday afternoon Bible classes at Stoneleigh Abbey for local young men had continued for some time as, indeed, they were to do for most of her life.

Her diary thus begins with acknowledgement not only of her family's activities, but those of the estate workers and of the preparation for war being undertaken by local dignitaries. It indicates clearly how her family saw a real need to do whatever was possible to further the war effort.

1914 Diary Entries

12. Aug. 1914.

My intention, if I have the time, is to write a short record of this time of War as it appears to a private individual living at Stoneleigh Abbey, in the Midlands – thinking it may possibly be of interest to members of my family at some future time. If I have to use the personal pronoun a great deal, I hope it may be forgiven, as of course this is not meant to be an historical account, such as appears in the newspapers, but only a private record of a few personal experiences.

On July 25th my friend Alice Skipwith (living at Leamington) accompanied me in one of my brother Dudley's motors to Worcester, where I was going on some business connected with Sunday Schools. It was a glorious day, and we enjoyed ourselves thoroughly with light hearts, except for a little anxiety respecting the state of Ireland, for everyone was thinking and talking of the possibility of Civil War. That day, for the first time, there "arose the little cloud out of the sea like a man's hand", for there appeared on the newspaper posters in the towns the ominous words "European Crisis", but so little did we realize coming events that we asked each other what this could mean! By the following Saturday, Aug. 1st, all here were in a state of intense anxiety, hoping against hope that a way to peace could be found.

That day (Aug. 1st) Dudley, Mabel (Mrs Rowland Leigh) and I went to a children's play at Mrs. Guthrie's: and here we were told by certain people, such as Lord Grenfell, who were certain to know, that it was inevitable that England should go to War. And then began a strange time, which is difficult to describe; all one's thoughts and interests were changed, former interests forgotten, thoughts concentrated on the one great matter which filled all minds, we went to bed at night to dream of it and awake with the weight of it in the morning.

On Sunday (Aug. 2nd) Mrs. Hand at the little Stoneleigh Post Office had to keep the office open all day and night for possible telephone messages – a small local incident which seemed to bring matters home very closely to us.

Monday, Aug. 3rd, was Bank Holiday, and as far as the banks were concerned the "holiday" lasted till Friday.

Tuesday, Aug. 4th. That morning I received a typed circular letter from the Central Office of the London Country Holidays Fund[1], saying that the arrangements for sending out the second party of holiday children were cancelled, and the first party were to be sent back, as previously arranged, on the 6th. I took my tricycle as soon as possible to the village to pay off the cottage women who had holiday children, and to inform all who were expecting the second party. There did not appear to be undue excitement anywhere; one woman, indeed, said "When I think of the War I cannot eat my dinner!", but another, living in a cottage in a field rather far from anywhere thought I said that the children could not come because of the water, instead of the War, and asked "Is it bad then, something like it was the other day at Kenilworth?"

Dudley, who had been attending a meeting at the House of Lords, came back here on Wednesday, and set to work to see the different Assistant Commissioners for the Baden Powell Boy Scouts, as General B. Powell sent a telegram to him as Chief Commissioner for the Northern District asking if 1,000 Scouts could be supplied for various offices and odd jobs.

I cycled into Leamington, and saw little boys marching solemnly along after a miniature Union Jack, armed with sticks and toy guns. I heard that all German waiters were dismissed from the Leamington Hotels, and that a number of German governesses were returning home hastily. I met Miss Murray, the Ashow Schoolmistress, who had come over with some difficulty to Ashow from Birmingham, where she was spending her holidays; she said that at Coventry women were crying at the Station, seeing the departure of their husbands and lovers who were going off on active service, but at Birmingham Station they were not allowed on the platform.

On Wednesday evening we had a dinner party, which had been arranged before the trouble began, and could not easily be given up: but it was the strangest dinner party in its way that I ever remember, though I think that we were all glad to meet together and talk things over. Twice in the course of the dinner Dudley and I were called out to speak to young men from Stoneleigh village; one was John Thorley, who had only been married about a fortnight, and was off to Warwick to join his Yeomanry regiment; he, and young Morris, both came to see us about a number of C.L.B. lads whom they thought would be willing to volunteer for service in the Territorials. Morris afterwards got them to meet together in the Reading Room, on Friday evening, where D. addressed them, and about 20 boys of about 17-22 volunteered to do what they could. 14 bicycled over to Coventry next morning, to the Territorials' Drill Hall, and were placed on the waiting list.

As further urgent messages came from the C.C.H.F., begging us who were country correspondents to get the London children back in the best way we could, I settled to take the whole party up myself on Thursday 6th, viz. 11 from Stoneleigh and 11 from Ashow. Beatie (Mrs. Rupert) who was also going up, kindly helped, but we had no difficulty, and were only 40 minutes late; we were kept a little time outside Euston while trains with troops went by. In London I called on an American lady with a message from Mabel Leigh, and she said "I only wish you English could hear us talking among ourselves about you! I cannot tell you how we admire your calmness and courage; if you could hear us I know it would give you courage if you needed it – but you don't! We are proud of you." This lady was with a cousin who had just lost her Son, who had died of a specially bad kind of typhoid in a London private hospital.

The London streets were remarkably quiet on the whole. I got into London about 6 p.m. and wandered about the streets a bit between 6 and 7, ending with dinner at my Club, the Alexandra Club[2] in Grosvenor Street, where, as the Club was closing that evening for cleaning, I was the only guest; I was charged only the usual price for dinner, but I noticed in the windows of Restaurants that a dish of eggs and bacon usually 4d was raised to 8d, etc.. In Davies Street I saw men in khaki going hurriedly in and out of Head Quarters, and for a few minutes had an odd sensation as if I were watching a scene in a Theatre, awaking to the grim reality, "No, it is real, it means War!" And I heard newsboys shouting and bugles sounding till I went to sleep. I was glad to get away by the 11.5 train next morning; the usual slip carriage[3] was on, and we ran into Leamington up to time.

On arrival at home I found all the family collected in front of the stables, together with the head gardener, foreman, and other heads of departments, and all the horses were drawn up, and being examined by a veterinary surgeon (Ringer) as Alex Parker had come to enquire about horses for Government use, an office which he very much disliked! Three farm horses were taken, and later a 4-year-old which was out at grass. Our useful horse "Durbar", and the small horse "Rufus" which Agnes and I drive in our 4 wheeled cart have not, so far, been commandeered.

Directly after luncheon D. and I motored to pursue researches after Scouts; we went to Stockton and Coleshill, and ended with the Meeting at the village to which I have already referred. We passed Meriden, where a few people were carrying on the Archery Meeting, but we heard that the Meriden Ball was given up, for the first time in its history.

On Saturday we called on Mr Cairns, the Vicar of Kenilworth, to ask him to superintend the Scouts in that district. I took the opportunity, as he is a very sensible sort of person, to consult him as to how far it was advisable for me to attempt to carry on my usual Sunday School Sec. work; he advised me to return to it in the course of a fortnight or so, as he thought it was impossible for people at home to continue indefinitely at the present high state of tension.

A special Service of Intercession was held on Sunday, 9th. A special short Epistle and Gospel were used at the early celebration of the Holy Communion at Stoneleigh, and appropriate prayers were used at the 11 o'clock Service: two of the Psalms for the "9th morning" – "O God we have heard with our ears", and "God is our hope and strength", came in with wonderful appropriateness. Mr Kendall, a clergyman who took the place of the Vicar, Mr Cooke[4], who was away, preached a splendid and very solemn sermon on "If one member suffer, all the members suffer with it", and the Service concluded with the singing of the National Anthem.

Agnes wrote out a notice and fastened it to the Reading Room door[5], inviting any women who wished to sew or knit for the Hospitals receiving the wounded, or soldiers on active service, to send in their names; she received a ready response, and is distributing materials in the village.

I had a curious task on Monday morning, which was to take our German lady's-maid to the Chief Constable's Office at Warwick to be registered, failing which she would have been liable to a fine of £100, or 6 months' imprisonment as an alien enemy. She had to give her name, age, birthplace, and present and past employment, and also was asked for her photograph, so that I took her to Leamington to be photographed. She may not travel without a permit, which will be sent to her. Two boy scouts were at the Constable's Office ready to carry messages. I also had to take a letter from D. to the Yeomanry Head Quarters, which was full of officers and men in uniform, very busy; indeed I had to explain that my business was urgent, otherwise I do not think I could have seen Col. Wiggin.

On Tuesday I drove the pony cart to Coventry to hunt for an Assistant Scout Commissioner for D. and was fortunate in finding a Mr Horner, Education Office Sec., who like everyone else was "anxious to do something." On the road home I offered a lift to a poor but very clean looking woman who was toiling along with a small bundle; she turned out to be the mother of a Reservist's wife at Leamington; he had been called out, leaving the wife and two little children; the mother wanted to visit her to cheer her up, and was walking from Coventry to Leamington, as most of the local trains were taken off, so she was glad to be saved a few miles.

[1] the London Country Holidays Fund: *set up in 1884 by the Rev. Samuel Barnett and his wife, Henrietta, as "The Children's Fresh Air Mission", with the name being changed in 1886 to The Children's Country Holidays Fund. Its aim was to give invalid or disadvantaged children visits to the country, of not less than two weeks, and within a 50 mile radius of London. Children were boarded with local "cottagers" who were paid by the Society, along with a parental contribution. Presumably, Cordelia used her contacts to extend the radius of the holidays to include Stoneleigh.*

[2] the Alexandra Club: *a ladies-only club that opened in Grosvenor Street, London, in 1884. It was restricted to those eligible to attend Court. Residential accommodation was available for those undertaking short visits to London. In 1899, Mrs Millicent Fawcett, President of the National Union of Women's Suffrage Societies, was made an honorary life member.*

[3] the slip carriage: *a railway coach, or carriage, that was uncoupled from an express train while still in motion and guided into a station by a guard using a hand brake. It allowed passengers to alight at a station without the main train having to stop, thus keeping journey times down. Some trains carried a number of these coaches, which were 'slipped' at different stations.*

[4] the Vicar, Mr Cooke: *the Rev. Herbert Edward Cooke arrived in Stoneleigh in 1910 and was to remain as vicar, and Hon. Canon of Coventry until 1948. During this time, he exerted an enormous influence on the community, particularly at the outbreak of World War I, when he joined both Lord Leigh and the Headmaster of the school, Mr Wells, in encouraging young men to join up. It was the Rev. Cooke who began the popular Church Lads'*

Brigade in Stoneleigh. He himself served with the 1st Battalion King's Own (Royal Lancaster Regiment) and Cordelia sent parcels at his request for the men. His son Wing Commander Humphrey Desmond Cooke was killed in June 1942 and is commemorated at Stoneleigh.

[5] Reading Room: *the Stoneleigh Reading Room was established in 1856 with the object of "Reading, Recreation and Refreshment". It grew from a building that was originally the coach house for the Leigh family when they attended church in the village. Later, William Henry, Lord Leigh, provided books and a number of dramatised readings were performed there, including one from Shakespeare given by the famous actress Mrs Kemble, who was the mother-in-law of Cordelia's Uncle James. The Reading Room became the Village Club in later years, and is now the only licensed premises, the last public house, the Stoneleigh Arms, being closed by Lord Leigh after cyclists from Coventry allegedly shouted abuse at his daughter - Cordelia! The Leigh family provided similar establishments in the neighbouring villages of Ashow and Westwood Heath.*

It is now **Friday, Aug. 14th**. I have not had much to record of the last 3 days. Public news is scanty, for (as my readers of the future, if I have any, will read in History) the War Office and the Admiralty are very careful to keep everything as quiet as possible. The weather has turned very hot, and beautiful for the harvest. My Brother Rowland and his wife went to London yesterday, and Mrs Rowland, who is American, called at the American Embassy, and kindly asked if a letter or message could by any means be conveyed through the Embassy to a niece of our German maid living at Hanover, about whom Louise (the maid) is desirous to hear news; Mabel was told that Louise's letter could only be sent round by way of Washington. Our Cousin Charles Leveson Gower[1] is at Homburg, and his wife has heard nothing from him for a fortnight.

I had a lesson this morning from Alice Skipwith in rolling bandages on a machine; I hope to roll a good many for the Warneford Hospital, which is to be used as a Base Hospital, and is reserving two large empty wards for the purpose.

[1] Charles Leveson Gower: *Cordelia had over a hundred cousins and second cousins. Charles Leveson Gower was the son of her aunt Sophia Leigh, her father's youngest sister. He is referred to in Cordelia's scrapbooks as "Uncle Charley".*

Saturday, 15th. There was a large Meeting at the Shire Hall at Warwick this afternoon, presided over by the Lord Lieutenant, Lord Craven, to settle about the Relief Committee, Red Cross Committee, etc. and to arrange for a County Organisation to work in conjunction with the Prince of Wales's Fund[1] and other central organizations in London. The High Sheriff, Col. Wyley[2], Lord Denbigh, Lord Willoughby, Mr. Cay[3], Sir Michael Lakin, Mr. Pollock (M.P. for Leamington), Dudley and others spoke.

We hope to arrange for Mills, the Head Keeper, helped by Fish, the Electrician, to give the young men of Stoneleigh lessons in shooting.

The Church Congress which was to have been held at Birmingham in October has been put off.

We feel very sorry for the Leveson Gowers, as Charlie was at Homburg before the War broke out, and his wife can get no news of him. There is an account in the "Daily Telegraph" to-day of a party of English who have arrived back in England from Homburg after great difficulties, and Charlie L. Gower's name is mentioned in the list of a few other English people who have not returned – he is probably a prisoner.

[1] the Prince of Wales's Fund: *the Prince of Wales's National Relief Fund was launched on 7th August, 1914, with a view to raising money for the relief of distress caused by the war, soon defined as that to be found among the families of soldiers and sailors, as well as that arising from industrial disruption caused by the war. A quarter of a million pounds was raised on the first day of the appeal. The appeal initially cut across other attempts to raise money, for example by the Soldiers' and Sailors' Families Association, as well as local initiatives.*

[2] Col. Wyley: *Colonel William FitzThomas Wyley was Lord Mayor of Coventry in 1911 and High Sheriff of Warwickshire in 1914. A great benefactor to the city of Coventry, he lived at the medieval Charterhouse which he left in his Will to the city.*

[3] Mr Cay: *Albert Cay was a wealthy glass manufacturer who lived at Woodside near Kenilworth; his only son Albert Jaffray Cay was killed in 1916. [Albert Jaffray Cay 9/719 Lieutenant in the 1st/1st Worcestershire Yeomanry (The Queen's Own Worcestershire Hussars) 5th Mounted Brigade. He was killed in action at Oghratina, Palestine on the 23rd April 1916, aged 36.]*

Sunday, 16th. Dudley addressed some men in the village after Church this morning, at Stoneleigh, and Rupert (Major Leigh) the men at Ashow, on the importance of all men and boys learning shooting, in view of a possible invasion by the Germans.

Monday, 17th. Rather a busy day. Early in the morning Alice Skipwith telephoned to know if D. could see Mr. Leeke, the husband of a Cousin of hers, who was anxious to try for a commission in an Infantry Regiment, and he arrived at 10 a.m. – 6 ft 4, and broad in proportion, and a champion weight thrower! D. wrote a letter of introduction for him to Lord Kitchener, and Rupert who was just going to London promised to call at the War Office and see if he could promote matters.

Lord Ernest Seymour came to luncheon to talk over a Recruiting Office for Kenilworth.[1] A recruiting agent came over from Rugby, with posters inviting men to join Lord Kitchener's "Second Army"[2], and these were posted about the villages. In the evening D., Agnes and I went to see the shooting practice in the Church Field at Stoneleigh; they shot at black paper targets fastened on to a board on the river bank. Tom Walton (the carpenter) told us that he had an old gun in his house, which had belonged to the famous village character, the tailor Job Lee[3], and that there was the tradition that it had been used for the shooting practice in that very field when invasion was expected by Napoleon. Three young villagers told D. that they were willing to enlist in Lord Kitchener's Army for foreign service. Later D. motored on to Kenilworth, and I left him at the Ashow turn and went to see the shooting at Ashow. Nothing could have looked more peaceful and calm than the little village as I walked through it, and it felt strange to see the little gathering of shooters and hear the shots in the beautiful meadow outside Bericote. D. came up later and gave the men a solemn "talking to" in the Reading Room. Our good little groom, James Amos, who was there, declared himself willing to enlist, there and then. On our return home we were told that both footmen were willing and later a keeper and three gardeners offered.

[1] Lord Ernest Seymour: *a former Lord Lieutenant of Warwickshire and Chairman of Royal Enfield, Ernest Seymour lived with his wife, Georgina, at The Firs, Abbey End, Kenilworth. He was also Chairman of the local Conservative and Unionist Club and active in the recruiting campaign that followed the outbreak of war. See also Constance Seymour (P. 66).*

[2] Lord Kitchener's "Second Army": *on 6th August, 1914, Parliament authorised an increase in the size of the Army by 500,000 men and the call for the first 100,000 appeared on 7th August. Early references appear to have been to a 'Second Army', in order to distinguish it from the pre-war regular Army. Subsequently, the volunteers who responded to this call were being referred to as members of 'Kitchener's Army' or the 'New Army'. Kitchener was the newly appointed Secretary of State for War.*

[3] Job Lee: *a tailor by trade, Job Lee has almost mythical status in Stoneleigh Village to this day: he achieved a great age and the hill known as Motslow Hill today is still called "Job Lee's Hill" by older residents, after his cottage which lies at the foot of it. He also did odd jobs at the Abbey, and Cordelia recalled reading from "The Pilgrim's Progress" to him when he had become old and blind.*

18th. D. and I motored to Westwood Heath[1] to see what could be done about a shooting range there. Our under chauffeur, the footmen, groom, keeper, and gardeners went to Coventry, and were all passed, except one gardener whose teeth are bad. D. spoke to them all outside the dining-room, and promised to keep their places open. Life now is rather like living in a stage play!

[1] Westwood Heath: *now an affluent area of Coventry adjacent to the University of Warwick, in 1914 it was a small village within the Stoneleigh estate. Cordelia's grandfather established a church there, and her father a reading room and a school.*

19th. and 20th. Comparatively peaceful days here. The 10 men from the house, garden and stables have gone off, after a short visit to their homes, amidst cheers from their friends; they go to Warwick now, and on to Salisbury Plain, for training. We learn to disbelieve all rumours of news not officially stated in the papers; last night for instance the postman said it was announced that a great naval battle was in progress in the North Sea, but the papers only record "desultory fighting". I am interested in a sailor boy who was some years ago in Camberwell, and who is my Godson; his mother wrote to me that she might not receive letters from him, but one could write to him, to "H.M.S. Ajax, C/o The General Post Office"; she only knows that he is in the North Sea. We have heard of people receiving letters from friends on active service; but the post marks are obliterated, and the writers are not allowed to say where they are. Curiously enough, we as a family here have no very near relations at the front; the brothers are too old and young Rowland and Robin are too young. The courage of wives and mothers who encourage their husbands and sons to go is beyond all praise. Mrs Leeke, for instance, telephoned the details about her husband to me without a tremor, though it meant that he would be leaving her and two small children.

The Bishop has suggested that where possible the Church bells should ring a few strokes each day at noon, to remind everyone to offer a prayer for our sailors and soldiers and the restoration of peace.

21st. Observed throughout our Church, and I believe the R.C. and Nonconformist Churches also, as a day of Intercession in connexion with the War. At Stoneleigh and Ashow there were three services – Holy Communion early, another service at 10.30 or 11 a.m., and another at 7.30 p.m. D. attended a great Service at St Michael's Coventry in the morning, at which the National Anthem was sung kneeling. At the conclusion of the 10.30 Service at Ashow, Mr. Reid Cuddon read out a very good letter from the Bishop, chiefly on the duties of loyalty, unselfishness, union between class and class, and prayer. The largest congregation at Stoneleigh was in the evening; the Vicar being away, no arrangements had been made for any singing, so I volunteered to play the National Anthem at the end, on my little American organ, which is kept in the Chancel, and the congregation sang it kneeling. The last time I played it at the end of the Service was in our Chapel at home, at the time of Queen Victoria's Jubilee.

One pound notes are issued now[1], and Postal Orders are accepted as common currency, no commission being charged on them.[2]

I am told that my pony-cart horse "Rufus" is not likely to be commandeered yet, as chestnut horses are not taken at first, their colour being too conspicuous.

A small comedy here in the middle of much that is serious, is the constant presence of "Florrie Wright"! – a little London girl who is a protégée of my niece Peggy Leigh[3], and is lodged at the village for a 3 weeks' holiday. She is to be seen about on all possible occasions, on the lawn, or in the village, or in the road, smiling at you when you are hurrying along with some important message, or looking at the shooting practice, and thoroughly enjoying life, whatever her neighbours may be doing! Also, at any critical moment you may hear Louise's parrots screaming "Polly!" or "Hulloa!"

[1] One pound notes are issued now: *the first pound notes were issued by the Treasury on 7th August, 1914. This was done in order to supplement coinage, which was becoming scarce as people hoarded gold sovereigns and half sovereigns. Ten shilling notes were issued on 14th August. The original notes were simple in design but were replaced by a more complex design in October 1914 (pound notes) and January 1915 (ten shilling notes). Carrying the signature of the Permanent Secretary to the Treasury, Sir John Bradbury, the notes were soon nicknamed 'Bradburys'.*

[2] Postal Orders are accepted as common currency: *the Currency and Bank Notes Act, which authorised the issue of bank notes, also stated that postal orders were to be temporarily accepted as legal tender and that no charge would be imposed on the sale of them. In other words, they could be used to pay for goods in the same way as coins, or the new Treasury notes.*

[3] Peggy Leigh: *Margaret Ethel (Peggy) Leigh (1901-1962) was the daughter of Cordelia's brother Rowland and Mabel Gordon. Like so many members of the Leigh extended family, she became an author, using the pen-name Jane Gordon.*

Sunday 23rd. Another fine sermon from Mr Kendall, on "I came not to send peace but a sword."

24th. D. and I went to Westwood Heath in the evening and he addressed some men in the Reading Room on the subject of recruiting. The 10 men from the house, garden and stables, and 2 young men from the village (Ernest Thorley and William Rose) came back for Sunday, and went to their homes, as Budbroke Barracks were too crowded to receive them; the arrangements there seem very bad.

25th. I had occasion to go to London for the day, which I found very quiet and rather empty; trains rather empty also. Many shops were flying the Union Jack, French and Belgian flags. Some shops had notices in the windows saying they would accept American money. Several taxi cabs, omnibuses etc. carried placards with notices in large letters, "Join Kitchener's Army for the period of the War only."

This evening the papers contain news of the first great battle, and 2,000 British casualties, but no names are yet given.

26th. Rupert came this evening, and assured us that Namur is not really taken. Also he is sure that the War Office feels that all will go well. But my impression is that people in general, especially in the villages and small towns, do not in the least realize the gravity of the situation. My old chiropodist at Leamington, for instance, (Kimberley) when I remarked that many more young men ought to volunteer for Lord Kitchener's Army, said "Why, Miss, you'll see, in another fortnight the Germans will be completely crushed", and it seemed a new light to him when I reminded him that Lord Kitchener had said the War might last 3 years.

Sept. 1st. The last few days I have been too busy to write in this book. On the 29th there was a rumour that a large quantity of Russian troops had come round by the Arctic, landing in Scotland and coming down through England, some of them shunting at Leamington Station. D., Agnes, Rowland, young Rowland, and Miss Hutton, the Governess, quickly got into the motor, and I took Peggy in the pony-cart, calling for Alice Skipwith on the way, and we all assembled at the Station, but did not see any Russians, though assured by various people that the rumour was true; according to one account, two Russian Officers had been seen in the streets, and another of our gossips said trains had passed with all the blinds down. All that we saw were some Yeomanry Recruits going to Hereford, with a great number of horses.

I had another letter from my sailor Godson at Devonport with the censor's pencil mark on the envelope; he said he was not allowed to "wright" anything about the War, or more than once a week; the last rule was in order to save the "senser" trouble.

Mr Batchelor, of Greystoke, has had a number of cards printed to form a "Roll of Honour" for the different villages, on which may be inscribed the names of the men from the village serving in the Army or Navy. D. and I are busy now taking them round. At Dunchurch, the Vicar, Mr Harbord, was just back from a lengthy journey from Switzerland; he was met with great civility but tedious delay. At Amiens he had talked with several English Officers wounded in the great battle of Mons; they said their men had surpassed themselves in courage, and their spirit is magnificent; they could hardly be induced to obey the order to retire. A Swiss Officer said to him when he was leaving Switzerland, "I want to salute you, because in you I salute a great nation, which is fighting, not for glory, for of that you have enough already, but for duty, and to help a smaller state"; and as the train moved off the Swiss stood to salute. Mr Harbord had been out in the Boer War and said the spirit of the English soldiers was just the same.

Netley Hospital[1] is moving some of its invalids to the Warneford Hospital[2] to make room, I suppose, for the more badly wounded cases from the Front.

[1] Netley Hospital: *the Royal Victoria Military Hospital at Netley, near Southampton.*

[2] the Warneford Hospital: *in Leamington.*

2nd. Eight more young men volunteered today for the Army at Stoneleigh. I met them in the village just as they were returning from Rugby, waving a flag and cheering. They have all been passed for the "Oxfordshire and Bucks" regiment, and go into training next Monday. They are Albert and Walter Morris, George Thorley, Sam Gallimore, Tom Ward, Harry King, Reggie Worrall, Fred Smith.

I have made up a leaflet calling on men to join, and have got 4,000 copies printed by Tomes.

3rd. Seven more village youths offered today, and 4 have been accepted, viz. Edward Wooding, A. Craddock, Tom Mills, Charles King.

D. and I went to every house in Westwood, including 2 public houses, "The Bell Inn" and "The Peeping Tom", leaving my leaflets. D. handed one to a passing young waggoner! And we pressed it through the key-hole and under the door of one house which was shut up. We found Tredgold lying on his back in his invalid chair and knitting socks for soldiers, who said he would be glad to distribute them among the people who called at his house.

My Cousin Channy (Chandos Leigh)[1] is reported among the "Missing".

[1] My Cousin Channy (Chandos Leigh): *Major Chandos Leigh DSO, 2nd Bn The King's Own Scottish Borderers, was the elder son of Edward Chandos Leigh, Cordelia's uncle and a prominent local solicitor. He died of wounds received at the Battle of Mons, on the 29th August 1914, and is buried at Hautrage Military Cemetery, Belgium.*

Sunday, 6th. Mr Cooke is back, and referred in Church to the splendid response Stoneleigh has made to the call for more recruits. I felt rather sad at my Boys' Bible Class as I had to say good-bye to George Thorley, a very old friend, who was among the recruits, though he is only 18. 10 out of the 12 are "old boys" of my Class, and I have given each a small knapsack Bible,

Why are we at War?

Because, in spite of the earnest efforts for peace made by the British Government, Germany invaded Belgium, which was a neutral country, and attacked France, which we had solemnly promised to help in time of war.

How long will the War last?

Nobody can say—perhaps three months, perhaps three years.

Shall we win?

Yes, by God's help, if every Englishman does his duty.

The Belgians have done their duty nobly. Our brothers from Canada, Australia, South Africa, and India, are doing theirs. What about *you*?

What is my Duty?

If you are between 19 and 35 years old, not under 5ft. 3in. high, and your chest not less than 34 inches, go and offer yourself at once for Lord Kitchener's second army! You can find out how to set about it at the nearest Post Office, Police Station, or Recruiting Office.

Remember, it is a matter of overwhelming importance. Shall your village and your home remain peaceful and happy, or shall it be over-run by the King's enemies? Shall the British Empire stand, or the German Empire stand? Which will you choose?

GOD SAVE THE KING.

Tomes, Printer, Leamington.

Cordelia's recruiting leaflet, of which she had 4000 copies made. See Diary entry for 2nd September 1914.

very light weight in a khaki binding with a gilt Union Jack on the cover.

The children and I cycled over to the village at 8.15 a.m. on Monday to help to give them a send-off. They went in 3 motors to Rugby, Mr Cooke's, Mr Metters'[1] and the Estate motor. The Union Jack was hoisted over the School, and all the School-children were assembled, as well as a great many of their grown-up friends. We all gave them a great cheer as they went off.

[1]Mr Metters: *was one of the most prosperous tenant farmers on the Leigh Estate, living at Manor Farm in Vicarage Road, Stoneleigh.*

Tuesday, 8th. I rang the "Peace Bell" at 12 at Stoneleigh Church to-day, happening to be at the Church at the time.

Thursday 10th. There are 27 names now on the Stoneleigh "Roll of Honour" of men serving in the Army or Navy. A recruiting Sergeant in uniform has gone down to Ashow this evening to see if he can enlist anyone. Poor Victor Billington at Ashow is lying in bed very ill, with the different flags of the Allies pinned on his nightshirt; he says "It is all I can do!"[1] Westwood is sending a good number of recruits now.

We are sending some clothes to Belgian refugees.

[1] Poor Victor Billington etc: *Victor Billington's death is recorded in September 1914, aged 29. The cause of his death is unknown; an Ashow man, he had previously worked as a nurseryman in Norfolk. In the 1911 census, he is shown as "married 2 years".*

Sunday, 13th. John Thorley was home this morning at the village from Newbury, for a few hours; he expects to move tomorrow, but does not know whether the Warwickshire Yeomanry will be sent to Egypt or to the Front; he says the men are all very well, and always have a great appetite for their food, which is plentiful though not specially well cooked. He saw some of the Russian troops, and knows as a fact that a great many have passed through England, though the report has been denied.

Four friends from Stoneleigh after joining up: James Craddock, Fred Smith, George Thorley and Walter Morris.

A letter published in the papers from a private says that Channy Leigh fell wounded, in a trench, and when two men tried to help him said, "Never mind me, go on" – so his fate is quite uncertain: this was at the battle at Mons.

An American family, Mr., Mrs., and Miss Sherman, are staying here till tomorrow, and, like all Americans, are full of sympathy for the English side.

We have all felt much more cheerful during the last few days, the news of the successes of the Allies filling every paper; though nobody seems able to form any opinion as to how long the War is likely to last.

16th. The War seems to feel very near to me to-day as an Ashow boy, Fred Newton, (one of my old Bible Class boys) has been killed in action.[1] His Foster Mother has just received the intimation from the War Office, with a printed circular letter from Lord Kitchener saying the King and Queen command him to express their true sympathy. She had only a few days before received a post card, which the soldiers are allowed to send, with certain printed sentences, "I am quite well", "I have been wounded and am in Hospital", "I was wounded and am now out of Hospital" etc. – one of which can be left and the others erased. In his case "I am quite well" was left, and also "I have received your letter."

[1] Fred Newton: *died on 9th September 1914 as a result of wounds, probably received either at Mons or during the Retreat, and is buried at Coulommiers Communal Cemetery, Seine-et Marne, France.*

17th. Went to Birmingham for the afternoon to a Diocesan Meeting. The streets were crowded near the Town Hall where recruiting seemed to be going on, and a military band was playing loudly. The Bishop's Meeting was held at the Queen's College near the Town Hall, and the noise in the street was so loud that we had to move from the large hall into a small room on the quieter side. Though the Meeting was entirely on Diocesan affairs the Bishop (Worcester) opened it with a prayer for victory and final peace.

18th. Had a letter to-day from the sailor boy, Harry Miles, on H.M.S. Ajax. He said he was not allowed to say where he was or what he was doing, but they had "plenty of work." The letter is undated, and there is a large black smudge in place of a postmark.

27th. The Harvest Thanksgiving has been held to-day at Stoneleigh, and we have every reason to be thankful for an extra good harvest. There is to be a Memorial Service at Ashow for Fred Newton.

Oct. 8th. There has been nothing of any special interest to note lately; but the following extract from a letter shown to me to-day is worth entering. The letter was written to old John Spiers at Stoneleigh by Mr. Macmillan, formerly a farmer near here, and now in British Columbia – dated Aug. 29:- "Out here, though 6,000 miles away in the far West, we are deeply and intensely interested in this wanton, wicked War into which the German Emperor and his gang of fellow murderers and assassins have plunged almost the whole of Europe, and this week Rossland and Cities in British Columbia sent off a strong contingent of soldiers to help uphold the honor and integrity of Britain and her glorious Empire." This is only one of hundreds of expressions of sympathy from distant parts of the Empire.

Rupert had a letter from an officer at the Front, dated Sept. 30th. "Your parcel arrived to-day addressed to Adjutant. At present there is none. The 3 Squadrons A. B. and C. acting as Divisional Cavalry to the 1st, 2nd, and 3rd Divisions respectively. The parcel turned up with A Squadron, with the 3rd Div. who also have a Head Quarters of Regiment attached, so have been divided up and the men much appreciate it. It was too far to send to the other Squadrons. Young Roase Broughton, a real nice lad, was the only remaining Officer with this Squadron, but Courage came from C Sq, 1st Div. and Ritchie and myself old timers from England to fill-up. All Squadrons I hear did well and gallant work, but now the infantry on both sides are entrenched there's little to do but observation post and patrol."

17th. I have had a letter lately from Albert Morris who is with 17 others of the Stoneleigh young men at Purbeck Camp near Portsmouth, and one from George Thorley who is with 3 others at Codford near Salisbury; both say they are well and happy; Mrs. Worrall told me that her Reggie wrote that they are "as happy as Kings". John Thorley also wrote from Newbury that he thinks the Warwick Yeomanry will move somewhere abroad in a fortnight. Weather is rather gloomy, and there has been some rain, but it is not cold enough to affect men camping out much at present, I imagine.

Charles Leveson Gower came back to England a short time ago, safe and well. No reliable news of Channy.

20th. A porter at Leamington G.W. Station told me that some magnificent Indian cavalry had been through the Station yesterday, with some fine mules. He described with great admiration how one had jumped on to a bar high up on the train and scrambled into the railway carriage, fearing lest he should be left behind. He said that one very big Indian grasped a railway porter by the hand saying "We fight for the King!" and that the boy was so frightened that he ran away! He said the Indians were so careful of their horses that they travelled with them, 2 men in each horse truck, and that the horses had gorgeous trappings.

At Paddington Station in the evening I saw some Belgian Refugee peasants, with children; I bought a few chocolate sticks and gave them; they looked pleased but made no remark.

Black sort of caps or coverings are put over the street lamps in London, and the people are asked to burn as few lights as possible, not to attract unnecessary attention on account of the danger from Zeppelins, etc.

21st. A dentist at Leamington, Mr Curle, told me that his son, a surgeon, was telegraphed for to-day to join a Hospital Ship for the Indian troops, sent out by the India Office, but he was not told the destination.

31st. Stoneleigh village is anxious to keep some Belgian Refugees; Mr. Carley, the farmer at Stareton, has generously offered his cottage at Stoneleigh rent free till Lady Day [March 25th] and D. offers a cottage of his. At a Meeting the other night a great many of the people came forward with offers of furniture, cups and saucers, saucepans etc., and weekly subscriptions in small sums which finally mounted up to about £1. Agnes has been to the Refugee Office at Warwick and finds that at present the peasants who have been sent from the Birmingham Depot so far are provided for, but more are expected soon. The difficulty will be that they are so far from a Roman Catholic School that we must have either all grown people or children too young for School.

Capt. Kay writes that a fresh urgent appeal is made for recruits, and an official enquiry is now to be made everywhere concerning the number of eligible men who have not yet volunteered; is this a preliminary step towards conscription?

In answer to Mabel Leigh's enquiries the American Consul at Berlin has written, through the Embassy at Berne, that it is believed that Channy died in Belgium.

Nov. 8th. Our Cousin Maimee (Lady) Mordaunt read us letters to-day from her two daughters, Winnie and Cicely[1], who are at Dieppe; Winnie is driving a motor ambulance, and Cicely is nursing wounded French and Flemish soldiers in a Hotel which has been turned into a Hospital. They are well and very busy, and find the soldiers most grateful – generally brought in very tired, and very dirty, requiring a good deal of washing, and sometimes hair-cutting! The Mayor has given Winnie a badge to show that she may drive her ambulance where she wishes. Cicely says that various French ladies come in to volunteer assistance who do not know much about nursing.

[1] Winnie and Cicely: *Winifred and Cicely Mordaunt were distant cousins of Cordelia, being the daughters of Sir Charles Mordaunt of Walton Hall, Wellesbourne, by his second wife Mary Louise Cholmondeley, Cordelia's cousin. Both girls joined the First Aid Nursing Yeomanry; Winifred became a Driver and was awarded the Croix de Guerre.*

12th. A Belgian family is at last settled in the village, sent over from Whitley; a nice looking man who has been a market gardener, his wife, a girl of 12, one of 10, one of 6, one of 3, and a baby; he speaks a little French, and the others only Flemish. The village has contrived to make the cottage most comfortable, and at present Mrs. Cooke is helping the man to make his purchases at the Co-op-Stores.[1] We hope that soon he will be employed on Mr. Metters' farm. The wife and children are very lively and cheerful.

I have called on the party of Belgian middle-class refugees at Kenilworth; there are about a dozen men, including an old Canon of Malines, and another younger priest, and about a dozen women, all living together at "Bridge House". The old Canon was well off, but now has lost everything; and one or two of the women told me that their troubles could not bear thinking of, but they were grateful for all the English were doing for them. A tiny Chapel has been fitted up for them in the house. Mr. and Mrs. Cairns give them lessons in English. We have lent them some French books. They told me they speak Flemish among themselves.

Also I have met two Belgian ladies, a mother and daughter, at tea at Mrs. Skipwith's, who are being put up at Mr. and Mrs. Corbet's at Leamington; they had to fly from Brussels, and came over in the last boat which took refugees to England; the husband is supposed to be still at Brussels. It was touching to hear the poor little lady say about Alice's little collection of jugs, "Mademoiselle tient beaucoup à ses petits pots – et moi, je tenais beaucoup à mes petits pots, et maintenant, ce sont touts perdus – tout!"

[1] The Co-op stores: *the Co-operative Stores in Stoneleigh were started in 1867 by the Reverend James Wentworth Leigh and were one of the first village co-operative stores in the country. In 1881 they were run by William Hewitt and family. At the time of World War I they were run by Joe Morris, three of whose sons served in the war and who corresponded with Cordelia.*

23rd. A former Stoneleigh boy who enlisted some time ago has been sent wounded to "Mercer's Hospital" at Dublin; Jonathan Prime by name. Agnes' friend, Miss Ward, has kindly been to see him, and writes as follows to his Mother:-

> "He was some time on the field before the stretcher bearers came, and they eased him to a great extent by cutting off the sleeve and freeing the poor arm, and putting on the field dressing then and there, and antiseptic pads. He told me that there were some poor cows that had been shot by shrapnel, and bleeding, and they had been tearing about quite near him, and looking very savage, but happily they did not touch him, though they were near enough for him to notice that their sides were wounded with shrapnel, and bleeding. When the stretcher bearers moved him they took him to the nearest regiment, which was the Black Watch, but it had been a fierce fight, and there were so many men of the B. Watch, very seriously wounded, that they could not send him on at once, but kept him there that night and looked after him. On account of the enemy, it was impossible to move the wounded except at night time, so he had to wait till it was dark the following evening, and then he was put into a horse-ambulance, which he found very shaky, as the roads in that part of Belgium were very rough. On their way they came to a farmhouse, and here he came across a great friend, and he was able to get a nice hot cup of tea made for him here – and two eggs – which he remembers with great satisfaction. That

night brought him to his own regiment – the Coldstreams. The following day they sent him to Boulogne. Here he was attended to and made as comfortable as was possible, and then he was put on board the Oxfordshire, and had a calm passage straight from Boulogne to Dublin and was well looked after. ... The X rays made it clear that his shoulder was seriously hurt, but he is very brave about it, and can think of nothing but his thankfulness in having his right arm as sound as if it had never been in the War at all."

Last week a Mrs. Archibald Little (authoress of several books, chiefly about China, where she lived for 20 years) stayed here 3 nights and gave a Lecture on the War each evening, at Stoneleigh, Westwood and Bubbenhall in succession, the first two nights with lantern slides. The Lectures were excellent, simple and impressive. There are very few unmarried men of the right age left at Stoneleigh to go, but a young footman here was moved by the Stoneleigh Lecture to offer himself again (having failed to pass before) and was passed, and 3 recruits were brought in by the Lecture at Westwood.

George Thorley writes very much pleased because he has been moved to Oxford into a comfortable house, the nights being too cold now for sleeping under canvas.

28th. Margaret Jersey sends us copies of Arthur's letters to see. In one, dated "Oxfords. Yeomanry, British Expeditionary Force, Nov. 5th" he writes:-

"We left the town where we had been for a few weeks on 30th Oct. at 7 p.m. and marched 30 miles arriving at a town about 7.30 a.m. We left there at 9 and half of us occupied some trenches, the other half advanced to surround one side of a town on a hill. There was fairly heavy shell-fire going on all the time, but we only had 2 men wounded. As soon as it was dark we took up a position all round one side of the town about 300 yards outside it. Then in the middle of the night we went inside the town and lined a barricade at one end of the street while the Germans were at the other end with a small gun at about 500 yards away. The Germans occupied the town the next day and we had to prevent their advancing

BRITISH TOYS.

To the Editor of the Manchester Guardian.

Sir,—I wonder if I might be allowed to express what I believe to be the feeling of a fairly large section of the public by saying how glad I am that with the capture by the British of the German trade in toys there is a good prospect that the reign of "ugly toys" will come to an end? May we hope that the hideous and vulgar golliwogs, gladeyes, drunken policemen, and the like will now sink into oblivion and no longer vitiate and vulgarise the taste of the helpless children, who are just as happy with toys which (without being necessarily beautiful) are at least pleasing to look at?—Yours, &c.,

M. CORDELIA LEIGH.

Stoneleigh Abbey, Kenilworth,
September 30.

OCTOBER 5, 1914.

Cordelia welcomed the end of the reign of "ugly" German toys.

more than a little way out of the town. We then held some trenches which were being heavily shelled. There were, of course, other British troops besides ourselves but the Germans were in far greater number; but they are said to be so done in that they cannot advance to attack. We had to do much the same kind of work all 4 days though on the 3rd Nov. the firing on both sides was most violent. The Kaiser was said to be about and this was for his edification. One regiment got awfully knocked about, but though we were in exactly the same line we escaped with very small losses – 2 killed and about 10 wounded. There is a good deal of luck in whether the big guns get the range of the trenches. The noise is terrific like a very bad thunderstorm but as there is no possibility of doing any good by jumping about everybody keeps very cool. I did not see anyone really scared though there was a certain look of bewilderment on many faces. It was so unexpected to most of them. Many had previously believed that they would rather enjoy it but I think they are now undeceived. The aeroplanes are the nuisance as they keep giving away the positions of the trenches and guns. I have not yet seen a spy but one of our fellows saw a windmill moving despite the fact that there was no wind, and it turned out to be the work of a spy who was found by some other troops. After our 4 days we have been given a rest for a couple of days. It was rather a surprise to us to be sent up right into the front line but circumstances developed so quickly that there was no alternative. Personally I performed no heroic exploits and took advantage of every available cover. Some of our officers insist on walking about as if there were no bullets which not only is foolish on their account but shows the enemy where our men are lying and attracts shell fire. All our work was dismounted. There is no difficulty in getting beef and biscuits to eat but your chocolate and lozenges have twice been of great use. Drinking water is really more difficult to get than food. The country here is rather hilly and not unlike England. I have never been in better health and I was only once really tired."[1]

Under date 8 Nov. "Our allies look out of date with their blue great coats and red collars. The cavalry are better but they will never get off their horses and so they are not as useful as they should be. The artillery is, I believe, quite good though not as good as the Germans. However, the nearer one is to the front the more in the dark one is as what is happening."

Under date Nov. 13. "We are going to take the place of the composite regiment of the Household Cavalry in one of the cavalry regiments which people consider an honour for a Yeomanry regiment. The chief need out here is for infantry and as many of them as possible. We work in shifts a day or so on and the like amount off. We get parcels pretty regularly. Letters come and go very irregularly."

(Arthur is now a Captain. His regiment was thanked and congratulated by the General).

[1] We left the town … etc: *the letter describes the experiences of the Oxfordshire Yeomanry after they left St Omer ("the town"). After marching 30 miles, they arrived at Neuve Eglise, before becoming involved in the fighting at Messines ("a town on a hill"). The trenches to which they subsequently retired, and in which they were heavily shelled, were at Wulverghem.*

Dec. 1st. Albert Morris and the other 7 Stoneleigh men in his party are in comfortable quarters at Clarence Barracks near Portsmouth. I also hear a good account of Albert Worrall, who is under canvas near Brighton; he and Tom Walden enlisted about a fortnight ago.

D. and Agnes planned to go to Boulogne, with Mr Reid Cuddon (Rector of Ashow) and a Mr Barker of Leamington who would have been able to drive D.'s motor; D. had intended to drive near the fighting line and carry away the wounded, and A. thought she might be useful in various ways to the wounded at Boulogne, writing letters for them, getting them food, etc. (she has not learnt nursing); but D. is at present unable to get permission to drive his motor anywhere near the front.

Their departure for France was announced in the "Leamington Spa Courier", so the mad woman at Hatton Asylum, called "Lady Godiva"[1], has written a long letter on the subject to A., telling her, amongst other things, that if she is in any difficulty with the President of the French she must write to her, and she ("Lady Godiva") will help her!

There are rumours lately that the Germans attempted a raid on England which was not in the newspapers and that it was repulsed by the Fleet; it certainly is an undoubted fact that the East Coast has been very strictly guarded lately. I was told yesterday of a lady who received a letter from her son, who is out somewhere with the Fleet, in which he said "You would be surprised if you could know where I am now"; one wonders what this means? Perhaps that they are very near the coast?

[1] "Lady Godiva": *Cordelia notes in her "Reminiscences" that her father had once met the lady there who called herself both "Lady Godiva" and "the Queen of France". Another gentleman, who apparently "seemed normal" was questioned about Queen Victoria. "Ah yes, you mean my mother," he replied.*

Dec. 4th. We went to Whitley Abbey[1] to-day to see the Belgian refugees – peasants – there. They seemed mostly happy and contented, though our Belgian family at Stoneleigh village were not contented and returned to Whitley. We saw a mother with her baby who had had to get out of bed and fly when the child was only a fortnight old; the baby had been very ill but was recovering.

[1] Whitley Abbey: *use of Whitley Abbey for Belgian refugees was offered by Colonel Oswald Turville-Petre. The Abbey, on the outskirts of Coventry, had lain empty since 1910. It was quickly adapted for use by refugees and about 120 had been admitted there by the end of October 1914.*

7th. We paid a visit to Mr. Phillips' Private Hospital for wounded soldiers, at Coventry.[1] Mr. and Mrs. Phillips have given up part of their large house, and take in 10 wounded privates, with a Nurse. They have strict military rules, which they find necessary, as otherwise there would be endless trouble; the soldiers must keep strictly to their time table, are not allowed out at night, must not smoke in their bedrooms, etc.. There are 10 there now, but we only saw one, as the others had gone, with the Nurse, to see a picture palace. The soldier we saw had had a finger shot off at Ypres. He did not speak as if the German private soldiers were specially brave as a whole; he said they can only be induced to charge if they were drunk, and will not advance except in closed up companies; if any get separated from their company and are fired upon they run away "squealing." They get easily excited, whereas our men keep their heads. He said he had seen many cruelties, but was not allowed to talk about them.

[1] Mr Phillips' Private Hospital: *Walter Phillips, one of Coventry's leading industrialists, had a wing of The Grange, his house in Davenport Road, Earlsdon, converted into a nursing home for wounded soldiers. One of the largest private houses in Coventry, it was demolished in the 1930s.*

16th. Had an interesting talk with old Steed and his wife in the village. They remember the Crimea, and how dear all food was at that time, and that the misery in the country was increased by a very severe winter, and deep snow, and that the sheep had sometimes to be dug out of the snow, also a very wet summer that caused the crops to rot in the ground. Mrs. Steed said that she and her family (father, mother, grandmother) were sitting at dinner one Sunday, and their dinner consisted of "tea kettle broth"; her mother had put a crust of bread in the kettle to improve the taste; when the then Dowager Lady Leigh (my Father's Mother) came in and asked what they were having, and, on hearing, went home at once and "sent the coachman down with a hamper – sugar, tea, butter, meat – and oh, Miss, we did have a feed!" We may indeed be thankful that in this War there is plenty of food; and the troops at the Front are reported to have an excellent commissariat.

D. has started for France to-day to help with the St. John's Ambulance. He is wearing a khaki uniform with St. J. Amb. Buttons, and a khaki cap. He takes the small "Ford" motor and Millar, the Chauffeur. He crosses to Boulogne this afternoon, and expects to go on soon to Amiens. He gets his instructions from Lord Norreys.

24th. A strange Christmas.

A nice looking Belgian family, carpenter and wife and 3 little boys, have arrived in the village from the Alexandra Park Refuge[1]; they came over from Holland 4 days ago. I went to Coventry Station to meet them, though they failed to arrive by the expected train, and found a great many soldiers travelling about, having a few days holiday; but to-day there is news that some troops are being hurried to the East coast, as another raid is expected to-morrow: so probably some holidays are being curtailed.

Dudley has come back, as he found his motor, not being an ambulance motor, is not wanted; but he may get one converted into an ambulance.

[1] Alexandra Park Refuge: *Alexandra Palace, in Alexandra Park, a former roller skating rink, was the largest of the clearing houses in London to which Belgian refugees were sent before being moved to more permanent accommodation.*

28th. Colonel Smith* has been exploring the Deer Park today. He is with Horse Artillery at Leamington, lately come from India, and has asked D's leave to practise them in the Park, as they have to practise for a time, and also get acclimatized, before going to the Front.[1]

We have heard a good deal during the last few days about Christmas leave being in many cases suddenly cancelled, and large quantities of troops being assembled on the East Coast, prepared for a raid, but it is difficult to learn the truth.

Our Belgian cannot get work as a carpenter, but I hope he will be employed usefully in the garden here. I took him in the pony cart to Leamington to-day to get him a great coat, and stockings for the little boys. I found him with Mr Wells, the Schoolmaster, consulting over papers which had to be filled in for the English Police[2]; he carries about a book with the names, ages, etc., of himself and his family, and his photograph attached.

* Col. Smith was killed at the Dardanelles, alas! June 1915.[3]

[1] Colonel Smith etc: *in the early months of 1915, the 29th Division was billeted in Warwickshire and north Oxfordshire, prior to being sent to a theatre of war. Most of its units were from the regular army and had been serving overseas in India, Burma etc. After returning from India in November 1915, the 17th Brigade of the Royal Field Artillery (rather than Horse Artillery) was initially put under canvas at Winchester, before being moved into billets at Leamington in December. In late March 1915, the 29th Division sailed for the Mediterranean and was involved in the landings on the Gallipoli peninsula on 25th April and the campaign that followed.*

[2] papers which had to be filled in for the English Police: *following an Order in Council, 28th November 1914, all Belgian refugees were required to register with the authorities. This was partly intended to trace Germans and other 'undesirables' who might have come into the country under the guise of refugees. Those hosting refugees had a responsibility to see that the registration process was enforced.*

[3] Col. Smith was killed at the Dardanelles: *Colonel Edmund Percival Smith was killed on the night 1st-2nd May, 1915, during a Turkish attack on British positions at Gallipoli. (The Gallipoli peninsula flanks the northern side of the Dardanelles Straits.) Colonel Smith is buried at Redoubt Cemetery at Cape Helles, Gallipoli.*

29th. Dudley has decided to be inoculated against typhoid, before going out again, and Millar the Chauffeur also.

June 25th, 1915. THE COVENTRY GRAPHIC. 9

Local Rolls of Honour (No. 10).—Stoneleigh and District.

The Call to Arms has been responded to in gratifying style in Stoneleigh, which, though only a small village, has sent a considerable number of men to the Colours. The above photographs show a number of men of Stoneleigh and district who joined the Forces, their names being as follow:—1, H. King, Oxford and Bucks L.I.; 2, J. T. Walden, Coldstream Guards; 3, A. Morris, Royal Garrison Artillery; 4, C. King, Oxford and Bucks L.I.; 5, E. Aris, Royal Navy; 6, J. Prime, Coldstream Guards; 7, A. J. Walden, Royal Fusiliers (killed at Dardanelles); 8, F. Smith, Oxford and Bucks L.I.; 9, W. Morris, Oxford and Bucks L.I.; 10, T. Wooding, Oxford and Bucks L.I.; 11, Pte. King; 12, J. Craddock, Oxford and Bucks L.I.; 13, R. Worrall, Oxford and Bucks L.I.; 14, T. Mills, 2nd Hampshires; 15, Sergt. J. Thorley, Warwickshire Yeomanry; 16, Corpl. A. King, Warwickshire Yeomanry; 17, E. Corley, Warwickshire Yeomanry; 18, B. Worrall; 19, G. Thorley, Oxford and Bucks L.I.; 20, E. Mason, Royal Warwicks; 21, W. Oldham, King's Royal Rifles; 22, G. H. Fardon, R.M.A.; 23, Sergt. A. Morris, Oxford and Bucks L.I.; 24, A. Worrall, Royal Warwicks; 25, S. Vickerman, Royal Navy; 26, J. Hewitt, Shropshire Regiment; 27, J. Scriven, R.F.A.; 28, A. J. Hubbard, Warwickshire Yeomanry; 29, Sergt. E. Steeley, Royal Warwicks; 30, Dr. H. Steeley, R.H.A.

Roll of Honour for Stoneleigh and District, Coventry Graphic 25th June 1915.

Chapter 3: 1915

Introduction

Cordelia's interest in her 'old boys' from Stoneleigh remained a major theme in her diary for the year. With her encouragement, local men continued to enlist, some under Lord Derby's Scheme, which was introduced in October. By December, Cordelia was proudly recording that every available man from Stoneleigh and Ashow had 'attested' (stated his willingness to serve). In the same month she was sent a recruiting badge as a memento of her work. Unofficially, she harangued the management of a department store for employing too many men. The local men who had enlisted at the beginning of the war were completing their training during 1915 and beginning to make their way to the front. Inevitably, some became casualties and the first deaths among village men occurred during the year. A member of Cordelia's extended family was another loss suffered, along with a family friend.

The family continued to help the war effort in whatever way they could. The Deer Park was used by troops training in the area, help continued to be given to Belgian refugees and wounded soldiers were visited, or were entertained at the Abbey. Rupert Leigh took a job in the Censor's Office and Rowland Leigh helped produce crutches. Cordelia collected sunshields that had been made locally and loaned a telescope to the National Service League. However, her pre-war commitments continued, for example to the Sunday School movement, to the Saltley Boys' Reformatory and to the Temperance cause.

It was a year in which government intervention in the lives of British citizens was increasingly apparent. Soldiers were billeted in the village, and lighting restrictions were introduced, along with the National Registration Form. During a visit to the Daimler works, Cordelia witnessed some of the transformation taking place in local industry. On her travels to different parts of the country, she was aware of other changes – whether it was the large numbers of men in uniform in London, or increasingly crowded trains, or a woman driving a hay cutting machine. Zeppelin raids were beginning to bring the war closer, at least to those who lived in London.

1915 Diary Entries

3rd. Jan. 1915. Sunday. Kept as a Day of National Intercession throughout the Empire, in France, and as far as possible in Belgium, and in some parts of America, by Anglicans, Roman Catholics, Nonconformists, and Jews. Unfortunately it poured with rain here all day, but our services were well attended nevertheless. At Stoneleigh there were celebrations of Holy Communion at 7.30 and 9.30 a.m. Intercessions at the usual 11 o'clock Service, special Service for Children at 3, another Intercession Service at 5.30, and Lantern Service, chiefly intended for men, at 7 p.m. I believe Mr. Cooke visited every house in his Parish and left notices, and papers saying that the King had asked everyone to join him in prayer. The Bishop of Worcester drew up an excellent "pastoral letter" which was read throughout this Diocese on the previous Sunday.

Three more (married) men from the Kennels Cottages have enlisted – John Garratt, Craddock and Parker. This brings the number of our Recruits up to 50.

Jan. 11th. Col. Smith brought some of his Field Artillery for practice in the Deer Park; they had no real ammunition, but practised directing their cannon on a mark – a certain tree on the top of a ridge; they practised near the large gate leading from the Stare Bridge road into the Park. An officer from Head Quarters came to inspect while we were there. Rupert's little boy, "Robin", aged 6, was an interested observer, and attached himself to Col. Smith with whom he has made great friends!

15th. Dudley has gone off again to-day, to Furnes in Belgium, to help the Belgian Red Cross.

Coming by train from Birmingham to Leamington this evening, I found that we were asked to draw the blinds after the lamps were lit in the railway carriage, and the middle windows which had no blinds were blacked over; this as a precaution against bombs.

Soldiers' wives and children are being given many entertainments; I was at an entertainment at the Bishop's Palace at Hereford yesterday, where Uncle Jimmy[1] (Dean of Hereford) presided in the Bishop's absence; there were songs, recitations, fiddle etc.

Margaret Jersey writes from Cannes:-

> "The journey across France is avowedly slower than usual, as the line to Paris was damaged near Amiens, therefore trains wander round Tréport and Beauvais, and one must sleep in Paris, as they get there too late to catch those to the South, but they were perfectly comfortable with dinner in a Restaurant Car.
>
> From Paris here we had the best sleeping compartments which we ever enjoyed – hot coffee and rolls at Avignon, and at Marseilles a Restaurant Car was attached with an excellent luncheon – while we drew up at the Cannes platform at 4.20 p.m., the scheduled time being 4.19. The train left Paris at 8.5 the evening before, not so fast as the special through trains of the usual Seasons, but, of course, with comparatively few passengers they stop at many of the smaller stations. I can now almost understand Mabel's story of her American ladies who travelled for a fortnight in France after War was declared without finding it out. Boulogne is full of Tommies, ambulances, etc. but once away from it France did not strike me as nearly as warlike as the Southern parts of England. There were occasional Red X people on platforms and we saw one or two Hospital trains, but not such swarms of soldiers as one runs across in many English places – fewer in Paris than London – and Paris not nearly so much darkened. Of course we were outside the military zone – it would be

very different if one went to North East France or Alsace, but it was curious to find a large part of an invaded country perfectly tranquil. We saw at the Invalides 8 flags captured from the Germans, naturally the centre of an admiring crowd.

Here all is quiet and provisions etc. plentiful and good. Many of the chief Hotels have been turned into Military Hospitals, and the soldiers are said to recover wonderfully quickly in this climate. We found the Paris-Lyon-Palace Hotel very comfortable – of course waiters are not plentiful, and much of the waiting fell on a funny under-sized but active Egyptian Jew, rejoicing in the name of Isaac."

[1] Uncle Jimmy: *the Reverend James Wentworth Leigh was Cordelia's uncle, being the youngest brother of William Henry, Lord Leigh. He was Vicar of Stoneleigh between 1864-73, later becoming Vicar of Leamington and Dean of Hereford. He married Frances Butler, the daughter of Frances Kemble the actress, and after the Civil War, they worked the rice plantations at her father's property in Savannah, Georgia, USA.*

17th. Rupert's little boy, "Robin", aged 6 and three-quarters, was walking with me through "Echell's Wood" today, and said "Aunt Cords, I shall always remember that seat; Mother sat on that seat with me that Sunday evening when the War began, and told me about it: and she drew a map for me in the ground with her parasol, and explained to me all about it."

19th. At a Meeting about Sunday School business at Canon Baillie's, at Coventry, one clergyman came in dressed in khaki.

Capt. Kay took me around the soldiers' ward at Coventry Hospital; there are 3 Belgians among them. I saw some X Ray photographs of a soldier's arm, taken in order to locate the bullet.

An advertisement I saw to-day at Kenilworth is worthy to be recorded in this work!

Délivré à titre permanent

COMMANDEMENT DE L'ARMÉE BELGE IIIe Section.

ÉTAT-MAJOR

LAISSEZ PASSER Monsieur le Lord Leigh attaché comme chauffeur au British Field Hospital. valable jusqu'à Dunkerque

GRAND QUARTIER GÉNÉRAL à Houthem, le 14 février 1915.

Pour le Sous-Chef d'État-Major Général,

Le Commandant du Grand Quartier Général,

Lord Leigh's pass, February 1915, enabling him to work as a driver in Belgium. See Diary entries for February 1915.

A very small tailor's shop had a large advert. in the window – "Business as usual during alterations in the Map of Europe."

There are persistent rumours that the King and Lord Kitchener are coming to Leamington next week to review the troops and visit the Hospital; and it is added that they will stay at Stoneleigh Abbey, but of this we know nothing!

22nd D. has arrived at Furnes.

27th. It was very interesting to-day to see the trenches which the soldiers from Leamington had dug in the Deer Park, by way of practice. They dug them a little way below the Deer Keeper's (Wooding's) Lodge. They dug them last night, and waited till about 11 this morning so that we might see. They came upon water in several places so that some trenches had water at the bottom. The guns were covered over with bracken and branches of larch to conceal them from the imaginary airships overhead. They dug about 8 small trenches. School children from Stoneleigh and Ashow were brought over by their teachers to see the sight.

Leamington is now following the example of larger towns and is very dark at night.

We have a second family of Belgians in the village, three women and a baby of 2.

Feb. 4th. Postal Orders are no longer to be used as current coin, and poundage is to be paid for them to-day.[1]

A very great number of horses and some mules are camped out in a very muddy field near Northumberland Avenue in Leamington.

[1] poundage is to be paid: *the overturning of the decision made at the start of the War when postal orders had been made legal tender. 'Poundage' was the charge imposed on the sale of postal orders.*

9th. D. writes very cheerfully from Furnes; the Belgian Field Hospital is well managed, and comfortable; the building is a Boys' School in peace time. He works a good deal with Sir Bartle Frere.

Mrs. Thruston has kindly visited a soldier in a Brighton Hospital who was formerly a Stoneleigh boy – Thomas Hewitt by name. He was 5 years in India, then went to the Front, and was sent back to England with frost bitten feet. Mrs. Thruston says that he talks quite quietly and naturally of going back to the Front as soon as he is well again, as an obvious duty!

The weather is very damp and there is a great deal of rain. The soldiers in England are suffering like everyone else from colds and influenza.

16th. Saw George Fardon to-day, who has enlisted, and is home for a few days suffering from bronchitis and laryngitis. Another of my old boys, Reggie Worrall, is now instructing 20 men in signalling!

22nd. Going to Fonthill[1] to-day by way of Basingstoke, found the trains full of soldiers – I think many of them going on, or returning from, a few days leave. At Banbury some Red X women were serving out coffee and bread and jam free to the soldiers on the platform.

[1] Going to Fonthill: *Fonthill in Wiltshire was where Cordelia's Aunt Octavia and her husband, Sir Michael Shaw Stewart, lived. Built by Cordelia's maternal grandfather, Lord Westminster, in the shadow of William Beckford's ruined abbey, it was considered a warmer alternative location to the Shaw Stewarts' other residence at Ardgowan in Renfrewshire. Cordelia was a frequent visitor.*

23rd. Saw my Cousin Walter Shaw Stewart's boy Niel, 20 years old, home for 10 days' leave, and anxious to hunt. He had been a long time in the trenches; said they were very glad of warm clothes sent out to them, and chocolate, gingerbread, etc. Another day at Fonthill saw my Cousin Archie Shaw Stewart, who had been 4 months helping to guard part of the Railway line near Salisbury; he and other officers had to walk along a beat of 10 miles, once or twice a day, and once at night, to see the men were doing their duty. He said that the Canadians were a good deal of trouble, especially the officers, who had no idea of discipline, and did not understand not being allowed to walk on the line just where they pleased. Archie's kit, uniform, sword, etc., had cost altogether £70, of which the Government paid £50.

1st March. My little Godson Aris is now in the "Queen Elizabeth", which I am proud to see has taken a leading part in the bombardment of the Dardanelles![1]

Emily Ward came over from Ireland last week, and her Irish boat was escorted by 2 destroyers.

[1] the "Queen Elizabeth": *commissioned in December 1914, the battleship Queen Elizabeth was the most powerful in the British fleet. She was sent to the Dardanelles to reinforce the British naval presence and to finish her 'working up'. Her importance was such that she was only sparingly used in the campaign.*

4th. Staying with Mrs. Twistleton near Box[1], I saw a sentry standing on the high road, guarding Box Tunnel, with a little sentry box and a warm stove.

This evening I was having tea with Alice Skipwith when her Parlourmaid came in saying "A constable has called, ma'am, to know how many soldiers you can put up." I helped her to interview the constable, who was standing ready with pencil and paper! She offered a room for two soldiers – privates – who, I hear now, (5th) arrived at the home this afternoon. 3/- a head is given for their food daily.

[1] Mrs Twisleton near Box: *the Leigh and Twisleton families were connected through various marriages; Cordelia's great-grandmother, Julia Judith Twisleton, was the daughter of the 7th Baron Saye and Sele.*

7th. Stoneleigh School door has a chalk mark on it![1] Notes have been taken of all the houses in the village, including the School and Reading Room, where soldiers could be billeted if required.

[1] a chalk mark on it: *to show that it would be used for billeting.*

April 3rd. Easter Eve. I have been in London since last Monday, staying here for Holy Week and Easter. London strikes me as altogether more warlike than last time I was here, some months ago. One sees soldiers marching through the streets, and drilling, signalling etc. in the Parks; one morning I saw a fine body of Scotch soldiers marching along with bagpipes. There are advertisements and notices everywhere urging men to join the Army – outside taxi cabs, large shops etc., and there are enormous placards put up supported by the lions in Trafalgar Square, where a recruiting band plays. Officers in khaki are to be seen everywhere, as well as men. About 7 p.m. one sees the search lights thrown out from the top of Hyde Park Corner Gate, searching for enemy aeroplanes, and looking like the tail of some huge comet. The streets and Park are very dark at night.

Aunt Katie (Lady Chandos) Leigh showed me an interesting diary kept by Eddie Leigh, who was at Neuve Chapelle.[1] There are rumours that there were muddles there, and that Lord Kitchener is very angry that so much ammunition was spent at N. Chapelle – more than we consumed in the whole of the S. African War – necessitating the sending out of some of the ammunition and big guns which had been reserved for the New Army; but one can never know the truth of any rumour; I suppose all will be revealed after the War! Aunt Katie sends out all kinds of provisions to Eddie from Fortnum and Mason in Piccadilly; I took Evelyn Codrington there who wanted to send luxuries to a nephew, at the Front, and we found various arrangements, such as Dutch Cheeses, preserved fruits, kippers, potted pheasants, etc., which they make a business of packing and sending out.

At the Holy Week Services which I attended I have heard addresses from "Father Bull", who has lately been with the troops, looking after wounded and dying soldiers. He spoke strongly of the sense of religion latent in almost all the soldiers' hearts, brought out by the horrors of the War, and also told of a great deal of quiet, unassuming self-sacrifice.

The Bishop of London is holding services out at the Front this week.

[1] Neuve Chapelle: *a British offensive on the Western Front, 10th- 13th March, 1915.*

Easter Day. At magnificent Services at St. Paul's, Knightsbridge, some prayers from the Litany were read from the pulpit after the Sermon, for the Allied Forces, prisoners, bereaved, wounded, etc., and for peace. In the evening 4 soldiers in khaki carried the Church Banners in a procession while "Onward Christian Soldiers" was sung.

Dudley telephoned from Dunkirk (France) to the housemaid at 31, Grosvenor Square[1], to say that he expected to cross on Monday night and arrive in London on Tuesday.

[1] Grosvenor Square: *was the London residence of Francis Dudley, Lord Leigh. His second wife, Marie Campbell, continued to live there during the Second World War, despite its being badly damaged during the Blitz.*

6th. D. arrived at Stoneleigh again this evening, looking very well. He says he knows no secrets, and nothing that we do not know, and can give no opinion about the probable duration of the War. He has had a most interesting time, and enjoyed the shelling of Furnes! He has kept a diary, so that future members of our family will read his adventures there, and I need not record them. He has brought back pieces of shells, tiles from a shelled house, broken glass and leads from a ruined Church at Reminghe, etc..

13th. It gave one a curious feeling to sit, peacefully in the Museum to-day, labelling and arranging the "instruments of death", and shattered glass from the Belgian wrecked Church etc., and to think of what is still going on, not so very far away. I wonder if any future inhabitants of Stoneleigh Abbey, who read this, will have a like experience, or will this be the last European War for many years to come, as some predict?

D. has said, and I have seen it noticed in the papers, that in many cases the Crucifix on the Church, or in the road, has been left standing alone with the Church and other building around it shattered and destroyed.

20th. Mrs. Charteris, Col. Charteris' Wife, who was at luncheon to-day, told me how she had been helping with the ladies who distribute coffee, soup, bread and butter and eggs to the soldiers passing through Victoria Station, who are given refreshments free. Many of the shops give butter, eggs, etc., gratis, and the ladies bring contributions with them. The hardest work is in the middle of the night and the early morning.

22nd. Rupert has obtained work in the Censor's Office in London, chiefly, I believe in reading and censoring letters from India. He is to work from 9 a.m. to 6 p.m. every day, Sundays included, and occasionally all night.

Harry King is the first of our Stoneleigh men who joined the New Army to go to the Front; he started about 10 days ago.

Wounded soldiers being entertained at Stoneleigh Abbey, May 1915. See diary entry for 8th May.

28th. I saw Tom Hewitt to-day at Stoneleigh, a nice looking youth, one of my old Bible Class boys; he was in India for some years, then went to Belgium, where he got frost bitten feet, and went into Hospital at Brighton, where he later developed slight typhoid, but is getting strong again now.[1]

I hear "little" Joseph Mills from Thickthorn Lodge has also gone into training at Portsmouth.

[1] Tom Hewitt: *see also diary entry for February 9th, 1915.*

Winifred Leigh, Channy's Widow, came for two days, and on Wednesday went with Aggy and me to Stoneleigh Church to choose a place for putting up a tablet to his memory.

She told us that her Brother said that the Prince of Wales is extremely popular with both officers and men, very anxious to share all hardships and dangers with the rest, and also very sturdy and strong though he is small.[1]

[1] The Prince of Wales is extremely popular: *Edward, Prince of Wales, joined the Grenadier Guards in 1914, although he was not allowed to go to the front. He was appointed to the headquarters staff of Sir John French, but found little to occupy him. He constantly tried to be posted to the front and share the hardships and dangers of those there.*

May 2nd. One of the little Belgians, Léon De Groote, came to my Infants' Sunday School Class. I had a letter from Harry King last week, my first from a Stoneleigh man actually in the Trenches – to acknowledge some chocolate I had sent. The letter arrived in one of the new green envelopes, on which the writer signs a declaration that it contains nothing which does not refer to family or private matters; it may be opened.

8th. We entertained about 100 wounded soldiers at tea, from Coventry, Leamington, Kenilworth, Birmingham, and one – J. Prime – from Stoneleigh! The day has been beautiful, and they were able to sit on the lawn and in front of the house, walk about, and some, sufficiently well, played croquet and lawn tennis. They had tea in the corridor, and an amateur musical society gave them a concert in the saloon. Eleven little "Church Scout Patrols" from the village had a happy day helping to wait and to make themselves generally useful! The men were extremely cheerful, though some were badly wounded, and 2 were on crutches. I was told that one had had a very bad arm from being inoculated with poison by an Austrian surgeon – he had recovered, but 29 others had died who had been poisoned in the same way. This seems on a par with the fiendish torpedoing of the "Lusitania", of which the news has come to-day.[1]

In the middle of the afternoon a telephone message came that the Matron of the Kenilworth Red X was wanted; I showed her the way to the tel. room and waited. She came out in a great hurry saying "I have got what I wanted! I am sent for to go to Malta, can I have the Kenilworth car at once? I must go back and start for London this evening." So I gave the order for her car, helped her to look for the other Ken. Sister, and in about 5 minutes I had seen her off flying to Kenilworth to make her final preparations! I suppose to nurse the wounded from the Dardanelles.

[1] the fiendish torpedoing of the "Lusitania": *the Cunard Liner Lusitania was torpedoed on 7th May, 1915, by the U.20, whilst en route from New York to Liverpool. It sank off the Irish coast at Kinsale with the loss of 1,198 lives, including 124 US citizens.*

Sunday, 9th. To-day De Groote's "Patron", a brewer from Belgium, now staying at Birmingham, came over with De Groote to see the house, rather an interesting middle-aged man, who talked a great deal in slow, incisive French. He stayed about 3 hours! And it ended by our all

WAR OFFICE,

30. June, 1915.

Sir,

I wish to express to you personally, and to those who have helped you in your recruiting work, my best thanks for the energy that has been displayed by you all in the matter of Recruiting.

I would ask you to take an early opportunity of urging all able-bodied men in your neighbourhood to come forward and enlist, so that they may be trained as soldiers to take part in the War, and help to keep our forces in the Field at the maximum strength.

I shall be glad to hear of any reasons that may be given you by young and suitable men for not availing themselves of this opportunity to see service in the Field, where they are so much wanted.

I am,

Sir,

Your obedient Servant,

The Hon: M. Cordelia Leigh.

Kitchener

Official thanks from Lord Kitchener for Cordelia's recruiting work – despite Cordelia being addressed as 'Sir'.

sitting down to tea together in D's morning room, including De Groote, the Belgian Carpenter! But War Time makes everything and anything seem to come as a matter of course.

14th. We heard of the death of Eddie Leigh[1]; he was shot through the body, and bound up by young Rodney, but death was probably instantaneous. The casualties are just now terrible, and especially among the Officers.

[1] Eddie Leigh: *Lieutenant Edward Henry (Eddie) Leigh, 2nd Bn The Rifle Brigade (The Prince Consort's Own), was the younger brother of Major Chandos Leigh. Edward was killed at Aubers Ridge on 9th May 1915 and is commemorated on the Ploegsteert Memorial to the Missing, Belgium. When the news of this, his only surviving son's death came, their father Edward Chandos died, apparently of grief.*

Chandos and Edward Leigh. The brothers were killed within a year of one another.

20th. Heard reports of the death of a Stoneleigh man, Tom Walden, son of the widow, Mrs. Walden, who keeps a small shop in the village.[1] A friend of his had written to her from Malta that he had been killed, but she had no intimation from the War Office. I telegraphed to Rupert to ask him to enquire, and he telegraphed back that he found he had been killed on April 14th while carrying documents. He was in the R. Fusiliers. I went down to tell his Mother what R. had telegraphed. Uncle Eddie's (Sir Edward Chandos Leigh) Funeral was being arranged for to-morrow while I was in the village. Poor Aunt Katie Leigh is mourning the loss of her husband and two sons at the same time.

We are waiting anxiously the news of Italy joining the War.[2]

I forgot to mention that at Malvern Station the other day I saw women collecting tickets; they wear bands with "G.W.R." on their arms.

[1] reports of the death of ... Tom Walden: *according to the Commonwealth War Graves Commission, Private Alfred Tom Walden of the 2nd Bn Royal Fusiliers was killed on 25th April 1915; he is commemorated on the Helles Memorial to the Missing, Turkey.*

[2] Italy joining the War: *on 2nd August, 1914, Italy had declared a policy of neutrality but was eventually persuaded to enter the war on the side of the Allies. Her decision was largely driven by the terms of the secret Treaty of London, which promised her large territorial gains at the expense of Austria-Hungary. Italy entered the war on 23rd May, 1915.*

28th. Another tragedy – Mr Henry Leeke, the fine, tall man who came over here in the early days of the War to ask D. to help him get a Commission – is dying of "spotted fever" (cerebral meningitis) at Aldershot. He was quickly made a Lieutenant, and had lately been put in charge of some machine guns, was very clever at gun work, and immensely popular.

An airship went over this afternoon, very high up, and making a great noise. I heard afterwards that it was from the Daimler Works at Coventry, on a trial trip.

June 1st. I was in Ashow School this morning when an airship – probably the same – went over, and all the children rushed out to see it, except one little girl who remained in her seat and cried! to the great amusement of the others.

2nd. Mr Leeke, who died last Saturday night (May 29th) was buried at Aldershot this evening, with full military honours.[1] I attended a little Memorial Service at St Mark's, Leamington.

Mills, the Painter, one of our first men to volunteer, is in Hospital at Edgbaston wounded, and suffering from the wicked poisonous gas.

D. and Aggy have been in London, to be near Margaret at Osterley, as George (Jersey) has died there – on May 31st – and will be buried at Middleton on Friday. There was a Zeppelin raid in London yesterday[2], but they did not see anything of it; but A. bought one or two respirators to be at hand in the house at Gros. Square if a bomb with poisonous gas is dropped thereabouts.

[1] Mr Leeke who died last Saturday: *Lieutenant Henry Alan Leeke, 9th Battalion Royal Warwickshire Regiment, died on 29th May, 1915, at the age of 35. He was the son of Mr and Mrs Henry Leeke, of Cliffe House, Leamington Spa, and the husband of Catherine Leeke. He is buried at Aldershot Military Cemetery* *(see P. 45).*

[2] a Zeppelin raid in London yesterday: *on the night of 31st May – 1st June, 1915, Army Zeppelin LZ.38 dropped about 90 incendiary bombs and 30 'grenades' (small high explosive bombs) on London, killing 7 people, injuring another 35 and causing more than £18,000 worth of damage. It was the first Zeppelin raid on the capital.*

21st. Tom Mills is in France, and Ernest Thorley and Stephens (the chauffeur) are either crossing or just going to cross; probably on the way to the Dardanelles.

A week ago D. and I attended the Annual Meeting of Saltley Boys' Reformatory[1], and the excellent boys' band had been used for recruiting purposes at Birmingham, and to play troops to the Station.

This afternoon Mr Reid Cuddon gave a tea-party to some wounded soldiers at Ashow Rectory; they came from the Warneford Hospital at Leamington and the Red Cross Hospital fitted up at the Parish Hall at Kenilworth. The Band from the Boys' Reformatory at Weston played in the field. I looked after one tea table in a small room where 8 soldiers assembled, and D. helped Mr. R. Cuddon in a larger room. My party were very cheerful, but those from the Warneford were inclined to complain of the restrictions at the Hospital, especially of being sent to bed at 8 p.m. in midsummer! One very nice young soldier whom I talked to a good deal, who had been wounded at Ypres, told me what a comfort hot baths had been which were provided for the men when they got a few days' rest from the Trenches; he thought the baths and good food made them "able to stick it", which they could not have done otherwise. He described how sometimes they would find a half burnt farm house, deserted by the owners, and sometimes they would find stores of apples, potatoes, etc., which came in very useful. In one farm house he had found a small dog which he tried to take away and make a pet of, but it escaped.

[1] Saltley Boys' Reformatory: *Saltley Reformatory School for Boys had been established in 1852, by John Ellis and Joseph Sturge, and moved to Saltley, in Smallheath, Birmingham, in 1853. It was renamed Norton Boys' Home in 1908, although continuing to be known by the Leighs by its former name.*

22nd. D. and A. are taking Italian lessons from a Greek R.C. Priest who is living at Leamington; he was with a Belgian Refugee family. They want to know Italian, as they both hope to get out to Italy later with a motor ambulance which D. has bought.

I hear that Reggie Worrall, the under-gardener's son, has become so proficient in signalling that he is teaching his officers!

25th. D. and I went to a luncheon given by Capt. and Mrs. Hoffgard at the Woolpack Hotel, Warwick, to some of the Yeomanry Officers who expected to leave Warwick the next day. Col. Beech and Arden Adderley[1] were there, and a Gen. Thornley (?) who was staying at Leamington, partly for recruiting purposes. After luncheon the men paraded in the Market Place, and marched to Leamington to try to get in more recruits.

[1] Arden Adderley: *Henry Arden Adderley was Cordelia's cousin, the second son of her Aunt Julia Leigh and Charles Bowyer Adderley, 1st Baron Norton, of Hams Hall, near Coleshill in North Warwickshire.*

July 9th. Staying for a night at Malvern I had to sign a paper at my Hotel giving my surname, Christian name, and nationality. Foreigners have to give their birthplace, year of birth, home address, etc.

I noticed a young woman driving a hay cutting machine one of these days in a hayfield near the Crewe Farm.

Rowland is making crutches for the wounded.

18th. Tom Mills has been invalided home, and is in a Hospital at Leicester, quite deaf.

Harry and Charlie King are at the Front. I was amused by a remark of Mrs. Worrall, in the village – "That old Kayser must be laughing in his sleeve when he finds it takes the whole world to beat him!"

24th. Alex Parker and Johnnie Arkwright came to luncheon (with their Wives) to consult D. about lending the Riding School for putting up some of the horses.

I forgot to mention that I collected about 400 sunshields early in the summer, made by different people, maids here, reformatory girls, etc., to send to the Victoria League[1] which collected them for the soldiers at the Front.

[1] the Victoria League: *The Victoria League was established in 1901 to promote a closer union between different parts of the British Empire and to foster hospitality, understanding and good fellowship – a "Society of Friendship". Although membership was open to both men and women, the first Committee was composed entirely of women. In the First World War the League organised beds and meals for servicemen on leave, food parcels for the families of servicemen and the collection of other goods for soldiers at the Front.*

Aug. 1st. John Walton, Reggie Worrall, Albert Worrall, and George Rose are at the Front now. The other day D. and I paid an interesting visit to the Hospital at Clopton[1]; Mr. Hodgson (Rev.

Patrons:
His Majesty the King.
Her Majesty the Queen.
Vice-Patrons:
H.R.H. The Duke of Connaught, K.G., K.T., K.P., etc.
H.R.H. Princess Christian of Schleswig-Holstein.
H.R.H. Princess Louise, Duchess of Argyll.

PRESIDENT, THE COUNTESS OF JERSEY.
DEPUTY PRESIDENT, THE MARCHIONESS OF CREWE, C.I.

HON. VICE-PRESIDENTS.

HIS GRACE THE ARCHBISHOP OF CANTERBURY.
THE RT. HON. H. H. ASQUITH, M.P.
THE DUKE OF NORFOLK, K.G., P.C., G.C.V.O.
THE EARL OF CROMER, P.C., G.C.B., O.M.
THE EARL CURZON OF KEDLESTON, P.C., G.C.S.I., G.C.I.E.
THE VISCOUNT MILNER, P.C., G.C.B., G.C.M.G.
THE VISCOUNT GLADSTONE, P.C., G.C.M.G.
THE LORD TENNYSON, P.C., G.C.M.G.
THE RT. HON. A. J. BALFOUR, M.P.
THE RT. HON THE LORD MAYOR.
THE RT. HON. A. BONAR LAW, M.P.
THE RT. HON. SIR GEORGE REID, G.C.M.G.
THE HON. THOMAS MACKENZIE
PROFESSOR M. E. SADLER, LL.D. C.B.
MR. RUDYARD KIPLING, LL.D.
MR. SIDNEY WEBB, LL.B.
THE RT. REV. THE MODERATOR OF THE CHURCH OF SCOTLAND
THE REV. THE MODERATOR OF THE UNITED FREE CHURCH OF SCOTLAND.
THE REV. THE PRESIDENT OF THE FREE CHURCH COUNCIL.
THE HEAD-MASTERS OF ETON, HARROW, AND WESTMINSTER.

HON. TREASURER, MRS. MAURICE MACMILLAN.
SECRETARY, MISS TALBOT

Victoria League.

Millbank House,
(Near the Houses of Parliament).

2, Wood Street,

Westminster, ________ 191__
S.W.

TELEPHONE: VICTORIA, 1541. TELEGRAMS { "VICTRIX, VIC, LONDON." (INLAND) "VICTRIX, LONDON." (FROM ABROAD)

OFFICE HOURS: 10 TO 5.30. SATURDAYS 10 TO 1.

TO VICTORIA LEAGUE MEMBERS.

We have received an urgent request for SUN-SHIELDS for men of the Artillery and Transport Services of the 11th Division, First Army. Can you help us to supply 1,000 within the next week?

I enclose a pattern of the shape. An elastic, 20 inches in length and ¼ inch wide (brown) should be run through a hem at the top and knotted, to go round the men's caps.

The SUN-SHIELD should be hemmed or machine stitched all round.

Any material will do, provided it is thick enough to keep off the sun and not too heavy. Light woollen stuff, or drill, are suitable. The colour must be khaki, though the exact shade does not matter.

MERIEL L. TALBOT,

Secretary.

Address:- Victoria League
Millbank House
2 Wood St

May 21st. 1915.

Instructions for making sun-shields, which were among the goods people produced at home to help the war effort. See Diary entry for 24th July.

Frank) and Mrs. Hodgson have kindly given up most of their house to be a Hospital for the wounded; they have just kept his study, one or two bedrooms, one end of the dining-room, and a corner of the garden, for themselves. They even pay for their own food in their own house, as they share the food provided for the soldiers and the staff which is partly paid for by subscription. Mrs. Hodgson was dressed in a red nurse's uniform with a red Cross. The wards are beautiful, airy, long kind of huts covered with asbestos.

[1] the Hospital at Clopton: *Clopton House near Stratford-upon-Avon was converted into a Voluntary Aid Detachment Hospital in 1914, replacing the Town Hall, which had initially been used as a wartime hospital.*

6th. I had a rather curious experience, as I was one of the organisers of a Sunday School "Summer School" held at Malvern this week, and this was the closing day. In the afternoon I went to a School building where some of the students were lodged, and Miss Flint, the Head of the School, said she had had all the resident students there registered according to the form prescribed for registering all inmates of Hotels or boarding houses; if British, they only had to give their names and nationality; but she asked me if I had remembered to have the students registered at another School building which we had also taken for the week. I had immediately to see about it, and ensure that the 30 students at "Mowbray" were registered before they left Malvern the following morning, as otherwise the Sun. School Association might have been liable to a fine of £100!

12th. I have just filled up the National Registration Form[1]; Morris of the Co-operative Stores has been distributing the Forms in Stoneleigh Parish. I have to fill in the name, age, address, and occupation, which I have entered as "Voluntary Educational Work", and have written "Clerical Work" as the other work I am skilled in.

One of the London boys who is here with the Country Holiday Fund children, Meginness by name, has 7 brothers at the Front, and his Father is serving in the New Army at home.

[1.] the National Registration Form: *The National Registration Act, July 1915, required a register of every adult in the country between the ages of 15 and 65. On Registration Day, 15th August, 1915, everyone within the specified age group had to have completed a form giving their name, age, nationality, marital status and employment details. The Register was intended to assist in the efficient deployment of labour. Information on males between 19 and 41 was copied onto pink forms and men in essential industries were 'starred' for exemption from military service. Those not starred could be visited by recruiting officers to enquire about reasons why they had not joined up.*

21st. Markey is getting into a house in Montagu Square, and is occupied with the furnishing; she has allotted a special room in it to Arthur Villiers[1], and sent out patterns of the wall paper to him at the Front to choose from!

Ernest Thorley, a Stoneleigh man in the 9th Batt. R. Warwicks, is suffering from a fracture at the base of the skull, but we have not heard particulars.

[1.] Arthur Villiers: *Major the Hon. Arthur Child-Villiers was the youngest son of Margaret Jersey.*

Sept. 1st. I am staying a few days at Tunbridge Wells with Alice Skipwith. It is the Headquarters of the Central Division of the 2nd New Army, and numbers of soldiers drill on the different commons, while the children are happy digging mimic trenches in the sand which abounds here! We are requested to let down the blinds in our rooms when the electric light is turned on; one evening Alice was knocked up and had a message from the Policeman that her light was showing as one corner of her blind had got twisted up.

3rd. Ernest Thorley has died in the Hospital at Cairo.[1]

[1] Ernest Thorley has died: *Lance Corporal Samuel Ernest Thorley, 9th Bn Royal Warwickshire Regiment, died of wounds on 25th August 1915 and is buried at the Cairo War Memorial Cemetery.*

9th. I went to London to-day for 2 nights. Last night there was a raid of one – or some say – 3 Zeppelins over London[1]; D. missed seeing the actual Zeppelin which I hear was a beautiful sight, like a shining silver cylinder floating along and burning with a red light, but he afterwards saw 4 different fires caused by the raid.

[1] Zeppelins over London: *on the night of 8th-9th September, 1915, three Navy Zeppelins were sent to bomb London. The L.13 was the only one to reach its target, dropping most of its bombs between Euston and*

Liverpool Street; these included a 660lb bomb, which was dropped near St Bartholomew's Hospital, the first bomb of that size to be dropped. The raid killed 26 people, injured another 94 and caused over £500,000 worth of damage.

10th. We thought that there was likely to be more last night, but last night was quiet. D. and I took a taxi all about the City this morning, to see the ravages – broken windows and remains of fires, etc., chiefly in Wood Street, Little Britain, near St Paul's, etc.. The National Penny Bank seemed completely demolished. In several places there were barricades across the streets, guarded by Policemen. I hear the firing of our guns was very loud.

I have been seeing Mary Longford at her house in Bryanston Square, very anxious about Longford; the War Office heard that he was wounded at the Dardanelles on Aug. 21st, but curiously enough she can get no further particulars, though various rumours keep coming in – some that he is severely wounded, some that he is dead, others that he is only slightly hurt.[1]

[1] I have been seeing Mary Longford etc: *Mary Longford (née Child-Villiers) was Cordelia's cousin, being the daughter of her aunt Margarette Elizabeth, Countess of Jersey. She married Thomas Pakenham, 5th Earl of Longford, who was killed on August 21st 1915 at Gallipoli. During the First World War Lord Longford commanded the 2nd (South Midland) Brigade of the British 2nd Mounted Division with the rank of Brigadier-General. The Division was initially based in Egypt but was sent dismounted to Suvla on the Gallipoli peninsula as reinforcements during the Battle of Sari Bair. On 21 August 1915 the Division was in reserve for the final attack on Scimitar Hill. When the initial attack by the 29th Division failed, the Yeomanry were ordered to advance in the open across a dry salt lake. Raked by shrapnel fire, most of the Brigade halted in the shelter of Green Hill but Longford led his men in a charge which captured the summit of the hill. As he continued to advance, he was killed. His last words before his death were, reputedly "Don't bother ducking, the men don't like it and it doesn't do any good...." Longford's body was never recovered. His grave is marked as a special memorial in Green Hill Cemetery at Suvla.*

22nd. Some veterans, chiefly of the Indian Mutiny but some Crimean, came over to tea, some dressed in the old uniforms, and were much delighted to meet Sir George Higginson, one of the heroes of Balaclava[1], who was staying with us. Audrey Liddell and I played Patriotic Songs and the National Anthems of the Allies to them, she on her violin and I accompanying on my little American Organ which we put out on the lawn.

[1] Sir George Higginson, one of the heroes of Balaclava: *General Sir George Higginson (1826-1927), a grand old man of the British army, was commissioned into the Grenadier Guards in 1845, and fought throughout the Crimean War. He participated in the battles of Alma, Balaclava and Inkerman, where his horse was killed from under him. He was also present at the siege and fall of Sebastopol and spent time in the United States during the American Civil War. His autobiography in 1916 was entitled "71 Years of a Guardsman's Life". A close personal friend of the Royal Family, he was associated for many years with the Gordon Boys' Home, now Gordon's School, at West End near Woking, Surrey, which was founded as the national memorial to General Charles Gordon, who was killed at Khartoum, Sudan, in 1885.*

23rd. Our party, including Aunt Sophie Leveson Gower, Audrey Liddell, Sir George Higginson, Mrs. Mackenzie, Annie Adderley, D., Aggy, self and Alice Skipwith, who came over from Leamington, were allowed to see a famous Airman, Mr. Dunn, take a short flight from the field near the Daimler Works at Coventry. The Airman was over from France for a short rest, and expected to be flying soon over Macedonia and perhaps Jerusalem! It was a very pretty sight to see him slowly ascend, fly gracefully away, and then come slowly down again to the exact spot whence he had started. We saw some wonderful huge motors at the Works made for carrying big guns, but as we were such a large party we were not allowed to linger at the Works.

25th. George Overton, the footman, who had been wounded slightly at the Dardanelles, came to see us from Budbrooke Barracks[1], looking very smart. It was curious that he and most of the servants from the house, gardens and stables have been together; he said "me and the under gardener heard Stephens holler when he was wounded, and carried him out of the lines; me and the first footman saw Ernest Thorley fall!"

George Thorley has gone to the Front; he was in my Bible Class till the last Sunday before he left home.

[1] Budbrooke Barracks: *the barracks of the Royal Warwickshire Regiment, situated to the west of Warwick and opened in 1877.*

29th. At Marshall and Snelgrove's to-day I had an argument with one of the Shop Walkers, saying that there ought not to be so many men there, and that it was ridiculous in any case that men should be serving lace and frillings; he said that all the men in the shop were either over age or rejected for some good reason, but I cannot believe it.

Oct. 18th. Going to Fonthill to-day, by Reading and Basingstoke, found quantities of soldiers travelling, and all trains late. I think many had been for a few days' furlough, and there were also many recruits going to their training camps.

Yesterday Mr. Field came to see D. about a telegram he had had from Lord Craven, who is really Lord Lieutenant, though he spends a good deal of his time as King's Messenger; Lord Craven had had a telegram from the King asking him to do all he could to encourage recruiting.

I was at Hereford last week with Uncle Jemmy (the Dean)[1] who went out lately on Lord Brassey's Yacht[2]; the Brasseys went to Lemnos[3], but the Dean stopped at Malta and then went to Alexandria and helped the Chaplains in the Hospitals.

My old boy, Tom Hewitt, has been killed.[4] Also there is a report that our little Groom, James Amos, is killed. George Thorley is in Hospital at Rouen ill with enteric.

The following was written to a friend of mine:-

> "Lady Anna Maria Cust (née Needham) had a sister Lady Mabella Knox whose daughter married Count Wilhelm Von Zeppelin, one of the richest men in Europe and totally blind. She was said to be the plainest woman in Europe with the most beautiful voice in speaking any language. It was quite a love marriage, he fell in love with her voice. They had one son, Count Conrad Von Zeppelin, and one daughter now Countess Von Adelmann Von Adelmannsfelden, and it is their first Cousin who is the inventor of these Zeppelin Air Ships ... I saw one Zeppelin very clearly on Sept. 8th. R. and I arrived here (in Lennox Gardens) at 10.15 p.m. just as the raid began, and R. went out at once as a Special Constable to keep people in their houses. I saw it from our roof, I and our Cook and Housemaid got out of the Bedroom window. It was like the keel of a ship high up, going very fast, dropping what looked like fireworks, but I was told afterwards that some of those might have been bombs, but not likely, as bombs do not light up till they explode on reaching something hard. The lights we saw were bullets from our Airguns."

[1] Uncle Jemmy (the Dean): *i.e. the Rev. James Wentworth Leigh.*

[2] Lord Brassey's Yacht: *Thomas Brassey, 1st Earl Brassey (1836 – 23rd February 1918) was a British Liberal Party politician, Governor of Victoria, Australia and founder of The Naval Annual. Between 6th July 1876 and 27th May 1877 he circumnavigated the world in his steam-assisted, three-masted, topsail-yard schooner "Sunbeam". This voyage is said to have been the first circumnavigation by a private yacht.*

"The Suffragette," July 9, 1915.

Registered at the G.P.O. as a Newspaper.

The Suffragette

Edited by Christabel Pankhurst

Official Organ of the Women's Social and Political Union

No. 109 Vol. IV. FRIDAY, JULY 9, 1915 Price 1d. Weekly

WAR SERVICE PROCESSION, JULY 17

QUEEN ELIZABETH.

QUEEN ELIZABETH TO THE WOMEN OF TO-DAY:

"I saved our country once—it is for you to save it now."

An unusual and intriguing entry in Cordelia's Scrapbook; no explanation for its inclusion is given.

[3] Lemnos: *an Aegean island, some 50 km from the Gallipoli peninsula; Mudros Bay was used as a base during the Gallipoli campaign.*

[4] Tom Hewitt has been killed: *Private Tom Hewitt, 5th Bn The King's Own Shropshire Light Infantry, was killed on 25th September 1915 at Bellewaarde. Tragically, his younger brother George, of the same regiment, was killed on the same day; they are both commemorated on the Menin Gate at Ypres. Cordelia had received a letter in which the writer believed George had been taken prisoner – an illustration of the difficulty of receiving accurate information.*

Oct 30th. Janie (Mrs. Broughton) Dugdale[1] brought two nice young New Zealand soldiers, brothers, (Lieutenants) over this afternoon. They had been wounded at the Dardanelles, and came separately to Hospitals in England; each thought the other was dead, till finally one of them heard that the other was alive, and staying at Wroxall, and he telegraphed to his brother there; the Dugdales then invited him to join his brother at Wroxall. One of them said to me "It is worth while being wounded to have the joy of coming home – we all call England home." I said "It is splendid the way all of you – all the Colonies – have come to our help", and he answered quietly, and almost shyly, "It is the least we can do."

[1] *Janie (Mrs Broughton) Dugdale*: lived at Wroxall Abbey, Warwick; her husband James Broughton Dugdale was High Sherriff of Warwickshire in 1907.

Nov 15th. I am lending my telescope to the National Service League, as a letter to the "Times" said that telescopes, as well as field glasses, are useful.

William Stoney and Leonard Worrall are with the A.M. [Army Medical] Corps, near Salisbury; they enlisted about 3 weeks ago. George Clifford will enlist as soon as Mr. Wright can spare him from the Farm at Ashow. Arthur Mills[1] from the Kennels is enlisting also.

I hear that Robin had the satisfaction of saluting Gen. Joffre[2] in the street in London the other day, and of being saluted by him in return!

Old Fardon[3] is much pleased as George Fardon[4] was praised by his officer for some of his repairing work to motors, in France.

[1] Arthur Mills: *the youngest son of Arthur Mills senior, a well-respected gamekeeper for the Leighs. Mills senior was to lose two sons, Henry and William, in the Great War.*

1915

Stoneleigh School

Christmas Presents to our Soldiers
and Sailors – Stoneleigh men.

Dear Sir (or Madam).

Your help is asked in raising a fund for sending each of our Stoneleigh men a Christmas present of some kind
There is no need to plead the cause, but it is necessary to get to work at once and despatch the parcels the first week in December that they may reach our men by Xmas Day. Will you please subscribe now, and if possible attend a meeting at the Reading Room, after the Temperance meeting on Thursday, (about 8·20) to decide what form the presents shall take and to elect a Committee to send them? Remembrance of nearly fifty old school-boys at the front is my apology for taking the initiative.

Yours faithfully,
William H. Wells.

The appeal by Stoneleigh School Headmaster, William Wells, for Christmas presents for ex-Stoneleigh Schoolboys now at the Front, 1915.

[2] Gen. Joffre: *Joseph Joffre was Commander-in-Chief of the French Army from 1911 to 13th December, 1916, when he was replaced by General Robert Nivelle.*

[3] Old Fardon: *Edward Langley Fardon had worked for the famous metal-worker Francis Skidmore of Coventry who created the Albert Memorial. He came to Stoneleigh in 1873 at the invitation of Lord Leigh and produced ornamental work at the Abbey as well as providing heating systems for Stoneleigh church and the Abbey itself. Reputedly, Edward built the first iron bicycle with rubber tyres and also the first suspension wheel for it. However, he did not patent his wheel and is said to have shown it to Starley, the cycle maker in Coventry, who supposedly 'cashed in' on the design.*

[4] George Fardon: *was the son of Edward Langley Fardon. During the War, he served as a mechanic in the Royal Marines Artillery Brigade, which was equipped with 15 inch howitzers, often deployed as single units along the Western Front. George used his skills as a motor mechanic, and perhaps also his family skills as blacksmiths, to repair guns and equipment.*

The Funeral of Henry Leeke: described by Miss Skipwith

It was a beautiful day, June 2nd, 1915, when with all the simple grandeur of a Military Funeral with "Full honours" we laid to rest in Aldershot Cemetery, in "sure and certain hope of the Resurrection", the body of Lieut. Henry Alan Leeke. The funeral had been postponed till 5 p.m. as the Battalion had been engaged in Manoeuvres, and the men could not be spared earlier from their duties.

We drove 8 miles from the neighbouring village of Hawley by motor, literally wrapped up in the wreaths and Crosses. We first went up to the Hospital, where the Procession for the Cemetery was formed. We had some little time to wait. The road along which the Procession would pass was lined on each side with soldiers, with the Band of the 11th Hussars. First came soldiers marching with arms reversed, then followed the gun carriage bearing the Coffin covered with the Union Jack. Each soldier, standing with bowed head and leaning on his rifle, saluted as the Coffin passed. Then followed the mourners, who were Mr Sam Leeke (Uncle), Etta Pickard, and myself. Then followed soldiers, carrying wreaths and Crosses; then came Officers, including General de S. Caley, General of the Division[1]; but as it was impossible to look behind, I could not see the order in which they followed. We marched to the music of Chopin's Funeral March; it was most trying, but very beautiful; one experienced a kind of pride when one realized that one was following with soldiers, soon leaving for the Front, to do honour to so good a man, and so efficient an Officer.

We marched on to the gate of the Cemetery, where Gerald Skipwith joined us and followed with Etta Pickard. The Coffin was lifted on to the Bier by the men of the Machine Gun Section, Henry's special men. The Bishop of Woolwich (Uncle), the Senior Chaplain, and the Brigade Chaplain, Mr Dixon, were the Clergy present. The Bishop read the Psalm and Sentences, but we could scarcely hear the words, as the Funeral March was softly played behind us. The Cemetery, which is on the side of a hill, is very pretty; rhododendrons grow there; and there is a pleasant view to be seen; the grave is in the part specially reserved for the Military; it was lined with moss and flowers. Mr Dixon read that marvellous chapter in Corinthians splendidly, with a note of triumph in his voice. The Bishop finished the Service. After the Benediction the volley was fired, followed immediately by a few bars of exquisite soft music by the Band; this was repeated three times. Then came the ritual of fixing bayonets, followed by the "Last Post", this was also done three times, and all was over.

The Bishop thanked the General for all that had been done, and the General, much moved, said he was glad to do honour to such a good man and good officer. R. I. P.

"Remember all those, the brave and the true, who have died the death of honour and are departed in the hope of Resurrection to Eternal Life. In that place of light, whence sorrow and mourning are far banished, give them rest, O LORD, the Lover of Man."

[1] General de S. Caley: *Major General W. de S. Cayley (sic) commanded the 13th (Western) Division from July 1916 to May 1918. At the time of the funeral, he was, in fact, in command of the 39th Brigade, 13th Division.*

Dec. 2nd. After a Temperance Meeting at the village, I was waiting outside the Reading Room in the road, in fog and half darkness, when an enormous soldier suddenly came up and shook me by the hand! I had to say apologetically "It is so dark I can't quite see who it is", and he said "Morris!" so it must have been Henry Morris, one of the older sons of Morris at the Co-op. Stores. He was very full of the devastation he had seen at Ypres and elsewhere, but seemed hopeful, as he said, "we have enough munition now, though it will be slaughter before we are done."

12th. In consequence of Lord Derby's Recruiting Campaign[1] every available remaining man in the 2 villages has "attested", including Mr. Cooke, the Vicar of Stoneleigh!

[1] Lord Derby's Recruiting Campaign: *Edward Stanley, 17th Lord Derby, was appointed Director-General of Recruiting on 11th October, 1915, and immediately introduced a programme, which became known as the 'Derby Scheme', to boost recruitment. Using the National Register established in June 1915, all eligible males between 18 and 41 years were called upon either to volunteer or to "attest" – state – their willingness to serve if called upon to do so, with the promise that married men would be called up last. The results were disappointing and the scheme was abandoned in December, leaving the way open for the introduction of conscription.*

17th. I am much pleased as Capt. Kay has sent me a recruiting badge, as a memento of the recruiting here. George Rose (Junior) was given a badge, and 7 days' leave, as a reward for some good work he had done – I believe in helping to take a dug out in France from the enemy, but I not did know he was home till after he was gone again, and could not make out the story exactly from his Father, who said he was very modest and would not say much.

25th. Another Christmas and we are still at war! George Thorley was at the early Service at Stoneleigh, and his family returned thanks for his return and recovery. Later I saw him and one very small schoolboy and two or three older boys, who, I suppose, were having a Christmas holiday from munition making, playing football on the almost disused football ground near the village!

Chapter 4: 1916

Introduction

As 1916 began, so Cordelia began another volume of her diary. Her concerns had broadened in the sixteen months since she had begun to record life during war-time: not only was she considering the welfare of those at the Front, but war was beginning to impinge all too closely on home life, too. Together with the perils of Zeppelin raids, both in London and Warwickshire, there was the vexed question of food supplies: she recorded the increasing necessity for women, in men's absence, to work in a variety of capacities, and provided an insight into living on rations. Despite the Derby Scheme's introduction in 1915, encouragement of recruitment remained vital, and Cordelia's brother, Lord Leigh, became involved in a Government Recruiting Party's visit to the Front. A visit to munitions works in nearby Coventry was made; the novelty of aeroplanes and their dashing pilots noted; the provision of hospital equipment and supplies commented upon.

Although 1914 and 1915 had seen the deaths of two cousins and several young men from Stoneleigh and Ashow, Cordelia continued to record the names of many more who were joining up as they became old enough to do so; life in the villages proceeded as well as possible, with a variety of substitute clergy being necessary in the churches. During the year, the loss of Lord Kitchener on board the *Hampshire* sounded a sad note.

Cordelia's many contacts also provided news of current events outside her compass, the most startling, perhaps, being an eye-witness account of life during the Easter Rising in Ireland.

1916 Diary Entries

Jan. 31. 1916. It is sad that my War Journal extends to a second Volume!

There has been nothing special to record during the earlier part of this month. The regulations with regard to darkening lights at Coventry and Leamington and in the neighbourhood generally have been made much stricter lately, and we have put shades over some of our passage lights, and a kind of brown holland blind over the top of a large window on the middle front stairs, as we were told that some of the lights could be seen from a long distance, and might serve as guides to Zeppelins making for Coventry. Coventry itself is very dark and mysterious looking at night.

Our electrician Fish, Fred Stoney, Harry Metters, Sam Wooding, are all wearing armlets waiting to be called up; Mr Cooke, the Vicar of Stoneleigh, has "attested" as a non-combatant.

Dudley has at last got his wish, and has been allowed to visit the Front with a small Government Recruiting Party, for four days; he started early on Friday 28th, & Aggy & Rupy saw him off from Charing Cross. Last Tuesday he motored to Salisbury, then Bristol, and finally Chester, to see various people who might give him leave to go! This is said to be the last Government party which will be sent out, to see what is going on and then to come back and stimulate recruiting.

About 80 magic lantern slides (Natural History) which I lent a year ago to H.M.S. "Black Prince" have been safely returned to me, only one being cracked, with a grateful letter from the Chaplain who took charge of them and said they had been very useful.

Feb 4. On the same evening as I made my last entry in this Journal (Monday, Jan. 31) Zeppelins passed very near here, in their raid of the Midland Counties.[1] I slept peacefully all night and heard nothing, but on going down to an early breakfast next morning (Feb. 1) Wyatt met me saying "There is no post yet and no newspapers; I expect there has been a raid; guns were firing last night." I went on to take a Class at Stoneleigh School, and found the whole School excited, and many people had heard guns and whistles and ringing of bells. Later we found that both Coventry and Rugby had stopped their munition and other factories working, and turned off all their lights; the Birmingham trains were stopped, and workmen walked home to Leamington, etc. So no damage was done at Coventry.

In curious contrast to the prevailing excitement was a quiet little Funeral which Rowland and I attended at Stoneleigh that Tuesday afternoon, when our good old gardener William Knight was laid to rest after a long and peaceful life spent chiefly in the garden – the peaceful English country life which our younger men are fighting to save for us.

[1] Zeppelins raid of the Midland Counties: *on the night of 31st January – 1st February, 1916, nine Navy Zeppelins, which should have attacked Liverpool, lost their way and ended up attacking a number of towns, including Loughborough, Scunthorpe, Derby and Burton-on-Trent, as well as the Tipton - Walsall area. 70 people were killed and 113 injured. Attempts at intercepting the Zeppelins were unsuccessful and costly, with six aircraft lost.*

Feb 6th. The evening Service at Stoneleigh to-day, Sunday, was put back from 6.30 to 5.30, as the "lighting orders" direct that no Church is to show lights after 7 p.m.

One hears of pheasants being out in the roads, and making a great noise on Monday evening, before the firing, but I thought an even more curious story was one told me the other day by Mr and Mrs Neale, the Schoolmaster and his wife at Westwood Heath; Mrs Neale said that they were walking in a wood near Tile Hill that evening, a little before there was any Zeppelin alarm, when they heard a strange cry, which at first they thought was from an owl, but Mr Neale knew that it was from a fox, which they had never heard before though they often walked in that wood rather late in the evening.

Feb 23rd. I took a hired motor car to-day from Banbury to Tysoe, where I had to address a

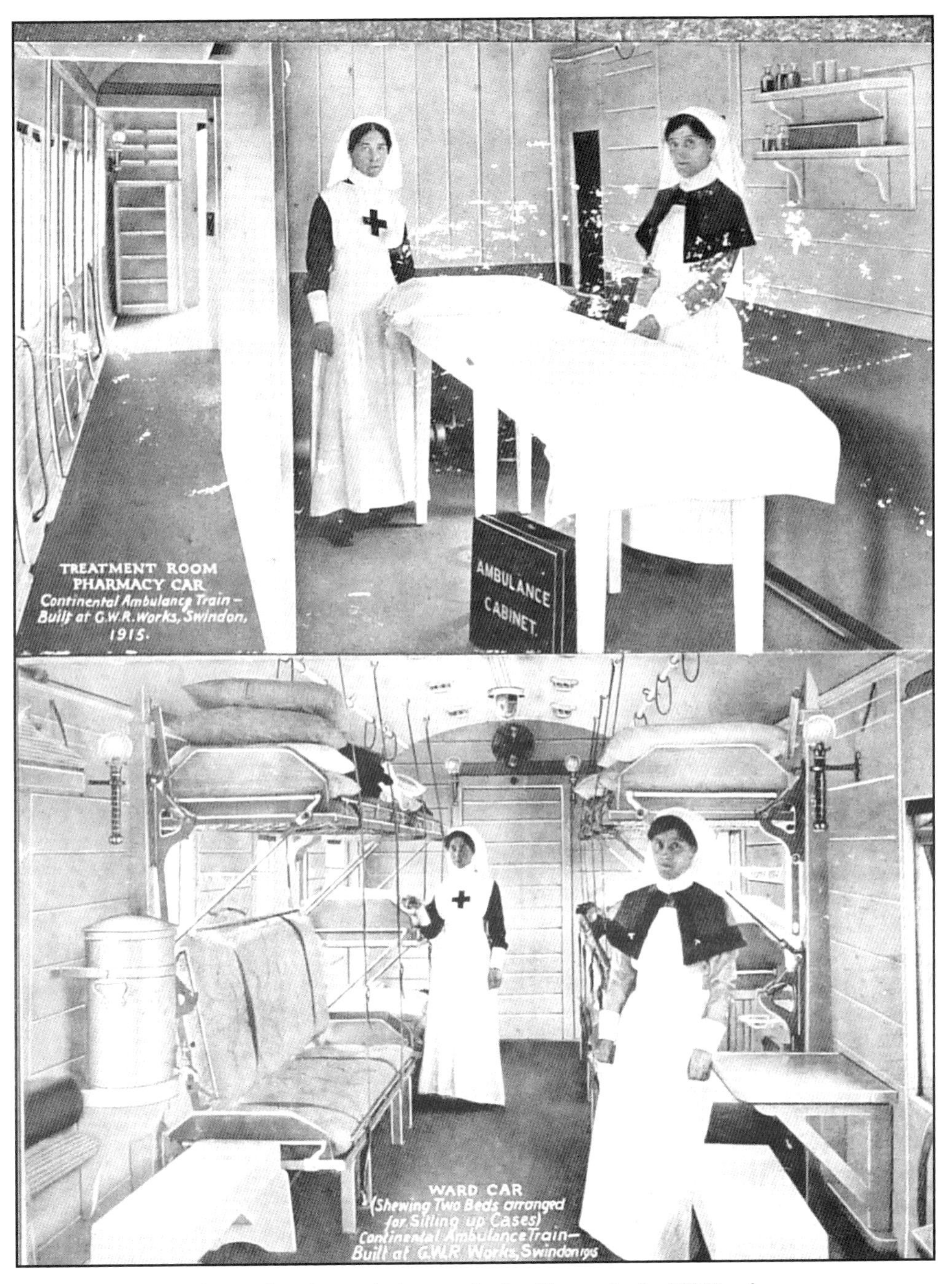

The interior of an ambulance train. See Diary entry for 21st March.

Mothers' Union, and had the new experience of being driven by a Chauffeuse, a nice, smiling, quiet young woman employed by a garage at Banbury; she drove most skilfully down the dangerous Sunrising Hill; and was quite indifferent to snow, and a biting N. wind.

I have not written anything here about D's adventures in France, as I am keeping an account of it which he wrote out for me, in a separate collection of papers and newspaper cuttings connected with the War.[1]

Mr Carley, the Farmer from Stareton, called the other day to ask me to undertake the canvassing of women in Stoneleigh Parish for Farm work; he is to undertake to canvass the Farmers to enquire who will employ them.

[1] D's adventures in France: *see Scrapbook section for 1916 (P. 99).*

24th. The papers have arrived from Warwickshire Agricultural Committee, with instructions as to how to canvass; but this would not be a good day to begin as snow is falling heavily and is thick on the ground!

March 7th. Nineteen Stoneleigh women altogether have allowed me to put their names on my list, as being willing to work in some way on the land, some for whole time, some for part time, and two would undertake haymaking or garden work.

Two nights ago we had a Meeting in the Reading Room to consider what measure of defence should be taken in the village in the event of an Air Raid. D. took the Chair, and Inspector Parkinson from Kenilworth addressed the Meeting. Then one Committee was formed of messengers who were to go around the village, and to Ashow and Stareton, to see that lights were sufficiently darkened, in case of an alarm; a second Committee to do Ambulance work in case a bomb fell in the village and hurt anyone; and a small Committee to watch in case of an unexploded bomb to see that no one went near it.

Last night, Sunday, I went to Stoneleigh Church for the evening service at 6 p.m., and Mr Cooke gave out that the Service must be shortened, on account of not showing lights after 6.30, as there had been a warning sounded that Zeppelins were about, though he did not know how near; we therefore had a very short Service, and the Nunc Dimittis and two hymns were sung without the organ. Mr Cooke himself had to hurry away to his duty as Special Constable, to help guard the roads and to stop all traffic entering Coventry so long as Zeppelins were about. We hear to-day that all trains were stopped; also that the Zeps came over Leicester, but we know no details.

By the way, the "Sors Liturigoe" fell out that the first Psalm for yesterday's evening Service was the XXVIIIth, beginning the "The Lord is my light, and my salvation, whom then shall I fear?" and continuing most appropriately throughout.

15th. I hear that four of our men were in the trenches together – Albert Worrall, Reggie Worrall, Craddock and Parker; the three in front pressed forward, and Parker shouted "Forward, Stoneleigh lads! Give it them hot! Parker is behind you!"[1]

[1] four of our men were in the trenches together etc: *the men were serving in the 11th Battalion of the Royal Warwickshire Brigade (37th Division) and were in the trenches at Hannescamps, in the Somme Department, about 10 miles south-west of Arras.*

21st. I went to a Meeting at Birmingham to-day, and at Snow Hill (G.W.) Station saw a very long Ambulance Train which was built for the French Government at Swindon, and was being shown at 1/- a head. I think the showman said it was about 960 feet long, and could take 750 patients. There were berths over each other in some compartments, and seats for less badly wounded men in others – no cushions were allowed. There was a small operating compartment. Also a dispensary, storeroom, and kitchen.

23rd. Said good-bye to William Allen and William Darlow, Ashow boys who are likely to be called up to-morrow; they were "old boys" of my Bible Class, 39 years old now. George Clifford and William Palmer are also being called up, and some more men from Stoneleigh, including the older Prime, who will be a loss to the village as he mends all the boots.

The following notice is now typed up and put in various parts of this house!-

"All persons using the light in this room must pull down the blinds before turning on the light and see that the window is completely covered so as to prevent the light showing outside. The Penalty if this is not done is £100 or six months hard labour."

April 20th. Monday in Holy Week. Streets in London, where I have come for Holy Week and Easter, darker than ever. I have actually to feel round the pillar box in Grosvenor Street at night to find the slit for posting letters. Hyde Park, which I walked across at 8 p.m. to attend a late Service at St Paul's Knightsbridge, looked very weird, with three great searchlights playing over it, the planet Venus like a little sun, and then the great Easter moon rose suddenly from behind very angry looking dark clouds.

Easter Sunday and St George's Day – April 23rd. Two soldiers in Khaki carried banners in the fine Procession at St Paul's, Knightsbridge, when 'Hail Festal Day!' was sung, and one carried a banner in the Procession in the evening service, and while 'God save the King' was sung at the end.

The Union Jack is hung behind a large Crucifix just outside the Chapel at St Paul's Church, and under the Crucifix is the Roll of Honour of the soldiers fallen in battle, with 'Greater love has no man than this' over the names, and wreaths, flowers, etc. arranged beneath.

The Sinn Feiners in Ireland[1]

Emily Ward writing to Agnes Leigh – Easter Tuesday* – says (address Beechwood, Killiney).

"I am wondering if you will get this letter! For we are in the most extraordinary state, as we have no post and no newspapers and Dublin is apparently in possession of the Sinn Feiners.[2] The telegraph wires are cut and no trains are running further than Kingstown. As you can imagine it is very disquieting, and we only hear by word of mouth every separate item of news.

We heard yesterday afternoon that the Sinn Feiners had got on the roofs of houses and were shooting down on the people below, that they had played havoc in Stephen's Green (a beautiful Square) and were digging trenches and cutting the trees for barricades – holding up motors, and using them as barricades, tearing up tram lines, raiding the Post Office and the Bank of Ireland and finally that they had seized the Railway Stations and shot Reynolds the station-master of our line whom we all know. ...

Mr Talbot was at the races yesterday and had the greatest difficulty in getting back. ... He believes that it has been splendidly organised (probably with German brains)[3] as all the entrances to Dublin appear to be barricaded. ...

If they set any buildings on fire we should see the glares from here, but they evidently have not! So perhaps things are less bad than we hear. ... No carts came to-day for orders – there is to be no meat market in Dublin this week and the

Butcher declares that – short of Dublin – we have only three days' provision for the population.

Now we hear – within the last two minutes that Troops are pouring into Dublin which sounds better.[4]

Personally I feel that anything is better than this feeling of suppressed and smouldering rebellion, which has now been going on among a comparatively small section of Nationalists – and this will bring it to a head and perhaps the Secret Sitting this afternoon will not only ordain Conscription for England, but also for Ireland.[5]

While writing this sentence we have heard firing which may be small ones at Kingstown or big ones in Dublin. ...

Wed: As far as we can gather by hearsay the S.F. still hold Stephen's Green and have actually dug themselves in – spoiling the greenest grass in the world – hacking the trees and trampling the bulbs (which were a sight in their number and colour).[6] ...

We are told that round St Stephen's Green are soldiers, but not in sufficient number to cope with the situation yet. The road between Kingstown and Dublin is shut to the general public – but 4,000 troops from your side have landed and are now marching along into Dublin. We get no letters, no newspapers and are cut off from the outside world, and are wondering how things fare in the North and how Belfast is and how the war is going on.

Jameson's Whisky Distillery has been looted and Jacobs' Biscuit Manufactory – and considerable looting of the shops down Sackville Street – and then there are wild stories of Dublin Castle being taken[7], guns mounted on top of it; the Archbishop's Palace being taken for the same purpose. ...

Mine sweepers are to be seen in the Bay, for they find this channel has been mined. ... I looked out in the night towards Dublin – but there was no glare in the sky – only searchlights from Kingstown Harbour darting brilliant rays in every direction.

We cannot change cheques and have just what money happens to be in our purses – the government have taken over the shops and we have not yet heard if we are to be given tickets to allow so much a head! This huge Army suddenly in our midst will have to be fed. ...

Weds: eve: Now Mother's doctor has come straight from Dublin, & he saw five old soldiers with armlets deliberately shot by the S.F. One of these will recover but the 4 others have died. To-day he was in again, and from the Shelbourne Hotel, the British troops were firing into St Stephen's Green, and he said the dead were lying in heaps. It is all very ghastly but the S.F. movement is the bane of Ireland and it has been growing and growing unchecked like a malignant disease. ... Now – if ever – it can be cut out root and branch.

We have had orders here that no-one is to be out after eight o'clock. ...

We hear that Sir Roger Casement &c is caught.[8]

We hear mails are going over tonight.

Thurs: The Baker brings the news that at Ball's Bridge (this side of Dublin) where their bread is baked – the dead bodies had to be cleared away from the centre of the road before the Baker's carts could come along.

Meat and butter are the only things as yet that are scarce for the bread has arrived as usual.

12 noon: The firing is horrible, and it is going on without ceasing – they must have some big guns for one hears each boom distinctly.

The last item of news is that a house we know quite well by sight, which stands at the corner of two roads – this side of Dublin, was filled to overflowing with S.F. who were sniping from all the windows as the soldiers came along the road – and they have been obliged to blow it up.

Friday, 28th April. To-day we have no Butter. The first pinch. It is a great question whether we shall get bread to-day. If the S.F. are able to – of course they will ravage the bread carts. …

Several buildings in Dublin are now on fire, and from my bedroom I was watching the fires through field glasses and the glare in the sky.

The whole rising is horribly well organized – by Germans of course and very hard to get under ….

Killiney conversation now is chiefly:- "Have you got a good supply of flour?" "We've run out of butter. …" "How are your potatoes lasting?" and we can't be heroic, for there is nothing we can do except obey orders, and have the house shut up by 8 p.m. … I think meat will be the next thing that will come short.

What we are longing to know is how much you know in England. … We actually heard of a Wednesday Daily Mail in Ballyrack. … This is the only paper that has come into Killiney since Monday.

Later: Kitty has seen to-day's Daily Mail and each house is allowed to keep it half-an-hour!!! So now we do not feel so absolutely vague as we have been for the last four days as if we were on another planet.

5th day. April 29. Saturday.

This is how we are situated now. We believe that our letters go to England (Note) as we hear that once a day they are collected and brought down to a ship in Kingstown Harbour – but not a single letter can get to any other part of Ireland. …

To-day no butter and only porridge as a breakfast dish, but bread is arriving all right. Talking of bread – a sleepy old scarlet bread cart, with baskets on top, was ambling out from Dublin, and was stopped by the soldiers. On opening it, it was filled with rifles. The driver was shot within two minutes – martial law.

(Every vehicle is stopped and examined. Mother in her drive yesterday was stopped six times.)

There are pickets all along the road to Dublin – one at our gate with a field kitchen.[9]

Among other things the rebels in the Four Courts got hold of all the Income Tax Records and Documents and threw them into the River Liffey which will cause endless trouble and confusion.

We also hear that if the Germans had succeeded in landing even a small force – the Rebellion would have assumed formidable proportions."

* (Note) All the letters from which these extracts are taken arrived at Stoneleigh together, May 3rd.

"You must realise what it is to be without any outside news – but to hear guns all day and see the sky red with the glare of fire at night – guns stuck in the hedge at your back door, armoured cars whizzing round corners, soldiers barricading every road – rumour deliriously wild – from mouth to mouth – no telegraphs – or telephones!!

For instance – a story that a little gun-boat in the Liffey[10] had sent a few shells in the direction of Liberty Hall, for intimidation purposes, arrived in Killiney thus: "There's a Dreadnought up the Liffey – and aeroplanes showering down Bombs"!

These leaders of rebellion – fancy two Schoolmasters![11] Can't you imagine how all the boys who have passed through their hands have been taught History?

May 5th. We have got a letter from London – the very first letter that we have received from England for eleven days. No newspapers get through – they can be got in – a messenger with a pass goes to Kingstown and we generally see one some time during the day. We cannot even get letters from Dublin and none from the North or West. ...

A good man, and a rich chartered a ship at Howth and sent it to Liverpool for provisions as they were very scarce, and it arrived back from Liverpool the day before yesterday – laden! Chiefly for the poor – but we got a pound of butter. One train runs daily but no private telephones or telegraphs yet.

(Note) They had difficulties especially at Dunsany.[12]

A man at Bray, three miles off simply HAD to be in Co. Monaghan before Sunday, and the only way he could accomplish it was by crossing over to Holyhead, going by steamer from Holyhead to Greenore and then from Greenore to Monaghan by train.

May 7th. There is great unrest still – the sort of swell before a storm, and only yesterday five miles from this a woman shot a soldier dead – and the soldiers have authority to shoot any who refuse to give up arms. The soldiers hate this work.

May 8th. This day week I hope to be crossing over and already am putting irons in the fire about it. You have no idea how odd it is to be under Martial Law, and how difficult it is to leave the country unless you are a prisoner. ... First of all I get hold of the Patrol Commander and he conducts me to the Town Hall in Kingstown where I swear I'm myself. Then I have to be very chatty and lay before them my reasons for leaving Ireland. Then if they consider I have urgent reasons, I am given a Pass. Then my luggage is searched and more catechisms and proving of identification on the steamer to the satisfaction of the Provost Marshal. ... This is all because they are catching S.F.s by dozens and have to be very careful they don't escape dressed up as women.

We can't walk into Kingstown – a mile and a half away – without a pass – and Kingstown people can't come here. Our little parlourmaid was very anxious about her family who were rather in the danger zone, so she went into Dublin yesterday to see how they were getting on. She found her mother had been almost shot and her sister quite.

The mother was on a wooden chair and the bullet went into the back of it making a hole, but the mother was not touched. Her daughter rushed across and actually her ear was hit by a second shot and has had to be attended to at a Hospital.

The poor parlour maid had great difficulty in getting back from Dublin and was felt to see if she had any arms concealed. She came out by tram, and soldiers came in at intervals and said "Any boxes on top?" which the conductor told her meant "Are there any people likely to be Sinn Feiners?"

Count Plunkett's three sons were all implicated in this business – two of their sentences have been commuted to penal servitude but the eldest was executed.[13] The pathetic thing was it was to be his wedding day – the day before he was shot – and Miss Giffard got leave and was married to him.

There were 200 leaders altogether but a good many have escaped. Most of them were visionaries, crankers, impossible in their childish folly – others were in the pay of Germany – all haters of England and bound together in this Secret Society – but the 15,000 rank and file were like the labour agitators and heaps of them not that – but just dupes of their leaders, thinking it fine to go against law and order – and especially England.

Another extract.

"The Martial Law gives great satisfaction and the soldiers' search for rebels and arms continue. Forty or fifty men were captured in Bray – in their beds at five in the morning (of the day they were caught). Stacks of arms were discovered and ammunition a mile and a half from this at Loughlinstown."

An incident.

"The Rev. Benjamin Plunkett, Bishop of Tuam was going to motor up to Armagh on Easter Monday to stay with the Primate for the enthronement of the new Bishop of Derry. Knowing nothing of anything in Dublin, he gaily motored into the middle of the rebels who were busily barricading Stephen's Green. "Your name?" they asked with cocked rifles. "Bishop of Tuam", he said blandly. Mercifully they thought he said "Archbishop of Tuam" (an R.C. dignitary) and they very politely said: "Father, we are very sorry, but we must ask you to give up your motor – we can't help it." Of course he bundled out, and with the words, "Father, send up a prayer for us," they added his beautiful Daimler to the barricade they were making, and he got back safely to Bray.

Mr Pitchford, organiser of the Amateur Ordnance Volunteers, on May 23rd, told us three interesting things, viz:

1. That a friend of his had informed him that during the previous week he had been employed in burying a great many Germans whose bodies in full uniform had been washed ashore on the East coast by many tides. It was said that we had sunk five transports that had tried to effect a landing to coincide with the attempt at landing in Ireland when Sir Roger Casement the traitor was taken prisoner.

2. The German crew of Zeppelin L.19 which had been left to its fate by the crew of an English trawler, who was afraid to trust the Germans, was rescued by an English ship in consequence of information given by the trawler. This rescue was not reported in the papers.[14]

3. Two German Zeppelins captured by the English are now in use as British air-craft, and we are building a very large airship on German lines."

[1] The Sinn Feiners in Ireland: *Emily Ward's account deals with the events relating to the Easter Rising in Ireland, when Irish Republicans seized control of much of the centre of Dublin on Easter Monday, 24th April, 1916, and declared a Provisional Government. In the fighting that followed some 450 people were killed and more than 2,600 wounded; most of the casualties were civilians. The fighting had effectively ended by 1st May. Plans for a more general uprising did not materialise, although there was isolated fighting in other parts of Ireland.*

[2] Dublin is apparently in possession of the Sinn Feiners: *the nationalist uprising was widely described at the time as a Sinn Fein rebellion, probably because Sinn Fein was the name most commonly associated with the separatist movement. Although Sinn Feiners were involved on an individual basis, the rising was actually organised by the Military Council of the Irish Republican Brotherhood (IRB), drawing support from the Irish Volunteers and the Irish Citizen Army.*

[3] splendidly organised (probably with German brains): *another widely held belief was that the rising was organised by the Germans, no doubt reinforced by the description of the Germans as "gallant allies" in the rebels' declaration of an Irish Republic on Easter Monday. The IRB had hoped for German involvement but a sceptical German government sent only a limited number of weapons. Even these did not reach Ireland, as the ship on which they were being carried was intercepted by the Royal Navy and scuttled by its crew a few days before the rising.*

[4] Troops are pouring into Dublin: *the British army had less than 2,000 troops in Dublin at the start of the rising, to deal with about 1,500 rebels. However, reinforcements were quickly brought from other parts of Ireland and, on Wednesday, 26th April, the first troops arrived from England.*

[5] Conscription for England, but also for Ireland: *introduced to the rest of the United Kingdom in January 1916, conscription had not been introduced into Ireland, although the possibility that it might remained.*

[6] The S.F. still hold Stephen's Green and have actually dug themselves in: *originally, the rebels did dig trenches on St Stephen's Green but soon abandoned them because the Green was overlooked on four sides by buildings.*

[7] wild stories of Dublin Castle being taken: *Dublin Castle, the traditional seat of British rule in Ireland, was not captured, although it might easily have been had a group of Citizen Army men pressed home their attack more vigorously, so small was the Castle's garrison at that point.*

[8] Sir Roger Casement &c is caught: *after a distinguished career as a British diplomat, Sir Roger Casement had embraced the Irish nationalist cause. He had been in Germany trying to recruit Irish prisoners of war for the intended uprising and to secure German support. A German submarine landed him on the coast of County Kerry on 12th April, 1916, but he and his two colleagues were soon caught. Casement was subsequently put on trial in London and executed for treason on 3rd August, 1916.*

[9] pickets all along the road: *small detachments of troops.*

[10] a little gun-boat in the Liffey*: the Helga.*

[11] two Schoolmasters: *Patrick Pearse founded the bi-lingual St Enda School in 1908; Thomas MacDonagh acted as assistant headmaster there.*

[12] Dunsany: *Cordelia's niece, Beatrice Child-Villiers, the daughter of her sister Margarette, married Edward John Morton Drax Plunkett, 18th Lord Dunsany of County Meath, Ireland and lived at Dunsany Castle near Tara. During the war, Dunsany, a prolific writer and friend of W.B.Yeats and Rudyard Kipling, served as Captain in the Royal Inniskilling Fusiliers.*

[13] Count Plunkett's three sons etc: *George Noble Plunkett (1851-1948), who had been created a Papal Count in 1884, was Curator of the National Museum in Dublin in 1916. His eldest son, Joseph, was executed on 4th May; George and John Plunkett were imprisoned in England, although released in 1917.*

[14] crew of the L.19 ... left to its fate: *the L.19 had been part of the raid on 31st January – 1st February. On its return leg, it came down in the sea and a British trawler captain turned down the opportunity to capture the crew for fear that they would outnumber his men and seize his vessel. However, no 'English ship' subsequently rescued the German aircrew, who all perished.*

May 24. We celebrated Empire Day at Stoneleigh, Westwood and Ashow Schools. At Ashow, a passing soldier – Airman – had kindly stopped and helped Miss Murray and Maggie Woodfield to hoist the Union Jack over the School, so we invited him to join in the little ceremony, and he stood solemnly in line with six little boys and three little girls, while D. made an address from the school steps, and then we sang God save the King, and saluted the flag!

In the afternoon about 60 Voluntary Munition workers[1] had a Meeting here – men and women – and a tea party. One youth, from St John's School at Warwick, had given up all his Easter holiday to working at munitions. They came from all parts of the country.

[1] Voluntary Munition workers: *in response to the demand for more shells, a movement was inaugurated in the autumn of 1915 to organise Amateur Ordnance Volunteers. Lord Leigh was appointed president of the Warwickshire area, which produced shell bases. The work was carried out by people who had access to a lathe and it was considered that the necessary skills could be learnt in about 12 days. Lord Leigh's electrician was appointed to supervise the work done by volunteers in the district.*

25th. Miss Leo Bonn brought over five soldiers, four with only one leg, and one with both legs off, who moved about on his knees; he was to have artificial legs later. He had started his career as a seaman on a merchant ship; and had been twice round the world. Afterwards he went to India as a soldier, before the War. Since the War he has fought at Mons, Marne, Aisne, La Bassée, Givenchy, and Neuf Chapelle – then landed successfully at Gallipoli, and was not wounded till Dec., one week before Gallipoli was evacuated.[1] Like all the others he was most cheerful – told us in fits of laughter how, while having a pillow fight with his chums, he forgot that he had no feet, tried to jump on to the ground and fell over – "it was fun!" he said, with a beaming smile.

[1] fought at Mons etc: *it seems unlikely that one man would have participated in this number of battles, though his wounds were real enough.*

28th. Harry King has been wounded again, but he is better, and in Hospital at Mhow India. Dennis Worrall has gone into training. One of my old boys, John Prime, Jonathan's brother, was here this morning, and is "called up" next week. Mrs Parker, at the Kennels, is to take Sweatman's place and milk our seven cows when he goes.

June 6. About 100 wounded soldiers were entertained here this afternoon, and a great number of attendants, Nurses, etc. Some played croquet and lawn tennis; and after tea Mr Thomas' entertainers from Birmingham gave a Concert and Conjuring performance in the Riding school. The Soldiers had their tea in the Corridor and old Housekeeper's Room, and the attendants and various people who came to help had tea in the Hall. There were parties from Leamington, Kenilworth, Berkswell V.A.D. Hospital, Coventry, Birmingham. The Stoneleigh Boy Scouts were to the fore – as they were last year – and spent a good deal of time playing croquet themselves, when not wanted for moving benches, waiting on the men at tea, etc! In fact they were left in possession of the lawn and enjoying themselves thoroughly long after the long procession of motors had carried off the wounded heroes and their nurses.

The tragic news of Lord Kitchener's death by drowning[1] was brought by Charles (Lord) Norton in the course of the afternoon.

I omitted to mention in its proper place that one week in March D. sent all the Stoneleigh and Ashow school-children (except infants) over to Leamington to see a good cinematograph performance called "Britain Prepared"; representing various scenes to do with the Navy and Army. The Girls' Reformatory were also sent, and some of A's G.F.S. [Girls' Friendly Society] Girls, and all our servants. They were sent in relays, in the Ford Motor, float, station cart, and pony cart, throughout the week, from Monday to Saturday.

I hear that three Stoneleigh women, Mrs King, Mrs Edmonds, and Mrs Chattaway (Junior) spread manure over 14 acres on Mr Barnes' farm in 4 days – a creditable performance for some of our Women Workers.

[1] Lord Kitchener's death by drowning: *Lord Kitchener died on 5th June, 1916, when the cruiser HMS Hampshire, which was taking him to Russia, hit a mine and sank off Marwick Head in the Orkneys, shortly after leaving Scapa Flow. The atrocious weather conditions meant that that there were only 12 survivors from more than 600 men on board the ship.*

9th. Mrs Craddock, Kennels Cottages, has heard in a letter from Albert Worrall that her husband was shot in the trenches on the third.[1]

[1] Mrs Craddock has heard ... that her husband was shot: *Private Alfred Thomas Craddock, 11th Bn Royal Warwickshire Regiment, was killed on 2nd June 1916 and is buried at Bienvillers Cemetery on the Somme.*

11th. Whit Sunday. Mr Cooke made the usual mention of Alice, Duchess Dudley in his Whit Sunday Sermon[1], and combined it very cleverly with a mention of Lord Kitchener!

[1] Alice, Duchess Dudley etc: *born in 1578, she was the daughter of Sir Thomas Leigh of Stoneleigh. She married Sir Robert Dudley, the illegitimate son of the famous Elizabethan Earl of Leicester. Later he abandoned her, living the rest of his life in Italy. Alice was a great benefactor to the parishes of Ashow and Stoneleigh, where there is a magnificent monument to her. Among her many bequests she decreed that a sum of money be given to the vicar of Stoneleigh for preaching a sermon on Whit Sunday in which he mentioned her name.*

13th. D. attended officially as Vice Lord Lieutenant, at a Memorial Service to Lord Kitchener at St Michael's, Coventry. Aggy, Beatie and Mabel went also.

There are three women at work now in the garden, weeding and doing other light garden work, and two others are helping beat the carpets.

I am distributing green Government armlets – green baize with red crown – to those who have worked on the farms as much as 30 days since the beginning of the War.

30th. Young George Rose has been wounded in the left arm, and is in Hospital at Bristol.

July 3rd. D., A. and I attended a Meeting at Westwood School to promote "War Savings". There were representatives from Stoneleigh and Eastern Green. Mr Carter, the County Secretary, explained the Government scheme for encouraging small investments.

24th. The Master of the "Victoria" L.C.C. School, Shepherd's Bush, writing to a lady who sends them flowers, etc, through my "Schools Mutual Aid Society" says: "At the present dreadful time matters are not too pleasant in the School, seeing that nearly all the 1500 children in this School have fathers and brothers at the front, and hardly a day passes without bad news of one and another. One widow has seven sons serving in the forces, all of whom attended this School. We have an Honour Roll of traced names of old scholars of over 500 serving in the forces. Many unfortunately have gone over for ever, but all have done well, many earned promotion, and we have just heard of one gaining the D.S.M. for which we are going to claim a holiday from the L.C.C."

Going to Durham on the 12th for three nights, I noticed women porters on the Midland Railway.

Albert Worrall has been wounded and is in Netley Hospital and I hear doing well. George Stephens is there too, in a different hut.

William Chattaway, formerly under chauffeur here, is missing.

27th. An Australian Airman, called Murray, testing his aeroplane, brought his machine down in Howe Meadow and came in to luncheon here. Afterwards he "looped the loop" and did various manoeuvres for our benefit. He said he was so well accustomed to flying that he could read a book while in the machine, only looking up occasionally to see he was in the right direction.

30th. Our Belgian, De Groote, called this evening to ask me to be Godmother to his little daughter born in Stoneleigh village about a month ago. He asked me to choose an English name, and wishes her baptised in our Church.

Aug. 4th. The second Anniversary of the Declaration of War. About ten people attended a Celebration of the Holy Communion at Ashow at 7 a.m., which I attended. At Stoneleigh at 7.30 p.m. a special Form of Thanksgiving and Prayer was used, and I played two hymns on my little American organ, "O GOD of Jacob; O GOD of love; O King of Peace", and the first verse of the National Anthem.

6th. The Belgian baby was christened "Elizabeth Mary" at 6.15 p.m. at Stoneleigh Church. The father was Godfather, and Mrs Wells[1] and myself Godmothers. Mrs Wells handed her to Mr Cooke, and I took her from him after the baptism and handed her back to the Mother. The only congregation were Aggy, Robin, and Mrs Wells' two daughters. She has a sensible rather refined face, with pretty blue eyes.

Albert Morris has been badly wounded, and is in a Hospital at Cambridge.

[1] Mrs Wells: *the wife of the village Schoolmaster.*

Emily Ward writing to Agnes Leigh, August 10th, 1916 says:

> "that her brother, Lord Bangor[1], who is in France superintending the supplies for the Royal Naval Division there, begins his responsible work daily at 6.30 ending generally at 11.30 p.m. ...
>
> He has to supply sixty units with everything except food – and applications received one Monday are invariably supplied the next Monday – and so on. ...
>
> He is at Ypres – a train from somewhere comes in <u>every morning</u> and he has four three ton lorries to distribute goods which are filled with extraordinary varieties – the day he wrote 14,000 anti-gas helmets had come – and eight ton of Horse shoes. The day before he had to procure hundreds of Sheepskins to prevent saddles galling the horses, and besides these, of course, all the everyday requirements.
>
> Sixty wagons from the different units come every morning for their requirements – and he has commandeered a field which he calls "The Dump" – and at the cross-roads he has had a sign-board put up "To the Ordnance Dump". ...
>
> He has several shops in the town – an Armourer's, a Bootmaker's, a

Tailor's &c., for daily repairs and lots of others – always as full of work as possible. ...

Tons of clothing came in from the Trenches, and the Field – all requiring disinfecting and washing – and the Laundry is on a very large scale – and he had to fly in his motor and collect all the sewing machines he could lay hands on to get through the work. ...

He says (metaphorically) everything goes on wheels, and everyone he comes across is most helpful.

Then he has a lot of office work with his clerks – directing the orders and attending to the hundreds of demands, and he has to visit the different units – to arrange things personally and report at Headquarters and so on – but having been able to run it in Gallipoli in many ways it is less difficult here."

[1] Lord Bangor: *Lieutenant-Colonel Maxwell Richard Crosbie Ward, the 6th Viscount Bangor, was the sister of Emily Ward and served in the Royal Garrison Artillery.*

Aug. 20th. Walter Morris has been seriously wounded in the thigh, at Salonika. D. has offered to cable enquiries, to satisfy his mother.

21st. Going to Fonthill to-day, I saw a great number of airmen at Basingstoke Station; they were drawn up in line on one platform, then told to carry their kits, which looked very heavy, and marched off to another platform.

28th. Albert Worrall, home for a few days, returned thanks in Church for recovery from wounds. George Thorley was at the Early Service also, and is helping in farm work for a month. It is now found that Walter Morris was only slightly wounded after all. Fred Smith is reported to be slightly wounded.[1]

In connexion with the National Mission of Repentance and Hope[2], three ladies belonging to the Pilgrimage of Prayer are going round these villages, sleeping two or three nights at each. They are dressed in blue, with blue hoods, a cross on the front of the hood, and a cross on the breast, and one carries a wooden cross which she sets up wherever they give an address. The three who visited Stoneleigh and Ashow came to luncheon with us on Sunday.

[1] Fred Smith: *Lance Corporal Fred Smith served in the 7th Bn Oxfordshire and Buckinghamshire Light Infantry and was wounded five times during the war.*

[2] The National Mission of Repentance and Hope: *the aim of the Anglican Church's National Mission was to re-Christianise the country, in part through the work of groups of Missioners – clergy, laymen and laywomen – who toured the country, although it was left to the decision of the local bishop as to the conditions in which women Missioners were allowed to speak.*

Sept 14th. A Party of us were shown round White and Poppe's Munition Works[1] at Coventry. About 5,000 women are employed there, and it is expected after a time 4 or 5,000 more will be employed. The rooms are extremely well ventilated, and the women as a rule looked well and cheerful. Of course there is a strong smell of petrol and a very great and continuous noise from the machinery. After we had left the rooms where the "bodies" of the shells are cut out, measured, etc., we were given special passes to the part where the high explosives are made; and before going into that part we were all given galoshes to put over our own boots so that there might be no danger of our boots striking some chance explosive fragment on the ground and causing an explosion. The works are very large and we were over three hours going round them.

[1] White and Poppe's Munition Works: *the Coventry-based firm of engine-manufacturers that became one of the main manufacturers of munitions components during the First World War; its workforce expanded from 350 to 12,000 in the process.*

15th. Capt. Murray, the Australian Airman, flew over the house again this morning, and brought his aeroplane down (a new machine on a trial trip) in the field just beyond the bog oak on the way to Stoneleigh village. In about five minutes time a crowd had collected, springing suddenly from every quarter! from the house, stables, farm, Kennels, and villages (being Saturday all the children were having holiday) and a little later Mr and Mrs Cay came hurrying from Woodside, just in time to see the machine slowly starting, first running along the ground, causing a great wind in the grass, and then slowly and gracefully rising and sailing away to Coventry.

25th and 26th. D. was out in his ambulance from about 11 p.m. to about 5 a.m. conveying wounded men from Stratford-on-Avon Station to Clopton Hospital. He conveyed nine men altogether, all bad cases, from the Somme.

The Stoneleigh school-children who are making crutches, bed-rests, hospital bags, etc., are now registered as "Stoneleigh Schools Working Party" at the British Red Cross & Order of St John Central Work Room (Regd No. 4523) where Markey (Dow: Lady Jersey) works as one of the Hon. Secs., and a Red Cross "Flag" is now put up in the Sewing Room at the School where they work.

Oct. 1st. "Summer Time" is now changed back to "normal time".[1]

Going back from evening Service this evening (Sunday) I saw searchlights playing over Stoneleigh village, for the first time that I had seen them out in the peaceful looking country-side.

[1] "Summer Time" is now changed back to "normal time": *at 2 a.m. on Sunday, 21st May, 1916, Greenwich Mean Time was advanced by one hour so as to make more effective use of daylight hours. Clocks were changed back at 2 a.m. on Sunday, 1st October. These alterations were made possible by Act of Parliament and were introduced for the duration of the War.*

3rd. Women are certainly working well. This morning I was talking to Mrs Smith and Mrs Upton, spreading manure in the Stoneleigh fields, while a procession of four more were going over from the village to work in our garden: Mrs Rench, Mrs C. Worrall, Mrs England, and Louisa Carter.

6th. De Groote's "Patron", M. Polverman, the Belgian, came over from Birmingham, bringing his wife to see the house, their son, a big man with a long beard who was Professor at Liège University, his (the son's) young daughter, and an Englishman, whose name I did not quite catch, with his wife. They gave us a warm invitation to visit Belgium some day after the war!

28th. A. and I attended Capt. Kay's Wedding at St Michael's, Coventry. D. was unable to attend as he was at Weston Reformatory[1], where the boys were being formed into a Cadet Corps and recognised by the War Office. Captain Kay married Miss Neville, Matron of some large Munition Works near Nottingham, where female workers make high explosives. There were a large number of soldiers present, including a party of wounded, also cadets, and women Munition Workers. By special request of Capt. Kay I wore his green Staff Badge! We went to a small "Reception" afterwards at the Gables, Kenilworth, where our host, Mr

Dudley Docker, told A. that his firm had been making the new "tanks", and that the secret was so well kept that even the workmen themselves thought they were making real, literal tanks for Russia[2]; the separate parts were made in different places, and finally put together and tested in a private ground closely shut in by barbed wire fences.

I lately met Col. Kenney Herbert[3], a nephew of Mrs Skipwith, who lost his right arm in an accident in the S. African War, and is now Commandant of a large internment Camp near Manchester where German civilians, living in England before the War, are interned. A great many are German Jews, and he told me amusing stories about some of their requirements. They objected to meat killed or cooked by Gentiles, and asked also for new cooking utensils which had never been touched by the gentiles' cooking. Also a Jewish Rabbi came to see him, called down many blessings upon him because he had been so kind in granting the prisoners' requests as far as possible, and then said that they wanted to keep the Day of Atonement – which turned out to be in three days – and to be left to themselves during that time, and to play on trumpets and howl. He told them that he must look in occasionally, to see that they were not boring tunnels to escape, etc., and that they must howl and play quietly, so as not to disturb other prisoners. He granted the Rabbi an escort for bringing the Book of the Law from Manchester for their ceremonies!

I omitted to record a visit from an Australian, Mr Whittle, on Sept 28th, who claimed to have invented a quicker way of loading munition trucks – I believe that is a roughly correct description of his invention? His introduction to the blind Capt. Pierson Webber, the poultry expert, whom he happened to meet here at Luncheon was very pleasing. He said something like this: "In my part of the world, Sir, there are soldier-ants, and if you put your stick into the ground near an ants' nest and shake it, all the soldier ants from a long way around come crowding in to defend the nest. The old country is attacked, and from all around we have been crowding in to her help." He asked me the date of the Gatehouse[4] here and said: "The old monks would stare if they could come back now and see a Briton had come from the other side of the world and was looking at their former home."

Rupert was summoned the other day for showing a light somewhere in his house in London – much to Robin's distress, who thought it was a "disgrace"! He was excused the fine when it was found that he was a Censor and entitled to wear H.M. uniform, and the writ was incorrectly made out.

Tom Steele has been wounded in the elbow, and is in Hospital at Leicester; William Palmer, who only joined a short time ago, has already been wounded in the hand, but not severely, and is in Hospital at Paignton.

George Lee is likely to be discharged soon, and too delicate to be of any use in the Army. William Chattaway, who was missing since July 3rd, is now officially reported killed.[5]

[1] Weston Reformatory: *according to Cordelia's "Reminiscences" her father William Henry, Lord Leigh, founded the Weston-under-Wetherley Reformatory. He took some trouble to find places for boys in the army or navy, which she said was "not easy".*

[2] literal tanks for Russia: *as a security measure to conceal their true purpose, the hulls of the early tanks were described as 'water carriers' or, alternatively, 'water tanks' for use in Mesopotamia and/or Russia. The name 'tank' stuck and soon replaced the term 'landship'.*

[3] Colonel Kenney Herbert: *Lieutenant-Colonel A. Kenney Herbert was in charge of an internment camp for German prisoners near Handforth in Cheshire. In fact, of the 2,713 prisoners there in April 1916, 2,399 of them were classed as military prisoners.*

[4] the Gatehouse: *the Gatehouse at Stoneleigh Abbey is the only explicit reminder there of the building's medieval Cistercian foundation, having been built in 1346 and surviving the abbey's dissolution in 1536.*

[5] William Chattaway ... is now officially reported killed: *Private William Henry Chattaway, 12th Bn Northumberland Fusiliers, is commemorated on the Memorial to the Missing at Thiepval, Somme, his death being recorded as 3rd July 1916.*

November 18th. Mr Wells has given me the list of things supplied by the Stoneleigh children for Hospitals within the last three months. In Oct: they sent 56 lbs of potatoes and 20 lbs of runner beans, grown by the boys in their own plots in the school garden, to Kenilworth V.A.D. Hospital; five pairs of crutches to Barford Hill Hospital; and they supplied Rowly's Depot with ten pairs of crutch sticks ready for heads; and the girls have made three sleeping suits, eighteen hospital bags and eighteen washers, for Kenilworth Hospital.

Sydney Rench[1] has come to England with a Canadian contingent, and is likely to be sent abroad soon; he looks very smart, and is speaking with an American accent.

Robin Leigh tells me that the Housemaid at 7, Beaufort Gardens received a letter from her sister in the Orkneys, which said that at about eight o'clock in the evening of the day that "The Hampshire" went down, a man was working in the fields and watching the Hampshire, which was going very quickly, when suddenly smoke came out of her sides, and in twenty minutes she sank. He got on his bicycle and rode at once to Kirkwall (capital of the Orkneys) to say what he had seen. At about two o'clock the next morning, a farmer called Brass heard someone knocking at his door; he waited for a long time, and at last, getting uneasy, went downstairs, and there found an exhausted sailor who, quite unable to speak, just pointed to the sea. Brass took him in, and ran towards the sea; on the way he met another sailor who also pointed in the same direction. Going on, and looking over some very steep cliffs, he saw at the bottom a round raft with forty-two dead men on it. When the other two sailors recovered sufficiently to speak, they again pointed towards the sea and said "Kitchener is drowned", adding that his Lieutenant plunged into the sea on finding that Kitchener was drowned. They were so convinced that the Hampshire had been blown up by a mine that mine-sweeping continued for another six weeks afterwards. In another of the islands a ship came in the day before, flying a neutral flag, purporting to have a store of coffee, but before she came into port she was seen to be lowering something black into the sea into the part where the Hampshire passed.

The mine-sweepers afterwards found a huge mine with spikes sticking out of it, which could neither be exploded on land or sea, so sailors were sent for from Kirkwall to come and explode it by electricity, and the force of the explosion was so great that rocks were shot up into the air to a great height. N.B. It is believed that spies from Russia gave the information that Kitchener was on the Hampshire.[2]

At least twelve of the Reformatory Girls (Kenilworth) are working for farmers.

[1] Sydney Rench: *Sydney Rench moved from Stoneleigh to Canada in 1911 to work with his brother James. In 1915 he joined the army and trained recruits in the 105th Saskatoon Fusiliers before returning to England in March 1916 to serve with the Canadian Expeditionary Force.*

[2] Spies from Russia: *the death of someone as prominent as Lord Kitchener inevitably prompted conspiracy theories. These continued into the post-war period – there was even a film released in 1922 entitled "How Kitchener Was Betrayed". There seems little doubt, however, that the sinking of HMS Hampshire was caused by one of the 22 mines laid by the U75 on the night of 28th-29th May, with the casualties greatly increased by the very bad weather conditions.*

Dec. 9th. I saw a Mr Ward and his wife at Box, Wilts (while staying there with Mrs Twisleton) who had as their guest a young man called Makeham (I am not sure of the spelling) aged nineteen, who had been a pupil of Mr Ward's at his private school, where a great deal of music was taught. This boy was on leave after being wounded, and had come back to see his old Master at Box, where he had been a very promising pupil in music. Though only nineteen he had helped in the capture of a German trench, and wandering outside the trench afterwards entirely alone, into a kind of "Nomansland", had come across two German Officers, and called on them to surrender! This they meekly did, and followed the boy back into the captured trench, to the great amusement of his senior officers. He took a beautifully made pistol from one of them; but he generously allowed them to keep their Iron Crosses.

I met the young man afterwards on the platform at Box Station, a fine tall youth, rather unwilling to talk about his exploits, but he let out that they belonged to the Prussian Guard; also he said that someone else had afterwards taken their Iron Crosses.

27th. Our third war Christmas. Very few of our Stoneleigh men have had Christmas holidays this year, but I met John Walton on the Stoneleigh path this morning, looking thin, home on ten days' leave. He said, as most of the soldiers who talk about it at all, that nobody who has not seen the horrors of the trenches can have any conception of what things are like out there. He prophesies that all fighting will be over by July, if not before!

Stephens is back as Under-Chauffeur; he is invalided out with a lame leg.

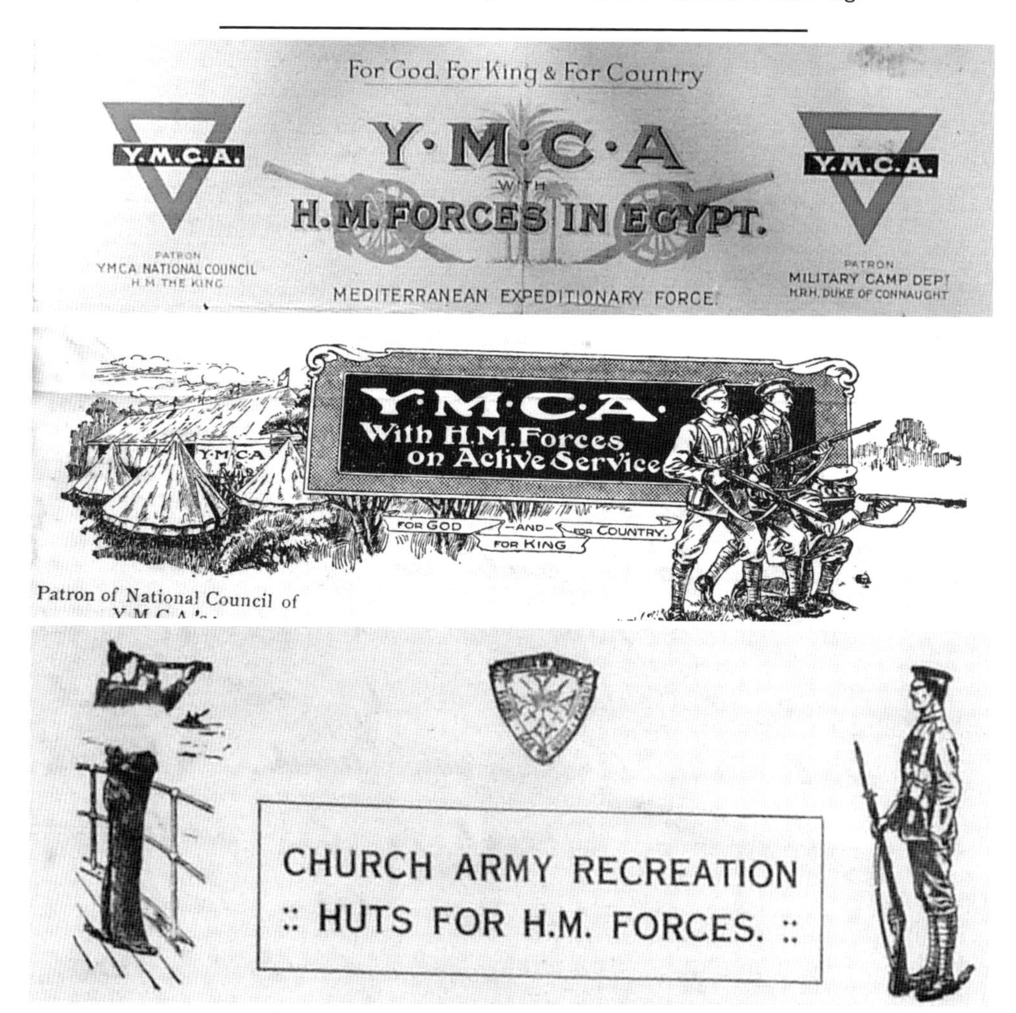

Letter-headings from Stoneleigh soldiers' letters to Cordelia.

Chapter 5: 1917

Introduction

The diary entries for 1917 are fairly scanty, on more than one occasion Cordelia commenting that there had not been much to record. However, she did introduce details illustrating the way in which the protracted nature of the war was affecting everyone and she recorded the presence of Canadian and Australian visitors, whether as guests or invalids; one of the most persistent themes is the occurrence of air-raids on London.

1917 Diary Entries

Jan 20. Miss Hutton's brother is a temporary Major.

Edward Carley and Alfred King are reported wounded, but the nature of the wounds is not stated; they were both in Egypt.

A Belgian R.C. Priest, "Aumayie", or some such name, an intelligent looking man, and "Mere Marguerite", Matron of the settlement of Belgians, formerly at Whitley, but now moved to a smaller house at Coventry, came over to tea lately, and the Priest told us terrible stories of German cruelties to Belgians. He also said that the Germans were prevented ultimately from getting to Calais, by the happy thought of a Belgian peasant, who advised the authorities to let the dykes loose near Dixmude, so that land was flooded and the German forces cut off from advancing.

22nd. As notice is out to-day that youths of 18 are called up, Bertie Rench, the youngest Stoneleigh boy to be called up, has to go to the Recruiting Office at Coventry this week.[1] He volunteered to go when he was not quite 16, with the first lot of Stoneleigh volunteers.

[1] youths of 18 are called up: *in January 1917 the War Cabinet decided to lower the minimum age for conscription from 18 years 7 months to 18, although the rule that no soldier could be sent abroad until he was 19 remained, at least in theory.*

29th. Having to be at Birmingham for a Meeting, I took a tram to go and see Ernest Walford, formerly a Stoneleigh boy, wounded and now at the "1st Southern General Hospital, Edgbaston". It took about twenty minutes from New Street Station to the nearest point to the Hospital, which proved to be Birmingham University turned into a Military Hospital. I then had about five minutes walk, to the entrance guarded by sentries, who however let me pass through without comment! and after crossing a large courtyard, I found myself in the great hall of the huge building, where I talked to a friendly hall porter. Walford's "B. Ward 6" was on the ground floor facing me, and the porter went to enquire if I could see him, but rather unfortunately he was out for a walk, and I had not time to wait for his return, so had to content myself with leaving a note and box of sweets.

Feb 19th. Last week, when I was staying at Hereford, Alice Butler[1] took me over a War Supply Depot where she works almost every day. They turn out peculiarly excellent swabs, in addition to all kinds of bandages, felt slippers, etc.

Lord Ernest Seymour's daughter Constance, who at one time nursed at the Red Cross Hospital at Kenilworth, has died of spotted fever at another Red Cross Hospital at Aldershot, and has been buried there with military honours.[2]

The V.A.D. Hospital "Hill View" at Warwick rang us up on the telephone to-day to ask for more of the crutches made at Stoneleigh School, which they say are the best they have had; some Australian soldiers there, who are very big men, say they suit them exactly.

We are trying to observe the new regulations as to food: 2½ lbs meat; 4 lb bread and ¾ lb sugar per head per week.[3]

[1] Alice Butler: *was the only child of Cordelia's uncle the Reverend James Wentworth Leigh, Vicar of Stoneleigh and later Dean of Hereford. Much admired by the American writer Henry James, a friend of the family, Alice married Sir Richard Pierce Butler, 11th Baronet of Cloughgrenan, Co. Carlow. He gained the rank of Honorary Major in the service of the 8th Battalion, King's Royal Rifle Corps and was twice mentioned in despatches.*

[2] Constance Seymour: *the youngest daughter of Lord and Lady Seymour, Constance Seymour was a*

probationer nurse with Queen Alexandria's Imperial Military Nursing Service at the time of her death, on 12th February, 1917, from cerebro-spinal fever. Before the war she had been honorary secretary of the Kenilworth Voluntary Aid Detachment of the British Red Cross Society. She is buried at Aldershot Military Cemetery and is commemorated on the Kenilworth war memorial.

[3] the new regulations: *following the German declaration of unrestricted submarine warfare, on 1st February, 1917, and the resultant increase in shipping losses, the Food Controller, Lord Devonport, launched a voluntary rationing scheme. Consumers were asked to limit their consumption of bread, meat and sugar. "Eat less bread and victory is secure" was the slogan and families adopting the voluntary scale were asked to display a notice in a prominent place stating: "In Honour Bound We Adopt The National Scale Of Voluntary Rations". The King and Queen were among those to agree to abide by the voluntary scale. Compulsory rationing of some foodstuffs was not introduced until 1918.*

March 15th. The Australian Airman Captain Murray was flying from Coventry, when his aeroplane caught fire; he brought it down in Howe Meadow, and just jumped out in time to escape being burnt himself. D. and I went to look at the charred remains this afternoon, in company with four Ashow schoolboys who had begged leave to run over and see it, saying to Miss Murray – "We will bring you back a bit as a keepsake, ma'am!"

16th. The Stoneleigh Schoolboys have leave from the Education Office to work in the women's gardens in their school hours – those whose husbands have gone to the War – under Mr Wells' superintendence.

I was pleased this morning when at the end of the religious lesson which I had been giving at Stoneleigh School, little Harry Fardon said: "Let us thank GOD for keeping that Airman safe yesterday".

17th. At a Sunday School Teachers' Service at Kenilworth this afternoon, Mr Cairns read Lord Nelson's fine "Prayer on the Eve of Trafalgar", the congregation joining in clause by clause.

Last night closed what will probably be known as "The Wonderful Week" – the week of the great Advance in France[1], the Advance in Mesopotamia[2], and the Revolution in Russia[3].

[1] the great Advance in France: *in March 1917, the German Army began to shorten the line they held on the Western Front by withdrawing to carefully prepared defences, which became known to the British as 'The Hindenburg Line'. As the Germans withdrew, so British forces advanced across the devastated zone that the Germans left behind them.*

[2] the Advance in Mesopotamia: *on 11th March, 1917, British forces occupied Baghdad, in what was then known as Mesopotamia.*

[3] the Revolution in Russia: *unrest in Russia led to the abdication of Tsar Nicholas II on 15th March, 1917, and the formation of a Provisional Government on 16th March. The overthrow of the autocratic Tsar was welcomed by many in Britain and there was hope that the new Russian government would reinvigorate the Russian war effort. On 30th March 1917, the Minutes of the School Council, Leamington High School for Girls (later the Kingsley School), recorded "Miss Leigh moved and it was resolved that the Head Mistress be asked whether it is advisable to include the teaching of Russian in the curriculum." (In July it was minuted that the HM had said it was not desirable.)*

26th. William Cleaver, Fred Stoney, Peter Wooding are gone or going now.

Miss Cobb sent me a nice letter to see written by the Head Mistress of a School in Dorsetshire, which corresponds with "Blackley Municipal School, Manchester", H. Master Mr Wilde, through our Schools Mutual Aid Society. The letter was written last June, but I think, though belated, the following extract is worth writing in here: "Mr Wilde told me he had 194

Miss C. Leigh 19/3/17

Dear Miss Leigh

Just a line to let you know I am getting on all right so far. I am writing to let you know that Willie and myself are still together here. I dont think he has written to lately, so I thought I would let you know he ~~is~~ is getting on all right. I cannot forget the way in which you looked after me during my stay at Kenilworth. Co. There is plenty of mud here, but we keep on smiling all the time. My address is 46 M.G. Company. B.E.F. ~~FA~~ FRANCE. if you would like to write to us. Please would you be so kind as to send the address on to Miss Hopgood as I have wrote to her twice and have had no reply. I must now close will write again later I Remain Yours Faithfully

Sammy Tuckwell (65254)

A letter from Sammy Tuckwell, a London soldier.

boys on the Roll of Honour, and he tries to keep in touch with them all, that must mean a lot of work.

Also three of his scholars are at Blandford Camp, and one boy wanted to see where the beautiful flowers came from, that he used to see once a month, and that made their Nature lessons so real. So I gave him an invitation to visit us, which he did and also spent a week-end with us last time my husband was home. You can't think how grateful the boy was and how he enjoyed the rest from camp life, he told me that he should often think of the nice time he had with us when he is out of England, he expects to be sent away soon."

April 2nd – 9th. Spent Holy Week and Easter Day in London again. There are many more women doing men's work now, most of the omnibus conductors are women, and Alice Dundas told me that she had seen two women window cleaners in khaki and knickerbockers.

Easter Day, April 8th. "Summer time" began, but it is the only sign of summer, as there is snow most days.

12th. Lance-Corporal W. Palmer came to see me, on ten days' leave.

Rowly works hard now in the "Soft Water" or "tank" room in the top passage, which has been turned into a work-shop where he can make crutches for wounded soldiers. He is spending a long time here, as his wife, who went to America to see her Mother who was dying, is kept out there at present owing to the submarine danger.

Millar, the Chauffeur, is devoting himself almost entirely to munition work in the munition room over the Dairy, the chauffeur work is done by Stephens.

Letter received by Miss Hutton[1] from her brother, (a despatch rider in France).

"<u>Easter Monday</u>

By the time you get this letter you will have heard the great news[2], so I will not be giving information "away" to the enemy. Easter Sunday smiled on us with sunshine. The Boche was very quiet though our guns were hammering away with their customary violence. Our H.Q. were in a dug-out under a heap of stones. Everyone was quiet unusually so busy with their thoughts, for on the morrow the do began at 3. I read the Royal Mag. being interested in a romantic yarn which would take my thoughts from the morrow. I never ended it, as a whizz-bang interrupted me making me dash for cover. My old bus standing a few yards away soon became a casualty motor bike as a shell went through the rear portion.

I slept in a stuffy crowded place; numerous messages all day long, Will shouting messages galore down the telephone.

At 4 a.m. I went outside and on the stroke it seemed as if every gun in the universe had opened on the Boche lines it was like one sheet of flame with mines going off, ammunition dumps going up and one mighty roar from our guns.

Soon machine guns and rifle fire marked the Jocks going over, the Germans going down in hundreds. Then batch after batch of prisoners came down the trenches unkempt undersized. Will stood by my side looking very proud. Brigade after Brigade poured forth under his direction through the telephone.

Then the shells became to[o] hot for us we had to retire to shelter for an hour or so.

Going to fetch a new machine I had to run a barrage, and for the first time I was utterly frightened. Some got through others did not and I was never more thankful than when I was back in the dug-out. Report after report came in, better and better news each time. The Jocks outraced the other divisions, nothing could stop them.

Fritz had had no food for many hours and was paralyzed by our bombardment.

Oh! it's so darned exciting.

Phil"

[1] Miss Hutton: *Dorothy Hutton was the governess of Rowland Leigh's children Peggy and Rowland.*

[2] the great news: *the opening of the Battle of Arras, which began on 9th April, 1917, went successfully for the British, especially by comparison with the opening of the Battle of the Somme in 1916. The most significant achievement was the seizure of Vimy Ridge by Canadian troops. However, the Battle soon developed into a costly stalemate.*

May 29th. Whit Tuesday. There does not seem to have been very much to record lately. I had meant to write in some time ago that Robin went into Hyde Park with his parents to see the King and Queen drive by to open Parliament, and he presented arms with a toy gun he had bought for the occasion, and was saluted in return.

We are much occupied trying to keep within the War rations. Personally I very seldom eat bread now, but much enjoy oatcake, and various barley and maize cakes which our cook produces, and as I greatly prefer eggs to meat, I have nothing myself to complain of, but it comes hard on people who cannot afford substitutes for bread.

Tom Mills is reported to be a Prisoner in Egypt, but at present there are no details.

The Ashow School-children gave us an excellent little performance on Empire Day, or rather on May 23rd, as D. had to be in London on 24th. Wilfred Swann, Bernard Beck, Bertie Patstone, and Willie Eiles held up the Flags of England, Scotland, Ireland and Wales, and sang appropriate verses; Gertie Webb was Britannia, and received the Union Jack from Swann; afterwards all joined in singing "Soldiers and Sailors".

The Infants had their own little performance also, superintended by Maggie Woodfield!

We were accompanied by Lady N. Bower, who had come to speak on Food Economy.

The following is written by Mrs Rowland Leigh:-

"June 11th. I left New York on Monday, May 28th, on the 'Baltic' of the White Star Line. I had bought a "Life-saving ever warm suit" in New York, and also had a "Gieve Waistcoat" which I wore during the day, for the two days we were in the Danger Zone. The suit was always beside my bed, and in the pocket, brandy, a whistle and chocolate, with an electric lantern.

General Pershing (the U.S. Commander-in-Chief) came on board in mufti, and at Governor's Island we picked up the rest of his party, about 150 men.[1] He had besides his Staff, experts of all sorts, the head of an enormous railway system, who had given up a salary of £20,000 a year, a most distinguished surgeon, various men who had invented arms being used in this war, and among the interpreters were men like Mr Bacon, who was American Ambassador in Paris under Roosevelt.

There were twelve women passengers, two with small children, and about fifty Englishmen, mostly soldiers, who were returning from Bermuda, or from sick leave. About the third day out, the Purser assembled us all in the saloon, and gave us a little lecture. He told us lists would be posted showing each passenger which would be their boat, we were then to put on life preservers (either our own or those provided by the Company) and go to the boat indicated. Should the boats on one side be disabled, we were told our alternative boats. Also we were told we would probably reach the danger zone, Tuesday, the 6th, and we should none of us undress until we reached the Mersey. This talk over, we all went up to the boats which were swung level with the library deck. Finding I knew no-one in my boat, I arranged with the Purser that I should be transferred to the boat in which were Major and Mrs Humphreys, with whom I had made friends. A few days later the Captain announced that some time during the day, five blasts of the fog horn meant that everyone must get into their suits, or life preservers, and see how quickly they could get on deck to their boat. Everyone was at their boat in seven minutes! Major Humphreys made me practise daily putting on my suit, and as it was difficult to fasten, we arranged that Captain Bickerstaff was to help him (Major H.) get upstairs, as he was lame, while Captain Phillip was to rush to my room and fasten me into my suit.

The night we reached the danger zone was a wonderful moonlight one, and as the Destroyers did not join us until 2 a.m. on Wednesday, we obeyed orders and slept in our clothes.

Without the Destroyers we were in real danger, for the Germans would certainly have shelled the life boats, and those that escaped would have had many hours in an open boat. The American Destroyers, "The Tucker" and "The Rowan", danced about, and raced around us, while we zig-zagged all over the place. I noticed the Destroyers had three men on the top mast, two standing and one kneeling, looking out for mines or submarines.[2]

We had the usual Ship's concert on board and collected £63, for the Seaman's Orphanage, and the night we reached the Danger Zone, the library was full of people, playing bridge or chess, as usual. We tied up in the Mersey at 10 o'clock, Thursday night, and were landed by 10.30 Friday the 8th after enjoying the reception given to General Pershing by the Mayor and Mayoress of Liverpool, the Welsh Fusiliers, and various Generals and Admirals. The Military Special left for London, and the rest of us caught an eleven o'clock train, and arrived comfortably in London about four.

It was an exciting, but uneventful trip. The previous trip of the Baltic, she was fired at twice. One torpedo at dawn missed her by 50 feet, the second in the afternoon missed her by 8 feet."

[1] General Pershing: *John Pershing (1860-1948), often known as "Black Jack" Pershing, was Commander of the American Expeditionary Force (AEF) in World War I. His party numbered 191 officers and men and the voyage to Liverpool in the Baltic was used to consider the future role and organisation of the AEF on the Western Front.*

[2] mines and submarines: *according to Pershing's biographer, Donald Smythe, 15 ships were lost in between 28th May and 8th June, the time it took for the Baltic to cross the Atlantic.*

Aug. 1st. We are having a few Canadian officers here as guests for a few days at a time – three not long ago, and two have come to-day.

Dr Tweedy, the kind and clever Kenilworth doctor, who had joined the A.M.C., and was "Major Tweedy" at a Birmingham Military Hospital, died at his home in Cornwall, and a Memorial Service was held for him at Kenilworth Parish Church on July 16th.[1] It was an impressive sight to see the great number of V.A.D. Nurses from Kenilworth and Birmingham Hospital, marching into Church, and a few Military Doctors were present also.

Arthur Villiers is a D.S.O. His achievement is recorded in my War Album.

[1] Dr Tweedy: *Reginald Tweedy died on 12th July, 1917, at the age of 48. He had been a doctor in Kenilworth for well over 20 years before relinquishing his practice in August 1916 and taking up duties as senior resident surgical officer at the 2nd Birmingham War Hospital. He held the rank of major in the RAMC. He died at Newquay and is buried at Kenwyn Churchyard, in Cornwall. His son, Captain Trevor Tweedy, had been killed in September 1916.*

The following is an extract from a letter written to Alice Skipwith by a cousin, Miss Doreen Kenney-Herbert, dated from Ealing, July 8th:

> "The experiences of yesterday were wonderful. I'm glad I have seen a raid[1], but I can dispense with a repetition. When we got to the office they said they had been warned of a raid at 10.30 (a.m.) there was a fearful din, and we all said "There they are!" and looked out of the windows expecting to see a few puffs of smoke in the sky, and perhaps a tiny speck which would not be distinguished from an aeroplane. What we did see was a thing like a great flock of birds, scarcely moving, flying quite low about ¾ mile away (we could tell from the buildings) and coming straight at our office. We counted 25 and there were shells bursting all round them, but they never got hit or seemed a bit perturbed, for they neither altered their pace nor their course, and they never rose higher or took the smallest notice. ... My face went flushed, and my hands went cold – nearly every man and girl in the room went deathly white, but there was no fainting or crying, or panic of any sort. The sensation I had was as if a cold iron hand had gripped my heart – I said to the girls: "Well! There's nothing to be done, let's do our work", and I shut my window and sat down at my table and began to write."

(Note: they were in a Government Office on sanitary arrangements.)

> "I then found my hands were trembling like ague, and I said to myself, "Don't do that – soldiers wouldn't tremble", and my hands got perfectly steady. Meantime the crashes and bangs were getting louder and nearer, and then the inner door opened, and our Head came out, and we all stood up to hear our orders. He told us to go down to the basement and out we filed into the passage. I picked up my little hand-bag and took it with me. When we got to the passage the lifts were tearing up and down, and the stairs thronged with a perfectly calm crowd of people quietly going down in order with no scrambling or pushing, and in less than 3 minutes nearly a thousand people were congregated in the passage and rooms of the basement. There was no panic, or screaming, or fainting. One poor girl had a heart attack, and two little 14 year old messenger girls were crying and clinging to big girls as the bangs grew louder and the brutes got over our heads. Our lot got separated, but three stuck with me and we got four into a large room where not many had penetrated, and I read aloud bits of my book to them out of my bag! It is one of Chesterton's and very amusing. We longed for a gramophone so that we could dance. One large batch of girls started singing the refrain of a song called "The long long trail" which has rather haunting words and a very haunting little melody, and it is "the rage" just now, and a great favourite with the Tommies who sing it on the march. I shall never forget the sound of those girls singing it

in the cellar room of a London office while the Germans flew over us and death dealing shells were bursting all round! We were down there ¾ of an hour, and then the order came "All clear" – "return in order according to your floors" and so we returned to work. About 20 minutes later Mother rang up to say she was all right, and they had been right over here. They came in massed formation flying low and slowly as they had been over London. They seemed to stop and hover just over the trees in front of the house, and then they all with one accord suddenly rose higher and higher and faster and faster, and were lost to view almost at once. They were flying so low over London[2] that I was told the pilots in them could be plainly seen through ordinary glasses – and as there were so many flying packed together – like a flight of rooks, and they were simply "meandering" they were going so slowly, and it seems incredible we never succeeded in hitting one of them while they were over London. The amazing thing is that they were over Parliament and the War Office and Admiralty and all the other Government offices, and they never dropped a single bomb on them. One of the theories is therefore that they were on an observation expedition and flying low and slow for observation purposes and that they will return another day "to make use of" their information gathered yesterday. Not nearly so many bombs were dropped or so much damage done yesterday as in the raid three weeks ago when there were not nearly so many raiders and they flew fast and high hurling down bombs the whole time."

(Part of the Post Office was wrecked in this Raid. Rupert was at work in his Censor's Office at the time.)

[1] I have seen a raid: *on 7th July, 1917, 22 Gotha bombers made a daylight attack on London, killing 57, injuring 193 and causing £205,000 worth of damage. The bombs fell in a rough triangle between Kentish Town, Hackney and Tower Hill. This was the second daylight raid on the city. One bomber was shot down on the return leg.*

[2] they were flying so low over London: *this appears not to have been the case, with the planes probably at a height of about 14,000 feet.*

Aug 29th to Sept 26th. I spent a few days at a little place in North Wales, Capel Curig – with Alice Skipwith who needed a little change after her Mother's death. One can hardly realize there that War was going on. Holiday-makers were racing up and down in motors, regardless of the waste of petrol. The only sign of war was that the fir trees had been largely cut down in some of the woods, and great motor trolleys passed our little "Cobden's Hotel" laden with the timber for Government use.

Sept 30th. Sunday. At last I have heard an air raid[1] myself! Alice S. and I were at the Alexandra Club, Grosvenor Street, and last night – Michaelmas night – we had gone up early to bed, about 9 p.m., when I heard a loud whistle, rather like a scream, which I was told afterwards was the warning given by the Police; almost immediately afterwards a gun fired, and I heard a man's voice in the street call out "Turn out that light!", a street organ which had been playing came to a sudden stop; and the Hotel servants ran up and down putting out all lights in the passages. Alice and I then went and sat at my open window to see and hear all we could. There was a brilliant full moon opposite my window, slowly and calmly coming out from behind a chimney-pot. For a minute or two the whole place was resounding with gun fire, now a long shriek, now bang! bang! and a sort of deep musical drum-like sound, quite indescribable; the only thing I can think of in the least like it would be a gigantic orchestra and a great thunderstorm rolled into one. By craning our necks we could see an occasional bright flash very high up, like a flickering star. At about 9.30 the noise stopped for a few minutes, and there was almost an uncanny silence, all street traffic was suspended. Then with a great clap of gun fire (I believe from the biggest gun which is kept over on this side) it began again; then we heard a whirring noise like a great humming top; which we were told afterwards was an enemy aeroplane; and the banging went on till about 10 p.m. The message "All Clear" was not given till much later, but it seemed safe to turn our lights on again about ten. We were amused to hear some workmen who were doing something to a neighbouring house every night begin hammering almost before the raid was over! We went early this morning to St Anselm's Church in Davies Street, and saw a hole in its roof made by a bit of shrapnel. But we have heard nothing for certain yet (7 p.m.) about any important damage.

[1] heard an air raid: *on the night of 29th-30th September, 1917, an attack was made by a force of four 'Gotha' and three 'Giant' bombers. Three or four machines reached the city and dropped bombs between 9 – 9.45 p.m., the other bombers dropping bombs in Kent. 40 people were killed in London, 87 injured and £23,000 worth of damage caused.*

Oct. 6th. I must add something to the above, as just after writing it, another raid took place. This time it began about 7.30, while we were having dinner, which we and other people in the Club dining-room calmly finished, as apparently there was no harm in keeping lights turned on so long as the blinds were down. After dinner Alice and I stood for a minute or two in the Club doorway, and the Club footman, a discharged soldier with his middle finger gone, told us a light we saw in the sky was probably an enemy aeroplane; then he said: "It's hardly safe to stand here because of falling shrapnel", and the next moment some shrapnel fell in the street close by. Afterwards we sat reading in the Library, where one is supposed to keep silent, and Alice and I and another lady there did not speak, even when the guns boomed! So one very quickly gets used to it – (at least I found I could read calmly, without taking much notice, that second night). On Monday we left London, so did not hear a third great raid which came on again in the full moon.

Oct 18th. A nice and interesting Chaplain of the New Zealand Forces is staying here on a few days' leave, from Sling Camp, Salisbury Plain.[1] "The Rev. Frank Dunnage", I came across him at a Sunday School Teachers' Summer School at Malvern last August, which he attended. Mr Cooke is now Army Chaplain in Devonshire; Mr Reid Cuddon is in charge of Stoneleigh Parish, and this being St Luke's Day, would have celebrated the Holy Communion at Stoneleigh Church, but he has a bad cold; so Mr Dunnage took the Service, and said afterwards what a joy it had been to him, coming from "a new world" to celebrate the Holy Communion in that centuries old Church in England.

[1] Sling Camp: *a camp adjacent to Bulford Camp on Salisbury Plain used by New Zealand troops during the War; it was called "Sling Camp" after the name of a wood known as "Sling Plantation".*

12 Nov. The Children's Country Holiday Fund are sending London children into the country to give them a little rest from the raids, and the shock. Nine girls and one boy are at Ashow (the boy is at the Grecian Lodge[1]) and attends Ashow School.

[1] the Grecian Lodge: *stands at the main entrance to Stoneleigh Abbey, on the Ashow to Stoneleigh road, and was designed in 1815 by C.S. Smith whose work includes the Pump Rooms at Leamington Spa.*

Chapter Five

Written by Emily Ward:

"Thursday Nov. 22nd. Good news to-day of Sir Julian Byng's successful Tank surprise[1] – followed by a five mile thrust into the Hindenburg line – a Victory! So let Joy-bells ring from the Church towers – of Stoneleigh and Ashow!

Round to the door comes Black Maria – a cruel name for that kindly coach – which is at present having a place in the sun, while the Rolls-Royce sulks in the stables – the triumph of Gas over petrol restrictions.[2]

Away go Agnes and Emily and Lord Leigh to Stoneleigh Vicarage. Mr Cooke has come home on five days' leave, and hears of the Victory with joy – and cordially encourages the idea of Joy-bells.

Now Mr and Mrs Cooke join Black Maria, who flies with us to the Village.

Wardell, the bell-ringer must be tracked to his lair, and we hear he is at the Cross Roads. In a moment we are there too, and he is taken aboard, and back again the gallant ambulance bears her seven occupants to Stoneleigh Church.

The whole School has been summoned, and they form a delightful semi-circle opposite the Church Porch – as peal after peal from the old Tower voice our thanks.

This bright morning is a happy setting for gladness – and the faces of the children shine as a half-holiday is proclaimed.

"GOD save the King" is then sung with fervour, and the bells are still ringing as Maria flies away with us to Ashow.

Here our news is greeted by great excitement – the Bell Ringer leaves his lunch, Miss Murray goes back into the School – and one by one the children come – till a very thankful little company stand alongside of the Church Tower – and while the bells are pealing merrily – treble voices are singing heartily "GOD save the King!"

'It is a comely fashion to be glad

JOY is the THANKS we give to GOD.'"

[1] Sir Julian Byng's successful Tank surprise: *the opening day of the Battle of Cambrai, 20th November, 1917, was very successful, with British forces breaking through strong German defences and advancing three to four miles, with relatively few casualties. One of the features of the British attack was the use of 476 tanks. Coming so soon after the costly stalemate of the 3rd Battle of Ypres, this initial success was understandably hailed as a great victory and was celebrated by the ringing of church bells on 22nd November. The celebrations proved premature: the attack soon lost impetus and the Germans subsequently regained much of the ground lost when they launched a counter-attack on 30th November. Sir Julian Byng was the Commander of the British Third Army that undertook the attack.*

[2] the triumph of Gas over petrol restrictions: *petrol shortages led to some vehicles being converted to the use of coal gas carried in containers.*

Dec. 29. Another war Christmas. Not very much to record lately, except that we have to be more and more careful about flour, meat, sugar and cream. At Rugby Station lately in the Refreshment room I asked for a second small cake and was told I must not have it. The other day I was going by train from Coventry to Kenilworth, and the train was so full of ammunition workers that I jumped in the Guard's van and had a very comfortable journey sitting on a hamper, in company with a perambulator, a kind, civil soldier, and the Guard!

Mr Cooke is to go abroad on Jan 1st.

Mr Powell, an old clergyman from Leamington, took the Services on Christmas Day.

Chapter 6: 1918-19

Introduction

Cordelia's diary became more fragmentary in the later stages of the war. The first entry for 1918 was not made until March and there were sometimes gaps of up to a month between subsequent entries. She also became more dependent upon the experiences and accounts of others, chiefly Emily Ward. For the most part, her concern was with the major events of the period. Foremost among these was the German Spring Offensive, when "one's thoughts are filled with the war as they have not been since the first terrible days of August 1914". At the time of the Armistice, she was "laid low" by the Spanish influenza, but shared in the "great excitements". The diary continues into the post-war period and contains accounts, usually written by others, of the surrender of the German fleet, the news of the signing of the peace treaties, in June 1919, and the Peace Celebrations, in July 1919, although the celebrations at Stoneleigh were not held until August 1919. Cordelia's contribution towards the war effort continued until the very end: for example, her work on behalf of the Victoria League and also the War Agricultural Committee. There were fewer entries relating to local village men who were serving in the forces, although, in December 1918, she noted the return of two Stoneleigh men who had been prisoners of war. Among those who died in this period were two of her godsons, as well as William Mills from the village.

1918-1919 Diary Entries

Easter Day. March 31st. In London again for another War Easter, & the greatest we have experienced, for we are in the very crisis of the struggle.[1]

One's thoughts are filled with the War as they have not been since the first terrible days of August 1914. I came up last Monday, 25th; on Tuesday Canon Hepher, preaching at St Paul's Knightsbridge, read out the Archbishop's fine call to prayer at 12 noon, & called on the congregation to unite in silent prayer for the allied forces on the Western front, and for victory. On Good Friday the Bishop of London conducted the 3 Hours' Service in that Church, and called it the most eventful Good Friday since the first Good Friday in the world's history. In the course of his fine address, he said that the Government had asked him to make an appeal for 30,000 more women to work on the land and set more men free to go and fight.

There seemed to be very few holiday makers about, & most people looked serious and preoccupied. I went to a "United Service of Intercession" near the Marble Arch in the evening, at which the Bishop and some other Church of England Clergy in their robes, and some leading Nonconformist ministers, joined in giving the addresses & reading prayers in connexion with the war; a Salvation Army band led the hymns, "There is a green hill far away"; "Rock of Ages"; "Glory be to Jesus"; and "When I survey the wondrous Cross"; the Bishop also read out a letter of good wishes from Father Vaughan, the Roman Catholic Priest. It was all very impressive, especially when the crowd joined in the Apostles' Creed and the Lord's Prayer.

The Victoria League has been arranging a number of lectures to be given in various military hospitals. Margaret asked me if I could manage any. I showed my set of Nature slides, "Nature's Year Week by Week", which I bought in years ago from "The Country Side", with extracts from the accompanying reading, at Hampton-in-Arden and Kenilworth V.A.D. hospitals, and the Military Ward in the Warneford Hospital at Leamington. The lantern provided at Hampton was a poor one and the slides showed up badly, but Mr Wells worked our own school acetylene lantern for it at Kenilworth and Leamington, & I think there it was a great success; we also showed Rowland's lantern slides of Stoneleigh Abbey & the garden & river & Deer Park.

The county Board of Agriculture is trying to organise motor transport of fruit and vegetables & cottage garden produce generally from the villages to the railway stations in the county. A great number of baskets called "Pot Hampers", will be required. Miss Verrall, of Walsgrave, has been giving lessons to some wounded soldiers at Hill House V.A.D. Hospital at Warwick, and Alice Skipwith is trying to learn from her that she may teach soldiers later, possibly at Leamington. They are made from long, stiff osiers, and great strength of hand is needed.

On Monday I passed a long train full of American troops near Banbury. May they soon hurry to our help.

[1] the very crisis of the struggle: *in the spring of 1918, the German Army resumed the offensive on the Western Front, with the first major attack being launched against British forces near St Quentin on 21st March. The rapid progress made by the German Army over the ensuing days posed a major threat to Britain and her Allies and led to fears that the war might be lost. Although this attack was finally halted in early April, it was followed by others.*

April 12th – 13th. About 11.40 p.m., was awoke by a great crash, apparently over the house. My first thought was "a thunderstorm" then "the mystery gun" then "an air raid"? and so it proved to be. Zeppelins attempting to get to Coventry and Birmingham[1]; at least, such was their evident intention, but they failed. I heard two more great crashes, but remained comfortably in bed, as I thought I could do nobody any good by getting up. Rowly & the watchman went round the house putting out lights, & Mabel took Peggy, young Rowland, & Robin down to bed in her room, as it was on the second floor. There were various rumours next day as to where bombs had fallen, & in the afternoon Dudley, Mabel & the children bicycled into Baginton & Willenhall, & saw a huge hole near Chantry Heath where one had been dropped, & two beasts lying near it dead. But mercifully very little damage has been done.[2]

Walter Morris has been killed in Salonika.[3] Mark Upton is dangerously wounded in the great battle in France, & John Walton is missing.

Arthur Villiers has been slightly wounded in the leg, & has been in hospital at Oxford, & now at Middleton.

I have had two letters from Emily Ward dated April 5th & April 13th about Lord Bangor's experiences.

> "I have had two letters from my brother one dated 26th & the other the 29th of March. He was at Villers Bretonneux at the Cavalry Corps Head Quarters. He had been for nearly a year at le Câtelet near Bapaume – in a hut amongst the ruins of a destroyed town. About 3 weeks or a month ago they were moved to Villers-Bretonneux & he described the curious contrast between a draughty hut & a luxurious Château where his next quarters found him. He described a palatial bed & the house centrally heated – peacocks under his window & every kind of beautiful bird in a large aviary. He has a natural love of birds & he said the ostriches followed him about – & strange Manchurian pheasants & white peacocks eat out of his hand – & he descanted on the extraordinary phases of this war.
>
> Then came the advance & the Head Quarters have shifted 5 times in 7 days – a tremendous undertaking & today comes a letter from the cottage by the side of a dusty road – pitiful groups of refugees endlessly passing with precious things lashed on to bicycles or perambulators or go-carts. He hears his château is in flames and his friends the birds probably eaten! While they are on the move – he says the soldiers carry the refugee children – they make room on lorries wherever they can to help the poor Fathers and Mothers.
>
> Was there ever such a strange 'Holy Week'?"

Letter No. 2

> "My brother has written two more letters & describes how sad & dreamlike it is to enter a nice town from which all the inhabitants have departed.
>
> He is again located in an interesting country-house with fine pictures & prints & a good library.
>
> The first book he happened upon was an old edition of Robinson Crusoe in French & beautiful illustrations "Les Aventures de Robinson".
>
> His friends the birds have all got loose he says. "Peacocks, Storks, Cranes & Ostriches I hear of all over the place. One bird came over here – & was sitting in a Tree last night – a sort of Yard-bird (Horn-bill)" which shows us that after all he is within a bird's flight from where he was stationed on March 21! The Château de Villers-Bretonneux is burnt, where he was living."

[1] Zeppelins attempting to get to Coventry and Birmingham: *on the night of 12th – 13th April, 1918, Zeppelin L-62 dropped bombs in the Whitley Common area of Coventry, although the L-62's target was Birmingham. It was part of the last major Zeppelin raid on Britain.*

[2] very little damage had been done: *about seven bombs were dropped, the first falling over Baginton sewage farm; the largest crater was in the grounds of Whitley Abbey, about 8 feet deep and 25 feet wide.*

[3] Walter Morris has been killed at Salonika: *Private Walter Morris, 7th Bn Oxfordshire and Buckinghamshire Light Infantry, was killed on 18th March 1918 at Doiran, Salonika and is buried in the Karasouli Military Cemetery in Greece.*

May 14th. Coming away from Church Stretton, with Alice Skipwith, en route for London, changed at Shrewsbury, where we came upon a Welsh soldier, a private, who was being sent from a Hospital at Llandindrod to one at Berrington, entirely alone; he had shell shock & could hardly move; as we had 2 hours to wait, I asked the porter who was supporting him on his arm whether he would like any help, & he seemed pleased with the idea, so soon I found myself going down in the luggage lift with a strange soldier and a railway porter, calling out to Alice "I will come back presently!" The porter then left me with him in the Refreshment Room, & I finally wheeled him out in the station carrying chair on to the platform, where we sat and talked for some time, till at last Alice and I got him a book, & went off sightseeing, returning in time to see him off by his train!

May 20th, Whit Monday. Mr Metters, our Stoneleigh farmer, has been up to say his son, "Lieut. Metters", has won the Military Cross in France! in the 8th Batt, Leicestershires; we do not know the details.

(Later, heard that his men had to retire, & he worked a machine gun in order to cover their retreat, having finally to run himself for his life when all his men were safely away.

Now alas – June 7th he is reported missing).[1]

[1] Lieut. Metters has won the Military Cross etc: *Henry Hands Metters was the son of Mr Metters of Manor Farm, Stoneleigh. He was one of three men from Stoneleigh and Ashow who were to be taken as prisoners of war during the Great War. First having served in France with the 8th Battalion the Royal Fusiliers, he was later discharged to a Commission in the 3rd Bn. Leicestershire Regiment and in 1917 returned to France. On 27th May 1918 he was taken prisoner near Cauroy and was eventually repatriated, arriving home on 30th December 1918. He wrote the following statement regarding his capture: "On the morning of the 27th May 1918 I was ordered to take a Lewis Gun and 4 men and block a Communication Trench so as to enable the remainder of the Battalion to take up new positions about 400 yards behind me. About half an hour afterwards I found that the enemy had penetrated the new positions, thus I was in an isolated position but I still held on as I had not received orders to withdraw. I still kept the Enemy at bay until all my ammunition and bombs were exhausted and eventually the Enemy rushed my position taking the 4 men and myself prisoner." Lieutenant Metters was awarded the MC for this action, as follows: "For conspicuous gallantry and devotion to duty during an enemy attack. He was sent out with twenty men and a Lewis Gun on to the flank of the battalion, and by his skilful handling of his men checked the enemy and caused them considerable casualties. He showed great pluck and endurance."*

> "May 24th. This is the 4th celebration of Empire Day in War Time – & by 10 A.M. we were all at Stoneleigh School to see these little patriots give evidence of their loyalty. The elder children sang part-songs charmingly – of Home and Country – Sacrifice and Victory – this was followed by a little performance by the Infants – which was the prettiest thing possible.
>
> Four of them were in costume, the Old Woman who lived in a Shoe – hobbling in – & walking forward slowly & painfully. Next came Mary Mary quite contrary – pensive & slightly sentimental – shouldering her rake. After her little "piece" was

over – Taffy tripped in – the light-fingered Welshman – and finally Simple Simon – (or rather the Pieman) – in Cook's Cap and Apron – alert, trim and business-like.

The rest of the Infants sat in their tiny armchairs opposite the actors – the little girls in front and the little boys behind – quivering with excitement & enjoyment as they took part in the entertainment.

For, you see, War-time morals have even crept into Nursery Rhymes – and under searching questions – (in rhyme) from the rows of earnest Infants – the Old Woman confesses the Rhondda Rations[1] make life in her Shoe increasingly difficult. No wonder our poor little Mary is pensive – as she realises that her cockle shells & silver bells – must give place to cauliflowers and beetroot – & her pretty maids all in a row must be fitted out with smocks and gaiters! Of course – Taffy the Welshman's crime is trebled by the present meat shortage – & as for the Pieman, notwithstanding his perkiness, his professional existence is no more. All these sad facts were conveyed to us by our very small friends as a huge joke – & the picture of their joyous faces is a thing to remember!

Then we trooped outside – & saluted the Union Jack as it floated to the top of the Pole and sang "GOD save the King" with all our hearts."

The above account was written by Emily Ward, who has since gone home to Ireland. She had a small photograph taken at Graham's, at Leamington, to stick on to her permit; Dudley had to sign a declaration, as a householder underneath, that the photograph really represented "The Hon. Emily Georgina Ward", and the Police Officer at Warwick had to sign a declaration that Lord Leigh was really a Householder, after which the Permit was forwarded to London for final endorsement. On June 8th Emily wrote as follows:

"On board R.M.S. Ulster:

Now we are in mid-channel. It was a very short journey from Chester to St Cubby's, & before the train door was opened – the porter asked "Have you got your Permit?" Halfway across the gangway they were examined one by one – a glance at the photographs – a swift glance at the faces with the words "Pass on!" It was a glassy sea, & on board an official was standing by a pyramid of Life belts. "The Life belts must either be worn, or in readiness to put on", he said; & people who intended sitting on deck – each clawed a life belt – & I found one as usual awaiting me in my cabin, but took the precaution of carefully studying which was back, & which was front, & took my hat off so that my head would go into the hole intended for it in a moment. I had luncheon in the saloon – two women & 32 men!

A General at a table near said to his neighbour "The two saddest men I have met during the past week are Lord Wimbourne & Sir Bryan Mahon!"[2] Now it is so cool, so calm – so bright that I am going on deck to see the loom of Ireland on the horizon – while the tops of the Welsh mountains are still clear, & if you receive this you will know that lifeboats were unwanted."

[1] Rhondda Rations: *Lord Rhondda was Minister of Food Control between June 1917 and July 1918. In January 1918, sugar was rationed, followed, in April, by meat, butter, cheese and margarine. Ration cards were issued and people had to register with a butcher and a grocer.*

[2] Lord Wimborne & Sir Bryan Mahon: *Lord Wimborne had been appointed Lord Lieutenant of Ireland in February 1915, a position he was to hold, except for a brief period in 1916, until 1918. Sir Bryan Mahon had commanded the 10th (Irish) Division, before being appointed Commander-in-Chief in Ireland.*

Chapter Six

July 6th. Harry Metters has at last been heard of; a message has come from an American Firm that he & other officer prisoners have sent cheques to be cashed. A post card has also been received from John Walton saying that he is a Prisoner. Albert Morris has won the Military Cross.[1]

Aggie & D. went up to London yesterday & attended the Service at St Paul's this morning in celebration of the Silver Wedding of the King & Queen.

[1] Albert Morris has won the Military Cross: *presumably this should be the Military Medal, as Morris was not an officer.*

July 28th. Mabel Leigh has shown me a letter from her brother Capt Arthur Gordon with the American Red Cross at Paris. Some extracts follow:

> "Sunday 31st March, Easter. On Wednesday I was told to go to the Gare de L'Est & take charge of refugees who were pouring in from the invaded districts. As I alone could talk French I assumed charge. ... The French soldiers were feeding when we arrived. When they finished we arranged the tables & benches & mattresses, pillows & blankets furnished by the Red Cross, & fixed up a big dormitory. And then they began to come. I shall never forget it as long as I live. No one in the prime of life – 112 of them (though we were only equipped for 90) children & old men & women, & middle-aged women. One woman had 7 children & a friend's child with her. They filed in, weary & footsore & despondent, bringing their movable possessions. ... I had to speak to them in French to quiet them. Towards morning they would come up to the cooking stove where we were, & we would give the old women a little hot coffee, which was intended for the soldiers the next day. One woman wept. She was about 60 & had her poor old father over 80 with her, & this is the second time all these poor people have been driven from their homes. I got supper about 1 a.m. at Mlle Richard's canteen. I take off my hat to these French women. They work without rest, cooking & feeding & helping the soldiers. No wonder the soldiers fight well. ...
>
> Thursday; we had a very strenuous night. Over 800 came, & we took care of about 150, mostly babies & small children. One baby was 4 days old. We sent the mother and child to a hospital. Another was 3 weeks old, another 3 months, & one old man was 92. Three old women were all lame & had to be helped.
>
> On Good Friday we gave them coffee & condensed milk & bread. The toilet & washing arrangements were horrible. Uncooked food for soldiers was stored everywhere, & rats as big as cats played about. ... Slept from 1.15 to 3.45 & was awakened by a heavy explosion. It was a shell from the German long range gun, which exploded in St Gervais Church, killing 75 & wounding 90, mostly women & children who were at Good Friday services.[1] They are trying to affect the nerves of the civilian population.
>
> At 7.15 a.m. Saturday a German shell exploded near by. The Gendarme said: "The Bosche are sending us Easter Eggs". I got my refugees off as quickly as possible. Three fell before they were finally evacuated, & I heaved a sigh of relief that my duties were over. No more refugees are to be taken care of at Stations.
>
> Easter Sunday, after luncheon went to see St Gervais Church where 155 were killed & injured on Friday. There was a crowd outside but a gendarme yielded to my French & let us in. The shell had come through the roof, tore down a huge stone column, & the whole stone quarry had dropped on to the praying people. As

This Form must accompany any inquiry respecting this Telegram.

POST OFFICE TELEGRAPHS.

C. OR B.

Delivery and Charges.

Means..................

Distance..................

Collected..................

Paid out..................

If the Receiver of an Inland Telegram doubts its accuracy, he may have it repeated on payment of half the amount originally paid for its transmission, any fraction of 1d. less than ½d. being reckoned as ½d.; and if it be found that there was any inaccuracy, the amount paid for repetition will be refunded. Special conditions are applicable to the repetition of Foreign Telegrams.

Sent, or Sent out

At......M.

To..................

By 14

No. of Telegram } 196

Office Stamp.

LEAMINGTON-SPA 11 NO 18

Prefix	Handed in at	Office of Origin and Service Instructions	Words 16	Received here at
S	10 40	London CTO	4 46	

C Leigh 1 St Marks Rd Leamington

Germany accepts armistice signed five oclock this morning

The Times

Received at From By

Charges to pay s. d.

B or C 3 M4480 Wt. 30690/F357 10,000,000 2/18 C & B (257)

Armistice Telegram, 11th November, 1918. See Diary entry for 11th November 1918.

> we looked, the Germans opened fire, & their first shell of the day exploded a few blocks away. The guards immediately put us out, & the crowd melted as if by magic & made for the subway."

[1] the German long range gun etc: *a siege gun (known to the Germans as the 'Emperor William Gun' but often referred to as the 'Paris Gun') bombarded Paris between March and August 1918, from a distance of 75 miles. The gun's barrel length was more than 90 feet and the gun's shells reached a maximum altitude of 25 miles. More than 300 shells were fired and some 250 people killed; the worst single incident was the shelling of St Gervais Church, which is mentioned here.*

Aug. 26th. The writer, Capt. Gordon, is here now – in England for a few days before returning to America. He is very interesting, & tells how German soldiers are giving themselves up as prisoners, with hardly any resistance, & apparently thankful to be taken; he thinks the fighting spirit is dying out of them. It is amusing to see Capt. Gordon & Robin gravely saluting each other; & rather touching to see them shaking hands on Capt. Gordon's arrival here – Capt. Gordon a rather fine type of American in his U.S. Khaki, Robin a good specimen of the English boy, intensely patriotic, standing out on the lawn with the Old Abbey as a background, saluting, & then gravely shaking hands. And almost immediately afterwards Capt. Gordon told me how much he was struck by the contrast between the War devastated France & our peaceful English country.

Yesterday I went to a very beautiful Memorial Service to the memory of Lieut. Kay, son of the Capt. Kay who had been Recruiting Officer at Coventry; he was in the 29th Div. & died of wounds received in action in France.[1] The Service was held at Holy Trinity, Coventry; a military band accompanied the organ for the hymns, & Chopin's Dead March; & 4 buglers sounded "The Last Post".

Mabel Leigh has been given a medal for her services to Belgian Refugees, the Médaille de la Reine Elizabeth.

Agnes collects books now for the War Library, which distributes books among wounded soldiers in Hospitals. I am contributing some of Aunt Georgie's Library, which she left me in her Will. I am also sending some to the British Prisoners of War Library – the Educational Dept.

Maimée Mordaunt came over one day, driven in a small motor by her daughter Winnie who was in Khaki ambulance driver's uniform & decorated with the Médaille de Guerre.

[1] Lieut Kay: *Lieutenant Noel Rawstorne Wilkinson Kay, 15th Brigade Royal Horse Artillery (part of the artillery of the 29th Division), died of wounds on 5th July, 1918, and is buried at Boulogne Eastern Cemetery.*

Sept 26th. Having meant to go to London to-day for a Meeting to-morrow I found myself suddenly stopped by a railway strike. I tricycled into Leamington to both Stations, to see what prospects I have of getting off early to-morrow. G.W.R. almost deserted; at last I found a civil girl in the Enquiry Office who said "We know nothing about the trains, or which are running till they are signalled!" The L.N.W. people said their trains are running much as usual, but a little late.

27th. Got to London punctually & with no trouble by L.N.W.

D. has been anxious to go to Italy to drive an ambulance, but Mr Carter, the Secretary of the County War Savings Association, implores him to stop in England to call, & preside at, Meetings, & D. has reluctantly consented.[1]

[1] Mr Carter, the Secretary of the County War Savings Association, implores him etc: *the National War Savings*

Association had been set up in 1917. The last of the war bond issues was introduced in September 1918 and is presumably the reason why Dudley's services were particularly required at that time.

30th. Albert Rench, home on leave for a few days, with the Scotch Canadians, looking well & handsome, expects to be sent to Russia to-morrow.[1]

[1] expects to be sent to Russia tomorrow: *the Bolshevik Revolution (November 1917) had been followed by the withdrawal of Russia from the war (Treaty of Brest-Litovsk, March 1918). Among other concerns, the Allies feared that the large amounts of supplies and equipment sent to Russia, and held in Russian ports such as Archangel and Murmansk, might fall into the hands of the Germans or of the Bolsheviks. From July 1918 onwards, Britain and other Allied nations sent forces to Russia, which remained there after the Armistice and supported the anti-Bolsheviks. Some 40,000 British service personnel were eventually involved in the campaign in Russia, which did not finish until 1920.*

Oct. 10th. Staying a few days at Fonthill, I find the Canadian Forestry Corps camped out in a field on the Tisbury road, for cutting timber in the woods, & a light railway put down.

I omitted to mention that German Prisoners worked for some of our Farmers during the harvest, & by all accounts did well.

In August I went round to the different Farmers in Stoneleigh Parish, as Village Registrar with a Circular issued by the War Agricultural Committee[1] informing them how they could obtain extra labour and where to apply for soldiers, Women Land Workers, & German Prisoners.

Alice Skipwith writes that on Oct. 5th she went to Southwark Cathedral to a beautiful Serbian Service with wonderful Serbian music. Father Velimirovic preached in a black cassock, & spoke gratefully of the English Church, & of all our King & rulers had done for Serbia.

[1] the War Agricultural Committee: *towards the end of 1915 the Board of Agriculture and Fisheries, realising the war could well be prolonged, set up County War Agriculture Committees. The first meeting of the Warwickshire County War Agriculture Committee had been held at Warwick on 13th November 1915. The scheme included appointing sub-committees in each borough and in each urban and rural district*

Nov. 5th. My Camberwell Godson, Gunner F. Davis, has been killed in action[1]; another, Harry Miles, formerly in the Navy, has died of pneumonia.[2]

[1] Gunner F. Davis: *Rifleman (sic) Fred Davis, 12th Bn Rifle Brigade (The Prince Consort's Own), died of wounds on 1st September 1918 and is buried at Aubigny Communal Cemetery, Pas de Calais, France.*

[2] Harry Miles: *Harry Miles had served on HMS Ajax.*

10th. William Mills, of the Kennels, has been killed.[1]

[1] William Mills: *Sapper William James Mills, of the 154th Field Company, Royal Engineers, was killed on the 22nd October 1918 and is buried at St Aubert British Cemetery, France. He was the second brother to lose his life in the war, and the last man from Stoneleigh to do so on active service.*

Nov. 11th. Great excitements! Laid low in bed at Alice Skipwith's, at Leamington, after severe influenza[1], I have been thrilled with excitements these last few days, waiting for the news that the Armistice is signed! A. telephoned the news of the Kaiser's abdication about 6 p.m. on Saturday (9th). This morning about 11.30 Alice rushed into my room crying "News! news! the Armistice was signed at 5 o.c. this morning!" A. had telephoned to her, adding that Wyatt was ringing the dinner bell to celebrate the event, accompanied by furious barks from Sandy!

A little later we heard the hooter which was to proclaim the news; & about one o.c.

the bells of St Mark's Church, opposite this house, rang out a joyous chime, with a sort of crash & clang of several bells together at intervals, with a most festival effect.

The maids are hanging out flags from the windows.

4 p.m. Alice has been out & says that every child, & bicycle, & horse, & most grown-up people, are decorated with flags. It is Gun War Savings Week[2] in the town, & a gun to "feed" with war savings is on view outside the Town Hall.

Fireworks at night.

[1] severe influenza: *the Armistice of 11th November coincided with the height of the Spanish influenza pandemic in Britain, during which more than 200,000 Britons died.*

[2] Gun War Savings Week: *11th November was the first day of War Savings Week in Leamington, to encourage local people to subscribe to War Bonds. A 6-inch howitzer, liberally covered in War Bond Certificates, was placed outside the Town Hall. The appeal was led by the Earl of Denbigh, whose speech to the inaugural meeting at the Town Hall was interrupted by news of the Armistice.*

Emily Ward has been asked to describe her journey on this GREAT DAY, November 11 from Ireland to England.

> "The night had been very stormy – the last night of war – and lo! as I came within sight of Dublin Bay – behold there was a great Calm.
>
> I went on board the "Ulster" – the trusty Mail Boat – who, with her sister-ships – the "Leinster" & the "Munster" had scarcely missed a passage throughout 4 years of war, notwithstanding the constant menace of the German submarines in the Channel. The fourth mail boat – the "Connaught" had been commandeered for troops and had long ago been torpedoed and sunk in the English Channel.[1]
>
> Only a month ago – on October 10, the "Leinster" had shared her fate, & sank with 300 of her passengers within 10 minutes.[2] It was a great tragedy, for nearly everyone in Ireland had some friend on board – & the weeks following were very sorrowful – as new details came to light.
>
> The "Ulster" left Ireland at quarter to 9, in the morning - & my friend, the Stewardess, spent nearly half an hour in my cabin – telling me the whole sad story from beginning to end – and then she left me – the life-belt spread out conveniently near.
>
> From time to time I looked out of my port-hole at the sunny sea – and presently came on deck. We were guarded by one, if not two destroyers & and Air-ship on either side. I was fascinated by one of these – which was behaving in an unusual manner making a sound like Tick-tick-tick-tick – and dropping things into the water. "What is it doing?" I asked a passenger. "I really don't know" said the man – "practising dropping bombs, perhaps!"
>
> The answer did not satisfy me – so I went to the other side – and there I saw Holyhead fluttering flags & the Air-ships – and the Decorations told us the great news!
>
> Still I was not satisfied, for I wanted the joy of hearing it by word of mouth – and so I said to the man in the gangway as I stepped on shore, "What are the Flags for?".
>
> He was patient with the Village Idiot, & answered "THE WAR IS OVER! the Armistice was signed at 5 this morning – our Wireless caught the news – 'Oly'ead knew it before Crewe or Chester!"

The Train waits at the Landing Stage till passengers and mails are ready to start, and, as I sat staring at the camouflaged Mail Boat – which had faced danger daily through these dark years – and while trying to grasp the bare fact of the words "THE WAR IS OVER"! and their mighty meaning & wide result – I was thrilled by a delightful sight.

Sailor after sailor came along, bearing on their shoulders Flags of Decoration – and as we steamed away from the Landing Stage – the sight of the gallant old Mail Boat – joining in the general rejoicing – as the flags were run up with a heart and a half – was a sight which will never be forgotten – a vivid illustration of the end of War! Part of the General Thanksgiving round the circle of the Earth."

A friend writes the following:

"The crowds round the Palace shouting for King George went on for days & even nights, but the first day when it began a man from the Admiralty was talking to him, and said 'Sir, the people are calling for you, will you not go out to them?' & the good King would not believe it – he said, 'no, no, they are only rejoicing – they don't want me.' The Queen came in & the man in despair begged her to make the King come out, & she burst into tears, she was so touched, & they went out together again & again: and so it went on day after day."

Another friend reports – with what truth I know not – that when Marshall Foch & Admiral Wemyss went to Paris to see Clemenceau[3], after they had dictated the Armistice terms to the German delegates, all three took hands & danced round and round!

[1] the 'Connaught' ... torpedoed and sunk in the English Channel: *the Connaught was sunk on 3rd March, 1917, with the loss of three lives.*

[2] the 'Leinster' had shared her fate etc: *the R.M.S. Leinster was struck by three torpedoes on the morning of 10th October, 1918, an hour after leaving Kingstown; 501 of the 771 people on board died when the ship sank.*

[3] Marshall Foch etc: *Marshal Ferdinand Foch led the French delegation in the Armistice negotiations, which took place in his private train. Admiral Rosslyn Erskine Wemyss, appointed 1st Sea Lord in December 1917, in succession to Admiral John Jellicoe, represented Britain at the negotiations. Georges Clemenceau was the French Prime Minister .*

Nov 24th. I have had a delightful letter from my Stoneleigh sailor, Ernest Aris.

"I guess you know by this time that things have been very exciting on board the Queen Elizabeth of late – with German Admirals coming on board at Admiral Beatty's[1] request, & then their Majesties the King, Queen, & Prince of Wales inspecting the Ship – & then the great day 21st November with the surrender of the German Fleet.[2] We left Rosyth at 4.30 in the morning & met the German Fleet at 9.40 a.m. which we escorted back to our base. Just after we got back, the Queen Elizabeth stood to let the other two Fleets pass, the German on one side of us & the Grand Fleet on the other, which gave three loud cheers for Admiral Beatty as they passed. We were flying the largest white ensign we could, also Admiral's Flag, which was extra large & made of silk, which looked very nice to the Germans no doubt. After all the [word illegible] which had passed, we waited a little longer – while the light forces came up. Then we saw a sight like a pack of Greyhounds. 50

German destroyers, escorted by 150 of our own. After we saw them all in safe, we left them in charge of the 1st Battle Squadron for the night. Then we went on our way to Rosyth, and we had to pass the U.S. Navy & our Battle Cruisers, who also gave us three cheers, all the Bands playing "GOD save the King", & others "Rule Britannia" and "Over There". It was a very nice sight to us. Then at 6 p.m. we had a Thanksgiving Service throughout the Fleet, on the behalf of the handing over of the German Fleet. We never did expect them to come in so quietly, we were all cleared for action in case it was necessary to open fire: but it was not needed. I was always proud to be on the Queen Elizabeth; but now I am prouder still, & thank God that we won that great Victory without losing a man or ship.

Your affectionate Godson. Ernest."

[1] Admiral Beatty: *David Richard Beatty, 1st Earl Beatty, had been appointed 1st Sea Lord in December 1917, in succession to Admiral Jellicoe.*

[2] the surrender of the German Fleet: *as a consequence of the Armistice, the Germans were ordered to surrender both their submarine and surface fleets. The surface fleet was escorted to the Firth of Forth, on 21st November, with Allied ships in column either side of the German ships. Between the 25th and 27th November, the German ships were moved to Scapa Flow.*

Dec. 29. First Sunday after Christmas. A "Peace Christmas" at last. The Christmas Psalm took on a new meaning on Christmas morning: "Lord, Thou art become gracious unto Thy land – righteousness & peace have kissed each other!"

Our two Prisoners of War, Tom Mills from Turkey & John Walton from Germany are home, & Harry Metters is expected. Walton was ill at first from change of food, after being half-starved in Germany. Aris, on leave from H.M.S. "Queen Elizabeth" came to see me the other day with his young wife. "The Times" of Dec 23rd gives the names of Major Child Villiers, D.S.O. amongst those mentioned in Despatches by Sir Douglas Haig.[1]

[1] Major Child Villiers: *the youngest son of Margaret Jersey, Major the Hon. Arthur Child-Villiers D.S.O. was mentioned in despatches: "for conspicuous gallantry and devotion to duty. He led his squadron dismounted in*

The Khaki Bible given to Joseph Charles King.

a counter-attack with remarkable skill and daring. Although wounded in the leg he refused to be evacuated to the dressing-station, but continued to lead his men, and sent back valuable information as to the situation, although in great pain. He set a splendid example of coolness and endurance."

Jan. 7th 1919. Tom Mills came to see me to-day; he said he was better treated than some of his fellow prisoners, probably because he worked in a hospital, but he was very badly fed. He showed me the little "Knapsack Bible" which I had given him, and said it was the only thing not taken from him. I have not seen Albert Morris, but his father told me that his decoration was given him owing to his having ridden backwards & forwards 19 times under heavy fire to carry rations to some of the men.

Jan. 26th. At Weymouth, where I am staying with Alice Skipwith to get well after influenza, there are a great number of soldiers constantly arriving from Havre; we have seen Australian, Canadian, & New Zealand troops marching by, as well as a large contingent of the Glos. Regiment. The streets are full of smart & smiling Japanese sailors from a Japanese ship in Portland Harbour. I have had my first sight of a camouflaged ship! She appeared to be made in folds or wavy lines & I am told she was a "razzle-dazzle".[1]

I have received a little pamphlet by Miss Soulsby called "What America means to an Englishwoman" in which there is this rather striking paragraph about America. "The older nations, with blood stained hands, needed to be cleansed by a baptism of blood; but the younger nation, who, like David's son, was to build the Temple of Peace, 'in a short time fulfilled a long time'. She gave her sacrifices – of her prejudices, her comforts, her sons – as whole-heartedly as Abraham gave Isaac; & now, like Abraham she receives her sacrifice back in order to do with it some better things."

[1] "razzle-dazzle": *a camouflage scheme widely used in World War I, although the purpose was less to conceal a ship than to make it difficult for the enemy to estimate its size, speed, course etc. Complex patterns in contrasting colours (usually black, white, green and blue) were intended to disrupt the rangefinders used by surface ships and submarines.*

Writing to his sister Miss Emily Ward in March 1919 from Germany, Lord Bangor told her 3 strange things.

Emily Ward writes:

"He was at Bergheim and lodged in a gorgeous German château. In his bedroom was a Kneller[1] – of a certain – Jones-of-Afton – Oxfordshire – but the curious thing was that hanging framed upon the wall was that beautiful hymn:

'LORD for to-morrow and its needs
I do not pray –
But keep me – guide me – hold me, LORD,
Just for to-day.'

Strange to find it in a magnificent German château & intact all through the war.

The next odd thing was, that, when last week the 10th Hussars returned to England the women & children in the village where they were billeted were weeping they felt so safe with them.

The third odd thing was this, in his words:

'The gate of the Château where I am staying is on the road side – and when the

German armies were going back after the Armistice – the owner of the Château had the gate removed – and the gateway blocked up & actually had ivy put over it, so the German soldiers should not see it & break into his place & perhaps wreck his home.

As soon as he heard the British Army was coming – away went the Ivy! away went the bricks! and the gate was rehung! The Germans trust us more than their own countrymen. Funny!"

[1] In his bedroom was a Kneller: *Sir Godfrey Kneller (1646-1723) was a significant Court portrait artist. Born Gottfried Kneller in Lubeck, Germany, it is perhaps not so surprising to discover one of his paintings in a German chateau.*

May 22nd. I have been at Folkestone & Canterbury with Alice Skipwith. One day at Folkestone an old Town Crier went down the streets ringing a bell & proclaiming "Extensive mine-sweeping operations are to take place, & there may be heavy explosions; all persons are advised to keep their windows open." We saw a column of smoke rise from the sea after an explosion. Nobody might go near the Harbour at Folkestone without a permit. But we had a good view of Dover harbour, with warship, & an overturned "monitor" across the mouth of the harbour.

Some flags of Canadian Regiments were hung in the Nave of Canterbury Cathedral for safe keeping while the Regiments were abroad. The old Church of St George's at Canterbury had a fine bronze memorial of the Action at Zeebrugge on St George's Day, 1918[1] & the flag which gave the signal "St George for England" had been presented to the Church and was hung near the memorial.

[1] the Action at Zeebrugge on St George's Day, 1918: *the attempt made by the Royal Navy, on 23rd April, 1918, to neutralise the port of Zeebrugge, which was being used by German U-boats. Block ships were sunk across the entrance to the port but only denied use of the port for a few days. Nonetheless, the daring raid was widely acclaimed as a success.*

June 21st. Most of the family are in London, the house is being cleaned, & carpets are being taken up; to-day I had a curious experience, for looking over the balusters I saw a man leaning over the carpets, with a round patch on his back! a German Prisoner at work!

June 28th. Saturday.

PEACE is signed![1]

Through nearly five long years one has wondered when this day would come; & how does one feel now that it is here?

Well, I think that the general agreement is, that there is very little of the excitement and exultation which attended Armistice Day in November.

Still, I, personally, felt a thrill when I heard the Stoneleigh Church bells ring out! I was down in the village about 4 o.c. & saw some of the children with little flags; then some one said that news had come to the Post Office that peace was signed, & some of the boys fired off squibs. About 7.40 I was sitting on the lawn when I heard the bells ring out – first Stoneleigh, which was answered later by Ashow. It is a cold, cloudy day, with gleams of sunshine.

[1] Peace is signed: *the Treaty of Versailles, which ended the state of war between Germany and the Allies, was signed on 28th June, 1918. The other Central Powers were dealt with in separate treaties. The treaties followed negotiations at the Paris Peace Conference.*

On **August 12th**, a large Garden Party in celebration of Peace was given at Stoneleigh Abbey to the villages of Stoneleigh, Ashow, & Westwood, & attended by about 800 people.[1] Fortunately, the day was fine. It was a sad day for us, as it was one of the last days of Rupert's illness, & he died on the 14th.

[1] a large Garden Party in celebration of Peace etc: *the Peace celebrations at Stoneleigh Abbey were held nearly a month after the national Peace celebrations, which had been on 19th July, 1919. The Leamington Courier for 25th July reported: "Lord Leigh decided that August 12th should be the day of the celebrations". Presumably, the family preferred to be in London on 19th July. It is quite likely that Stoneleigh was the only community in Warwickshire area that did not have its main Peace celebrations on 19th July.*

(Undated) Warwickshire Boy Scouts were represented at the Royal Garden Party for War Workers[1], by Samuel Cardall of Kenilworth, a "King's Scout". He had worked for 3 to 4 months making hospital requirements for the V.A.D. Hospital, and for 3 years belonged to the Local Volunteers.

[1] the Royal Garden Party for War Workers: *was held on 25th July, 1919, at Buckingham Palace.*

Oct. 12. A friend who has been reading this Journal remarks that the Palestine Campaign has not been once mentioned in it. Well, two Stoneleigh men went to Palestine, Edward Carley (the son of Mr Carley the Farmer at Stareton) and one of the King family: unfortunately neither of them went into Jerusalem; both have returned safely.

Margaret Jersey has just written me this about her grandson Charlie Rhys. "We are very pleased that Charlie has returned wonderfully well after sleeping on the ground in forests – sharing in battles, etc." (in Russia) "and he has won the Military Cross & Order of St. Anne (Russian).[1] I think his fellow-officers in the Grenadiers will be green with envy, as I believe they all volunteered and only Charlie was taken out of the regiment. Arthur has just gone off again on a visit to Cologne." Charlie left Sandhurst just before the Armistice.

[1] Charlie Rhys etc: *Charles Arthur Uryan Rhys, 8th Baron Dynevor, was the grandson of Margaret, Countess of Jersey, Cordelia's eldest sister. He was commissioned into the Grenadier Guards and in 1919 he was awarded the Order of St. Anne of Russia.*

Open Scrapbook

Chapter 7: The Scrapbooks

Introduction

As an accompaniment to her War Diary, Cordelia decided to keep scrapbooks of letters received and other printed material to do with the war. She eventually filled two books, which are now privately held in the archives at Stoneleigh Abbey. The scrapbooks are densely packed, with some material having been pasted in out of sequence, as Cordelia looked for space to include items that were of interest to her. The entries are not annotated and a good number of them, including many of the letters, are undated, although it is often possible to give an approximate date to them by studying their contents.

Despite these difficulties, the scrapbooks are a valuable supplement to Cordelia's diary and provide telling glimpses into the war work in which she and her family participated. In particular, they reveal that she not only encouraged young men to enlist but maintained a correspondence with them, which lasted the length of the war.

1914

Among the contents from the early months of the war, Cordelia's first scrapbook contains a statement of accounts of the Lady Lugard Hospitality Committee for the Relief of Better-class Belgian Refugees, including a list of donors; receipts are pasted in for the Harrods Belgian Relief Fund, showing that sugar, chocolate and arrowroot have been bought by the family. Cordelia's recruiting leaflet "Why We Are At War" was printed at a cost of 19/6 for 4000 copies, and a copy of the leaflet together with the bill for printing is included. "Anxious to do something" as she herself expresses it in the Diary, she sent her sister Agnes £5 towards the Overseas Emergency Fund, for a "Warwickshire" ambulance and duly pasted in the receipt; there is also a letter from the Reverend Farel Webber, a chaplain on HMS *Black Prince*, thanking her for slides she had sent as entertainment for those on board; touchingly, this is accompanied by a cutting from *The Times* reporting on his loss on May 31st 1916.

As stated, the scrapbooks are largely taken up by letters from "her" young men and one soon sees how Cordelia was doing what she could to make life comfortable for them. As early as October 1914 Jonathan Prime was writing to thank her for "the chocolate and the rest of the parcel" and later in the same month Albert Morris thanked her for several pairs of gloves; in November he wrote again to say that he had received the games she had sent. Ernest Aris joined the battleship HMS *Queen Elizabeth* following its commission in December 1914, and at Christmas wrote to thank Cordelia for the Christmas stamps and calendar. He also described Queen Mary's present to servicemen: tobacco, pipe, cigarettes and photo. Cordelia gave each of her Bible Study class a small "khaki" Bible when they joined up, and Joseph Mills, serving in an anti-aircraft brigade in Portsmouth, thanked her for this: "I shall always carry it with me and put my trust in God to bring me safe through this terrible war."

Several letters suggest that the young men wished Cordelia to know that her influence, both spiritual and practical, had not been forgotten: Joseph Mills continued "... it is every young man's place to join the army at this time. But I am afraid that the young men are not coming forward as they should do now. They do not seem to realise the terrible nature of this war. I think Stoneleigh and Ashow men have done splendid." George Paget, who had lived at the Abbey Home Farm, wrote from Royal Artillery Barracks in Woolwich that "I do

Church service on board HMS Queen Elizabeth in the Dardanelles. Cordelia's godson, Ernest Aris, served on the ship.

not think that Stoneleigh could do much more in supplying soldiers and it is to be hoped that members of the Temperance Society who have joined the colours will always remember the pledge." (Cordelia's father, William Henry, had been a keen Temperance man and she had evidently followed his example.) Harry Miles, a London boy from Camberwell for whom she had stood godmother, wrote from HMS *Ajax* "I still remember that walk through the Deer Park and the dogs' graves you showed us," whilst Harry's mother wrote to keep Cordelia informed of his whereabouts "in the North Sea with the Baltic squadron". She went on, "If you are writing to him tell him to always to think of his country he is serving and never to dishonour his flag, his father sets such store by his flag. Sometimes I wish I had a lot of sons, that they might do the same."

In the early months of the war Cordelia's correspondents were keen to keep her informed of their progress as they came to terms with Army life. The shortage of equipment meant that, in October 1914, Albert Morris was "wearing a scarlet tunic and blue trousers" but "expect to have khaki before long." Training involved "a good deal of marching and physical skill and night skirmishing". By November, he had moved to Clarence Barracks, in Portsmouth, and found accommodation much better than camping: "We are very comfortable here as we are in married quarters with a living and bed room and a little scullery and sink and a tap. It is almost like home. We parade close to the sea so we see plenty of cruisers go by." The improvement did not last, because he soon found himself billeted in a brewery: "it was really a shocking place to put us in but we thought we would be soldiers and make the best of it." Lance Corporal J. Mills, of the 4th Battalion Royal Warwickshire Regiment, was camping at Freshwater on the Isle of Wight and his description of life there was graphic:

"We have only 1 khaki suit each, 1 shirt and 2 pairs of socks each. I have had to send home for 1 shirt. Our pay is 1 shilling per day and out of this 8d is stopped for allowance for wife and children, leaving 4d per day for myself which is barely sufficient to buy the necessaries we require, viz; cocoa, sugar, butter, tobacco and stationery, stamps etc which we purchase for our own comfort as the allowance of food is not sufficient being half a loaf a day per man, with very little butter, meat, cheese."

Cordelia's correspondence was also with members of her family. Audrey Liddell, her second cousin, wrote from Peasmarsh in Sussex to tell of "Uncle Charley's" experiences, having been taken prisoner by the Germans; "Mama", "Auntie Etty", "Uncle Charley" and "Uncle Clem" were all Cordelia's cousins. Audrey's additional comments on recruitment give an insight into the life of the gentry in the early months of the war.

"The Germans seem to have behaved fairly well to him but it must have been very trying to work ten hours a day in convict's clothes and to get prodded in the back with a sentry's bayonet when one did not please him! He said one of the hardest trials was to be called up and hear news of German victories translated by an interpreter for the English prisoners' benefit. Mama and Auntie Etty are at Hookwood to say goodbye to Uncle Clem who left yesterday to be a conducting officer on some railway. I don't quite know what that is. How splendidly you have done with recruiting. I wish I could say the same for our village, but the men here simply won't see the necessity for training and argument is quite useless. They have no imagination and can't see farther than the nearest hop-field. But our chauffeur has gone to be an ambulance driver and we are quite proud of him."

Similarly her cousin Winnie Mordaunt of Walton Hall in Warwickshire wrote from the Military Hospital in Dieppe, where she was working as a chauffeur and theatre orderly:

"... most of the car work is in the morning, and the operations in the afternoon ... very messy jobs as one means so much cleaning, greasing and oiling and the other washing up, sterilising and mopping up endless blood and bits of bone! Tetanus and typhoid seem to be what the men die of after they're in hospital."

Winifred's sister Cicely Mordaunt, writing from the Hopital Lamarque, Rue de la Riviere, Calais, on 11th December, 1914, described some of her work as a nurse:

"Left Dieppe about a fortnight ago and came here to join the First Aid Nursing Corps of which Cousin Dudley is a patron. The Corps is running a hospital of about 100 beds in Calais for wounded Belgians because the Belgian wounded and refugees are badly neglected here – in spite of the great debt of gratitude they owe them, the French will do hardly anything for them! I hear they left a lot of Belgian children who had scarlet fever to get on as well as they could on the quay where they landed. Our people had to look after them in the end. Besides the hospital the Corps has a dressing-station up at Gostherde near Dixmude and they go up there in turns, two at a time for ten days. I wish my turn would come! They give clean shirts to the men besides doing the first field dressings. Just now I am very busy helping in the typhoid ward. It's hard work but most interesting – we are three girls and one trained nurse only – so when she is off duty we have to do her work – which is a great honour for mere probationers! She is going out tonight so I shall have to write the day report for the night nurses, which will probably cause a good deal of amusement. One lives and learns!"

A friend, Isobel Fitton, wrote from Newcastle in December about her brother Brigadier

General Hugh Fitton, “commanding the Division up here on the coast[1] … he has been having quite an exciting time. He is billeted in a little mining village 13 miles off, dreadfully uncomfortable as he is in an empty cottage with nothing but his sleeping bag on some straw. There was not even a chair at first but he says he is quite happy and content as there is a bath and hot water! We take him cooked food every day … my brother is busy entrenching and barbed wiring all the coast.” She concluded, optimistically: “It <u>must</u> be over by August.”

[1] Isobel Fitton etc: *The Fittons were a musical family well-known in Malvern. They were connected with the Elgars, and the mother and sisters had many pieces of music dedicated to them. Isobel Fitton inspired ‘Ysobel’, Variation VI in the ‘Enigma’ Variations, which is built on an exercise he devised for her, for crossing strings on the viola. She never married, and lived all her life at the family home, ‘Fair Lea’, in Malvern. Brigadier General Hugh Fitton subsequently died on 20th January 1916 from wounds received while inspecting trenches. He had been visiting the front line held by 16th Brigade near Vlamertinghe, north of Ypres, on the 18th January (only 11 days after landing in France) to learn about trench warfare when he was shot by a sniper. He never regained consciousness, died two days later at 1.20pm in No. 10 Casualty Clearing Station and is buried at Lijssenthoek Military Cemetery. The news reached his brigade as they were being inspected by General Joffre and Sir Douglas Haig. He was the first Brigadier General from the 34th Division to die in the War.*

1915

The Scrapbook entries for 1915 are dominated by Cordelia’s correspondence with the men from Stoneleigh who had enlisted and by the evidence of her continued gifts to them. Thus, Tom Mills acknowledged the receipt of a sunshield, and also books, which had been sent to France. The foodstuffs she sent off seem largely to have been chocolate, although Fred Smith wrote to say he would like “cake and cigarettes”, suggesting that Cordelia may have asked her contacts for their preferences. Arthur Cadwallader’s request, in September 1915, was for “underclothing”. Again, the men’s spiritual needs were not neglected. W. H. Stoney, in the RAMC at Salisbury, thanked her (6th November, 1915) for “the khaki Bible”, as well as “gloves and chocolate”. At the time, he and his comrades were living “in galvanised iron huts, each accommodating 32 men”, with “a large hut for a church”. Those who were injured probably received special attention. On 24th September, 1915, Thomas Bant Mills, in a Red Cross hospital in the Town Hall at Burton upon Trent, thanked Cordelia for magazines and jigsaw puzzles, adding: “My leg is almost well and my ears are better, I can hear splendidly now…”.

The Stoneleigh men were keen to tell Cordelia of their experiences. Joseph Mills was part of an anti-aircraft brigade at Portsmouth.

> “We are attached to the Royal Marine Artillery and drive armoured motors fitted with a pom pom gun and it is specially made for firing at aircraft though it can be used for firing on troops. It is quite a new gun like a maxim only larger and fires 120 rounds a minute and 2lbs shells. … We have to learn semaphore signalling and there are two drivers on each car and five marine gunners. We have to go out at night driving without lights which is very trying as the cars are very large. We are expecting to go to France this month. There has been a delay in the guns, but they are being fitted now. I met Tom Mills in Portsmouth.”

Tom Mills was with the 3rd Battalion of the Oxfordshire and Buckinghamshire Light Infantry, at Cambridge Barracks in Portsmouth, and reported that he was “digging 6 foot deep trenches”.

George Thorley found training physically demanding: "we have plenty of drill, about seven and a half hours a day". They were sleeping under canvas but found "we are all very warm at nights with 15 or 16 in each tent". Like other volunteers, they had to make do with temporary uniforms. However: "we are getting our new clothes next week ... I think I shall look a little better than in the blue." Harry Leeke, of the 9th Battalion Royal Warwickshire Regiment, was not a villager but he helped keep Cordelia informed of the progress of a Stoneleigh man in his unit. Writing from Aisne Huts, Blackdown Camp, Hampshire, on 3rd March 1915, he had this to say of Corporal Thomas Steele and of the conditions in which they were living:

> "He is in my 2nd machine gun company section so is constantly under my eye. I am in charge now of the two gun sections (4 guns) of the battalion. A most awful place here, all mud, and we are quartered in huts, none too clean. I believe this is our last one before France but I cannot say anything definite as no-one seems to know anything about it ... your man Steele is still Capt Coates' servant and looks very fit and well."

For the most part, the fighting was still distant for the men at this stage, although, in January 1915, John Thorley, with the Warwickshire Yeomanry, wrote from Drayton, near Norwich, to say that he had seen Zeppelins at Kings Lynn and Sheringham dropping bombs. He had also cut his head and had been kicked by a horse. Later, writing from Donington, near Newbury in Berkshire, he noted: "We have a lot of wounded around us, some attached as postman, orderly, and other light duties. They tell us the papers do not publish one half. We have one, as a postman, wounded in the shoulder in the retreat from Mons."

One who was soon in action was Ernest Aris on board the battleship HMS *Queen Elizabeth*. Early in 1915, his ship was still preparing for war and he:

> "will be glad to go for a change and see the world a little bit more before I come home again. ... I hope to be with better company than I am with at the present time – you hear nothing else only bad language with a lot of the Irish chaps and at mealtimes they throw the food in our faces for fun, they think it fun to put some down our neck and clothes and get us into a bother."

However, he was soon at sea: "I was a bit seasick when it was very rough".

He could not reveal his whereabouts, except to say that it was "like summer" and not like rainy Portsmouth. In fact, the *Queen Elizabeth* had been sent to the Dardanelles to take part in the naval attack on Turkish forts. This was soon public knowledge and Ernest was able to write, on 14th March, 1915, to say that he was "sorry that I did not write before but we have been very busy just lately bombing the Dardanelles which you will now see in the papers, which will make the food cheaper when it is done. We have been destroying the forts which are stopping the food coming to England – until they are done away the food will be getting dear in England." His birthday had been on 27th February but apparently he had not known what day of the week it was – until Cordelia sent a letter. Soon he was writing to say that: "we are getting a good name according to the papers."

Before long, other men found themselves in a theatre of war. George Thorley arrived in France, after being on a boat for 15 hours. He spent the next night riding in a train and hoped:

> "to come across some of the Stoneleigh boys. I am a little way from Morris and Smith but have not seen them while we have been out here. We are doing well for being on active service."

Charles McReay, with the 2nd Battalion of the Royal Berkshire Regiment, wrote from France to say:

> "we do not get many changes of clothing. We were relieved from the trenches the other night and are in reserve just behind the line and we are going in again tomorrow night, Sunday, I think, as the weather is all right and they are keeping us in for longer periods."

Harry King, in the Oxfordshire and Buckinghamshire Light Infantry, wrote, on 30th April, 1915, to say that he was adjusting to life at the front:

> "I have got quite used to bullets whizzing and shells bursting all around now. While in the trenches we could hear the Germans talking quite plain. All the French villages close by the firing line are one mass of ruins. Two chaps in my section come from Ryton so we generally have a talk about Stoneleigh."

Harry Jarvis in the 2nd Battalion of the Royal Warwickshire Regiment, writing from an undisclosed location, reported that:

> "we were in the trenches for five days ... we had quite a lot of shelling but they did not do much damage. One man in my company was wounded in eight places. The Germans are expected to make an attack here soon as they have been seen getting ready for it and have got guns here from some of the other fronts."

The countryman in him could not fail to note that: "The corn will soon be ready for cutting here." On 18th September, 1915, Arthur Cadwallader, in the 3rd Battalion of the Worcestershire Regiment, wrote to say that he had been in France more than 6 months and that:

> "I have been wounded once, that was in June but I am back in the trenches again now and am keeping well. ... The shells are flying all around us, we are having very nice weather."

George Thorley told Cordelia that: "I miss your class on Sunday afternoons". He was one of many village men who had attended Cordelia's Sunday school classes in their younger days and the religious beliefs they had absorbed are also reflected in their letters. George also told her that, close to his camp: "There is a very nice little church ... all their men have gone away so a lot of those who can sing have gone in the choir. I am one of them so I do not miss my singing in our old church." His brother, John, reported: "a very nice Church Parade at the village church this morning, they also allowed us leave, anyone who liked, to attend early Communion". W.H. Stoney, writing from Salisbury in November 1915, had also recently joined a choir. "The chaplain is a very nice gentleman indeed and one in whom a soldier might find a welcome friend." Thomas Mills, serving with the 1st Battalion of the Hampshire Regiment in France, was "so pleased I was in the CLB [Church Lads' Brigade] which I found so useful since I have been in the army, to trust in God and do what's right." A number of men were in the temperance movement and were keen to assure Cordelia that they remained true to their pledge. Thus, Thomas Steele hoped he would be: "worthy of my membership of the society and keep to the terms of the promise".

It was natural, of course, for Cordelia's correspondents to tell her what they thought she would want to hear and there were, no doubt, aspects of a soldier's life that would not be recounted to a lady, let alone one of her social importance. Nonetheless, the picture that emerges from these early letters is of earnest young men who were keen both to do their duty and to uphold what they considered to be the standards of their upbringing. John Thorley would be pleased to see "the German nation smashed for their excessive brutality" but also hoped "God will soon put an end to it, and bring us safely home". Likewise, Tom Hewitt, along with his brother, hoped "God will spare both of us to return to old England again", while Charlie McReay wrote simply: "Shall be jolly glad when it is all finished and I can safely return."

The Scrapbooks also confirm the other ways in which Cordelia, and the Leigh family in general, helped the war effort. There is an article by Lady Lugard, dated 26th March, 1915, on the work of the War Refugees Committee and a letter from the War Refugees Committee, dated 11th November, 1915, in gratitude for "excellent work done by your committee". Another letter (16th December, 1915) from the Bureau de Travail Belge a l'Etrange asks for help with indexing cards to assist Belgian refugees find work in England. R. MacLeod, of the National Service League, thanks her for the telescope "as telescopes are useful for seeing what the enemy is up to!"

The increasing human cost of the war is reflected in a copy of the Stoneleigh Parish Magazine for September 1915, which records the news of Ernest Thorley's death, and also in a letter from Mary Hewitt at Stamford, Lincolnshire, dated 8th October, 1915, in which she wrote: "I am sorry to inform you that my nephew Thomas Hewitt was killed in action September the 25th. His brother was also wounded and taken prisoner. His mother wished me to let you know." The letter was accompanied by a post card (21st October, 1915) from the Red Cross enquiry department for wounded and missing saying: "will do our best to make all possible enquiries."

An example of how rumours spread in wartime is contained in a letter from "Marky" (Cordelia's eldest sister, Margarette Countess of Jersey), dated 8th April 1915, Villa Luynes, Cannes.

> " ... I have heard a lovely story about the outbreak of war, which may be true – Kaiser loved the murdered Archduke with whom he had made deep-laid plots to take effect when Emperor F.J. died – when he heard of the murder he went mad with wrath – said he had lost his only friend, and (rather a la Henry II – Becket) sent frantic abuse to Austria for allowing it, and demanded vengeance – Austria, frightened of Germany, set to work to bully Serbia, and Kaiser found war much nearer than he bargained for, for he knew he was not ready – his brother Prince Henry at Cowes declared the Kaiser would never sign the Declaration of War, and really thought so – meantime Crown Prince and his myrmidons were delighted, and Crown Prince went to his father urging him to sign – Kaiser refused again and again so C.P. went away in the evening – got together all the war party leaders in full uniform and when morning came went to his father's room in the Schloss leaving the officers in the corridor. He sat on the table spreading the declaration before him and again asked Kaiser to sign, who again refused. Then he jumped up, exclaiming, "Sign or Abdicate!", threw open the door disclosing the crowd of officers, who all cried," Sign or Abdicate!" and the Kaiser gave in! Tell Aggy this and say I think it is even truer than the Russians! .... "

The 'Russians' is a reference to the widespread rumours of Russian soldiers being transported through Britain in the autumn of 1914, on their way to France.

1916

Early in 1916 the scrapbook documents begin by concentrating on the importance of recruitment. A very long letter, in February, recounts Lord Leigh's experiences with the War Office Recruiting Party, which he accompanied early that year. It takes the form of a diary entry:

> "The boat we came over in yesterday was crowded up to the eyes, about 1400 being the total – Malcolm Murray, Henry Guest and Lord Newton among them – the greater number were soldiers. From Boulogne we motored here, about 54 miles. Coming over we had as chaperon a destroyer (I think it was).
>
> Today we motored to Albert, about 90 miles, to the 14th Division of the 3rd Army. At Albert great destruction has been effected by the Germans. At the top of the tower of the cathedral the huge statue of the Virgin and Child stands out at right angles to the cathedral, poised above the city. We went into the trenches that are close to the town and went round them. They are very complete, with dugouts, mines, trench mortars, hand grenades, gongs by which to sound an alarm in case of a gas attack, wind vanes etc. A part of the trenches is paved, a part of them have wood flooring. Every few yards the ground is dug deep to improve drainage.
>
> Pretty heavy firing was going on, on both sides. In places the trenches run very close to the German lines. Part of the trenches were made by the French, part by the English. Keeping them in order entails much labour, as also does digging the mines under the German lines, and bringing up the earth in sandbags. The officer who showed us round said that owing to shortness of men those who had been sent back to rest were liable to be lugged back again before they had had proper rest, to repair the trenches. When coming out of the trenches the sloping of the ground towards the city hid one from the enemy and so we could come out in the open. The headquarters of the Third army where we called on the way to Albert are at Bocaine. As regards statues and the destruction of churches, when the statue alone is left intact, this has occurred so often that I hear that a book has been written in France about it. I saw practically two examples of it, at Oudecapelle and Reininghe. Owing to motor mishaps and delay, I got back to St Omer too late to dine with Sir Douglas Haig at headquarters, as I was to, but I went there late – the Duke of Teck was here, Major Heseltine etc.
>
> Jan 30th, Sunday. I went into the cathedral early – a fine church – mass was going on. We motored to the headquarters of the Welsh regiments, General Sir Ivor Phillips at Lebon. We went some way along their trenches, which leads to where the chief fighting was at Neuve Chapelle – going towards the trenches evidence is everywhere of the fighting in the battered roofs of houses and walls – at one place a tree had been cut in two – at other places crosses had been erected to mark graves – the wooden flooring had been covered with thin wire, making it less slippery. Some of us returned to see the Welsh battalions reviewed by Lloyd George, who was staying with Sir Douglas Haig. At Lebon two German prisoners had been brought in – their clothes were good, and they seemed in good condition and they gave no evidence of shortness of food.
>
> At one spot on the way to the trenches a number of crosses or memorials included one to a man in a Rajput Regiment.
>
> Jan 31st Monday. This day we went to see the Lancashire regiments. I myself

and others had been given to understand that we were invited to stay till Tuesday but on arrival in France we were told we were to stay till Monday only – also the Mayor of Liverpool, Mr Salvidge, was most anxious to see the Lancs Regt in which he was interested. I was able to get these matters put right through the Duke of Teck. We motored to Hallencourt, General Jeudwine, 55th Division. We also seem to have encountered the 114th Brigade 38th Division Major Crawshay; General Carter was, perhaps, one of those we met there. The Liverpool Scottish were at Hencourt – Col. Davidson. On our arrival some of the C.O.'s met us, and we divided up for luncheon. I had it at the 6th Liverpool Rifles, Col. Harrison. I motored in search of the battalion he wished to see with the Lord Mayor of Liverpool. The distances were great – at last we came to the London Scottish.

Juvenile Patriots.

Coventry Graphic Photo.

The photograph reproduced above shows a number of scholars and ex-scholars who are members of the Stoneleigh C.E. School woodwork class, with crutches and bed-rests, which they are making for the use of disabled soldiers. The class, of which Mr. W. H. Wells the head teacher, is the instructor, was established four ago by

Stoneleigh School woodwork class. See Diary entry for 25th-26th September 1916.

Here we found an officer who'd just returned after being wounded, and we saw practising at machine gun firing and bomb-throwing. The bomb they had was said to be the best – when set it did not explode until a spring was released – another or others they spoke of exploded without this catch, with, it might be, a very inconvenient result. We took cover when the bombs were thrown, and could see that the results were great on a tree that was struck. Bombs are sometimes, I understand, fired from a rifle. We saw the men's quarters and a football match.

I saw at headquarters Capt. Barry, 5th Lancers. This place is a long way back from the Front.

Feb. 1st. Tues. Motored to Boulogne en route for England: we missed the boat, and so had to wait for an afternoon one. I went to see Lady Hadfield at the Anglo-American Hospital at Wimereux – had luncheon with her – Sir Bertram Dawson there and two other ladies under Lady Hadfield, one of whom said that she saw at a distance the commotion of the explosion on the destroyer that had the accident a day or two before. The ship did not sink, but was got into harbour. I believe a boiler blew up. I went round the raised wall which runs inside the walls of the old chateau. We returned to England in absolute darkness, even down below the lights were out. The party I was with were eight in number."

The account is accompanied in the scrapbook by several newspaper articles detailing the itinerary and personnel of the party.

The cross over Ernest Thorley's grave at Cairo, for which Cordelia paid. See Page 102.

Other members of the Leigh family supported the war effort in various ways. Photographs in the scrapbook, from the *Coventry Graphic* for 21st April, 1916, show schoolboys at Stoneleigh School making supplies for soldiers – Cordelia's brother Rowland supervised this activity, along with the school's Headmaster, Mr Wells. A letter from her sister, Margaret Jersey (22nd August, 1916), an Honorary Secretary with the Red Cross, on Red Cross paper and headed "Central Work Rooms", details the way in which Stoneleigh school children could assist in making "necessaries and comforts for the wounded at home and abroad":

"My dearest Cords,

I enclose the leaflets about certificates etc – the schoolchildren could register as one working party and apply for two certificates, one for each school. As you will see, to entitle each worker in a party to a certificate there should be an average of 10 garments per person in 3 months, which is impossible to expect from children – so in several instances we have given a certificate to be hung up in school – you might, I should think, call it "Stoneleigh School Working Party" and you could put yourself or Headmistress as "Lady to whom re". I suggest that you should keep the "application form" which will be sent you if and when you register, till perhaps end of September and then send in your claims for certificates for September, June and July work. If you do not want to be troubled with information fortnightly please mention when you register. We close here next Thursday – re-open "Central Workrooms Royal Academy Piccadilly" Sept 4 – so unless you answer by return you had better not do so until that date."

Cordelia's care for individual local families is touchingly revealed in a series of letters concerning Samuel Ernest Thorley, who had died the previous year at Gallipoli. Edward T. Hull, a Church of England Chaplain with HM Forces, responded to a letter from her saying that "Yes, I think it is possible to get a cheap monument to mark the spot where poor Thorley lies. I remember a shop near the cemetery and am writing to Cairo for inquiry to be made." Evidently the Reverend Hull wrote to J.D.Hepple, the Senior Chaplain with HM Forces in Egypt, who wrote from Cairo on March 1st 1916 that a cross had been erected at a cost of one Egyptian pound; on the 29th he wrote again, "I enclose a photograph of Ernest Thorley's last resting-place. I am so glad the picture has come out so well and the words so distinctly, and I trust it may prove of some little help in consoling the parents." A year before the establishment of the Imperial War Graves Commission, Cordelia had obviously recognised the importance of seeing a marked grave. She received a letter of thanks from Thorley's mother, offering "my grateful thanks for your trouble for my dear son's grave." Perhaps Cordelia had acceded to the wishes of Reverend Hull, who had told her of his being with Thorley on the day before he died, when he had prayed with him and talked of home, and his mother. "I had great hopes of his eventual recovery that afternoon, but (perhaps you had better not tell his mother this) in his delirium he tore off his bandages and opened the wounds afresh."

Much of Cordelia's correspondence from 1916 includes instances of men continuing to receive parcels from her: magazines, socks, under-clothing, prayer-cards and Bibles are all mentioned. Receipt of news from home is warmly welcomed, and often Cordelia's birthday card served to remind them of the date! W. Tuckwell, writing from Hazeley Down Camp, Winchester, wrote "it is so lonely down here" and was feeling "so low down I am pleased to have a friend." No doubt the thought of leaving for the Front was frightening: her "Godson Willie", leaving for France, thanked her for the prayer book and continued "thanking you for all you have done for me through life." Driver A.J. Morgan wrote in October to thank her for a Bible "a great help to men on active service as we do not go to service very often. I often think of the Old Boys that would attend your classes and wonder if they will all return safe. I wish you every success with your Sunday School training and with the Harvest Thanksgiving. My only wish is that I could attend but my thoughts will be with you all at the little church on Sunday."

Several letters enquired after friends who were serving elsewhere, and others gave

Cordelia news of the writer – often about the progress of their wounds – which she was then at liberty to pass on. W. Darlow had had measles, and after a spell in hospital was sent to Plymouth to work with transport horses, before going to help with harvesting. Now with the 8th Dorsets in Blackpool, he described "a big review of the generals ... did look nice while the sun was shining on the sea front." An Ashow man, he told her news of two others: W. Allen was in Rouen, whilst Will Palmer had been wounded and was back in England. On 24th November George Fardon wrote that he was "glad to hear that Charlie [his brother] was doing good munition work." He added, however, a comment about life at war "I would like to explain to you but dare not as I am on active service and you are not allowed to speak the truth."

A series of letters from Victor Bonnard, serving with the Canadian Expeditionary Force, to Lord Leigh, provides an interesting insight into one man's attempts to remain positive. In one:

> "I am writing to you in my dug-out. We are having glorious weather and the time goes merrily along. You forget all fear – it is so intensely exciting."

On 14th June he wrote:

> "I'm now resting – having had a pretty rough time, some of the boys were buried alive. Some of the sights were too horrible to mention – nevertheless I still like the life, daily the beautiful birds sing to us – perched on leafless trees – their sweet notes being heard between the cannon roars. I am fit and *happy*. My father has just joined the AMC [Army Medical Corps] at Hull."

Ten days later, on 24th June "Somewhere in France" he:

> "Cannot mention my doings but am feeling fit and interested in my work. I often come across, while walking in various parts, doing fatigue work, a nice cross which marks the resting-place of either an officer or private – along a path or lane! I always stop to see whether he might have been a friend of mine. I have lost so many, which makes the whole battlefield sacred to me. The other night I noticed a cat waiting outside a wee cottage which was in ruins. I hope that my heart will harden in time to these sad sights! But as it is, it makes me want to remain – there is such a lot to be done, and I am quite a donkey in using a spade or lifting anything heavy. How were Major Chandos and Lieutenant Edward Leigh killed?"

On 27th July:

> "Have had a pretty rough time. Our trenches were knocked down and I only have three hours sleep ... but what is a few hours of hardship compared to the welfare and happiness of our homes for the near future? A while ago I dived into a dyke to get away from a shell bursting, and looked as though I had been clipped ... not feeling the worse for my adventures. PS Lord Brook is beloved by all the boys and officers. I can hear them speaking of his kind-hearted actions."

Matters took a darker turn on 24th September:

> "I am again in England. I shall never forget Friday Sep 15th inst. We could not have had a better morning and although we were unlucky having the bombing attack at 5 o'clock, being due over at 6, I was slightly wounded going over the first trenches and just before reaching our objective I was buried. The MO [Medical Officer] made me stay in bed today. I fainted a few times this morning but hope to be fit shortly. We lost very heavily and the awful sight of seeing my poor comrades killed has just about taken my heart. I did not have my rum and therefore had to light a cigarette! The Germans put up a very good fight at the start, but ran devilish

quickly when they realised we were after them! In fact losing an officer and going too fast we got under our own barrage, but as there were shells everywhere it made very little difference where one stood!"

And, on 2nd October 1916, at A7 No 5 War Hospital, Dorothy Street, Reading, he wrote:

"My shrapnel wound has quite healed and have got over the shell shock, except it has left me with a weak heart, which I believe in time will be all right too! Hope that your Lordship has not been troubled with the Zeppelin raids, everything seems pretty bright this side – I suppose owing to the excellent war news."

During the course of the year, many of the letters pasted into the scrapbook began to reveal increasing anxiety mixed with a determination to hold fast to the religious truths which Cordelia had taught. On 10th June A. Cadwallader of B Coy Machine Gun G Section, 3rd Worcesters wrote:

"We have had some hard fighting just lately. There were very few left of us, but I seem to be one of the lucky ones. My mother always tells me to trust in God's Providence and know it is God that protects me. And then dead or alive he will not forsake me. I should be grateful if you could send me some underclothing as I lost all mine in the last battle. The loss of Lord Kitchener must be a great blow to England but we shall have to sacrifice a great lot yet before the Huns are beaten."

Similarly, W. Worrall, 1st Battalion Royal Warwickshire Regiment, wrote from the Base Depot in France:

"I received the testament and prayer book you so kindly sent me before I returned to duty. I have got it with me always and often read it. You will see by this that I am in France. I left England on the 10th October and expect to be moving up to the line any day now, though I am some distance from the firing line I shall be there by the time you receive this. I shall fight like a British soldier should for his King and Country but I am also a soldier of the King of kings. I know Jesus Christ to be my saviour and I shall go forward trusting in God and doing what is right. I often think of the lessons I learnt at the Sunday evening Bible Class at the Abbey which you were so pleased to give us. I do thank you from my heart that you begged us not to have anything to do with gambling of which there is so much in the army and which I see every day. "'Twill save us from a thousand snares to mind religion young" is quite true. I hope I shall be spared to return to England again if it be God's will."

Worrall's quotation comes from a children's hymn by Isaac Watts, which was no doubt learnt in one of Cordelia's Bible classes. Its final stanza perhaps characterises an invaluable confidence which she had hoped to imbue:

"Let the sweet work of prayer and praise,
Employ my youngest breath;
Thus I'm prepar'd for longer days,
Or fit for early death."

(*The Advantages of Early Religion,* from "Book of Divine Songs" by Isaac Watts.)

1917

The 1917 correspondence continues the sense of anxiety intermingled with a determination to hold fast to faith: H. Waltham wrote in February, "Oft times whilst under fire I keep my trust in God and as you see I am still kept from death." H. Mills, writing from France in mid-June, and perhaps anticipating a forthcoming battle, asked for an Old Testament to be sent as he had read in the papers of how "before a very hot action" men had made a search for Bibles, and when one was found "at last they had to cut it into pages and every man had one which he eagerly read." Mills, along with other correspondents, kept Cordelia informed about the natural world which he observed: "the dog roses look nice in the hedges" and, the son of a woodman, noted how the enemy had cut down trees but the French were attempting to save them: "Those that have had a ring of bark cut off, they are putting a kind of bandage on, and those cut right off, they are grafting shoots on the stump. I hope they will succeed in saving them as it would be a pity to lose so many fine trees." Religious services were held with the brigade band, he told her, and he described the fine churches he saw on the march. In one: "As we stood in the church I thought of the old church at Stoneleigh. One more notable thing is that at every crossroad and grave yard there is nearly always a crucifix."

Several soldiers wrote of their difficulties or injuries. A letter from Charlie McReay reveals the growing necessity at that time to keep men at the Front for long periods of time. In May, he wrote that:

> "I have been hanging on for my leave ever since February 9th when I got to the railway station and then they cancelled it. Since then some other fellows have arrived and superseded me but I have had 10 days in England out of my 28 months stay in this country."

Later that year, in October, F.G. Clifford, hospitalised and awaiting a ship home, wrote:

> "I really have been frightened and shivering expecting some of us to get hurt badly with terrible shells. It is most wonderful how one comes through, it seems impossible sometimes one ever escapes being hit … there have been terrible storms and the sea very rough, I can see it from my bed in hospital. The nurses are mostly American but are very nice to all of us. I am able to see the water that parts so many loved ones. It seems very hard when the evacuation for England goes and you are not in, but of course we have to respect the motto "keep on smiling." I have no kit at all with me."

Others were in warmer climates but not in good condition: J.B. Mills, with the Mediterranean Expeditionary Force "somewhere in the desert" in June found the weather "very hot and trying", being "troubled mostly with mosquitoes and flies." Although Arthur Cadwallader had written in 1916 that he seemed to be one of the lucky ones, in 1917 he had had some near misses: not only had he received shrapnel wounds on one occasion, his little Bible "in my pocket" having prevented further injury, he told Cordelia, but in April, on board ship from Marseilles, he had been:

> "… on my way to Mesopotamia but unfortunately was torpedoed on the 15th. I was on board the Cameronia – I expect you have seen by the papers she has gone down. I was in the water about two hours but luckily was picked up by a destroyer. I was a terrible sight but I don't think I am any the worse for it now …"

This letter had been written from hospital in Malta, but later he wrote from the General

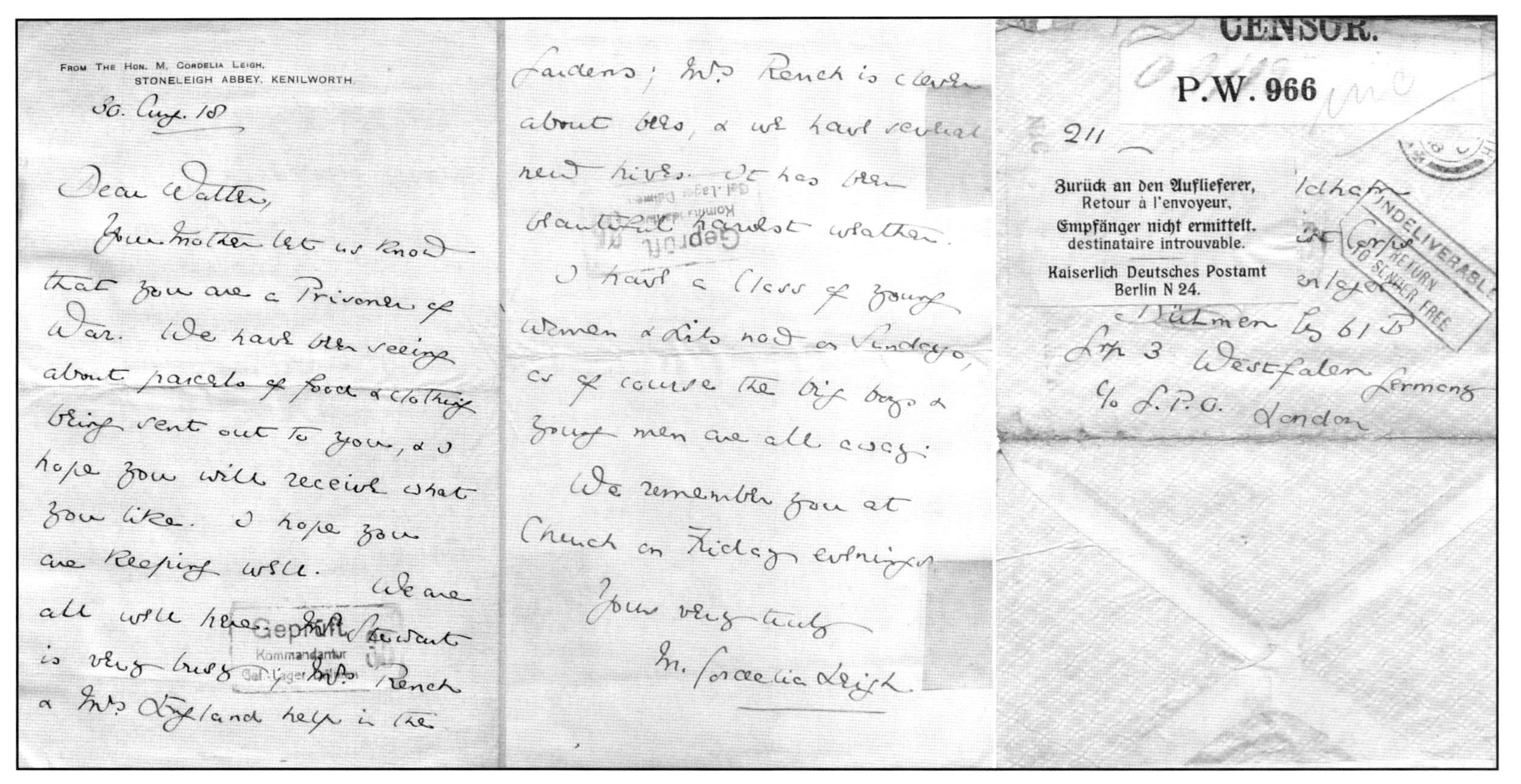

FROM THE HON. M. CORDELIA LEIGH,
STONELEIGH ABBEY, KENILWORTH

30. Aug. 18

Dear Walter,

Your mother let us know that you are a Prisoner of War. We have been seeing about parcels of food & clothing being sent out to you, & I hope you will receive what you like. I hope you are keeping well. We are all well here. Mr Stewart is very busy, Mrs Rench & Mrs England help in the gardens; Mrs Rench is clever about bees, & we have several new hives. It has been beautiful harvest weather.

I have a class of young women & girls now on Sundays, as of course the big boys & young men are all away.

We remember you at Church on Friday evenings.

Yours very truly

M. Cordelia Leigh.

CENSOR.
P.W. 966
211

Zurück an den Auflieferer,
Retour à l'envoyeur,
Empfänger nicht ermittelt.
destinataire introuvable.
Kaiserlich Deutsches Postamt
Berlin N 24.

UNDELIVERABLE
RETURN TO SENDER FREE

Dülmen
Westfalen Germany
c/o G.P.O. London

Cordelia's letter to Walter Oldham, returned by the German censor.

Hospital, Alexandria

"... I am suffering from the experience I had coming across. I have been in here six weeks now but I am pleased to say I am improving. I have still a long journey before me yet. I hope the war will be over by the time I get there."

1918-1919

The Scrapbook entries for 1918 and 1919 contain further examples of Cordelia's contacts with men from the village who were serving in the armed forces. One of the more unusual items is a letter that she had written to Private Walter Oldham, a prisoner of war in Germany. It had been opened by the censor and returned to her, although the reason for this seems hard to ascertain. It is undated but the reference to "beautiful harvest weather" clearly places it in the summer period.

"To: Pte W. Oldham, Army Cyclist Corps, POW Camp Dulmen, Westfalen.

Dear Walter, Your mother let us know that you are a Prisoner of War. We have been seeing about parcels of food and clothing being sent out to you, and I hope you will receive what you like. I hope you are keeping well. We are all well here. Mrs Stewart is very busy; Mrs Rench and Mrs England help in the gardens, Mrs Rench is clever about bees and we have several new hives. It has been beautiful harvest weather. I have a class of young women and girls now on Sundays as of course all the big boys and young men are away. We remember you at church on Friday evenings."

Various post cards and letters in the Scrapbook thank Cordelia for the books that she had been sending. In a letter dated 1st March, 1918, Harry Miles wrote to Cordelia, thanking her for letter that had arrived in time for his birthday:

"I was more than pleased to know that you had not forgotten it. Thank you very much for the little book. I hope you won't mind my asking you but if you have got an envelope large enough to hold a photograph like that one of the king I gave you, I would let you have another of our own little made-up church. We cannot get any large envelopes here... yes I would very much like to come to the Temperance Society meeting but it cannot be done. I would like to hear the birds sing and see some flowers, I miss all those sights of nature now. The only woodpecker we hear is the carpenter."

In similar vein, Driver A.J. Morgan wrote from Italy, on 2nd April, to thank her for the hymn book that she had sent him:

"I am pleased to hear that everyone at Stoneleigh is quite well. I am pleased to say I am enjoying the best of health. I trust I am still a recognised member of the Temperance Society as I often think and long for the time when I shall return and rejoin my old Bible class. Well, I am highly pleased at being in this country as it is much better than France, and the scenery is somewhat grand. I have just settled down after a fortnight's march and some of the sights I saw were beautiful, especially in the mountains. The civilians here are very nice and obliging, do anything for you, so you may guess it is a great help to Tommy."

On 15th September 1918 William James Mills wrote from the Western Front:

"Very many thanks for your most welcome parcel which I received yesterday with the socks and muffler, which will be very useful especially as the cold weather

3rd Batt'n West Yorks. Regt., Whitley Bay. Northumberland.
Dec. 1, 1918.

My dear Friends,

How much has happened since I last wrote! Words fail to express all that we felt when the news came of the Victory won. A deep sense of relief and thankfulness must have been in all our hearts, that the burden and strain of anxiety of the past years was over for a time. How wonderfully God has answered a peoples' prayer, our thankfulness if it is true, must be shown in our lives in the days that are before us. Let there be no slackening in our Intercession With all the problems in our own country, and those which will arise at the Peace Conference, we need that those in high positions shall have a right judgment in all they do. For this reason the Friday Evening Service, will, I hope, continue to be held whenever possible, and be well attended.

The sympathy of all will be extended to Mr. and Mrs. A. Mills and their family, who have been called upon to make the second great sacrifice during the War. On the eve of Victory, William James Mills fell in action on Oct. 22nd, somewhere in France. His was a particularly attractive nature; loving his games, always to be relied upon in all he undertook, he was a splendid example of regularity and punctuality in his School and Church life, where he gave of his best in the Choir for many years. He crowded a good deal into a life, short in years, but long when one considers the influence of a life like his. He, with the rest of that great army of heroes, who have given them may be assured of our prayerful sympathy.

I cannot say how gladly I send you my wishes for a Happy Christmas as I look forward to beiug with you again so soon.

Your sincere friend and Vicar,

H. E. COOKE.

An extract from the Stoneleigh and Ashow Parish Magazine.

will soon begin to be felt, and the Pocket Text Book is something which is always handy as when in these trying times, when danger is all around us, it makes you feel as if you want to read God's word to comfort you. I still have the Prayer Book you gave me some time ago and I have felt the benefit of studying it when I have been in danger and doubt. We do not get a service very often now; we had used to have one regularly every Sunday at one time but we can hardly expect a service where we are at present, we are following up the Germans and we are only staying in one place for a night and off again next morning, following the Germans on their retreat. It is surprising how near to the fighting game is found – partridges are very numerous just there, and it reminds one of England seeing them flying about. It is a shame to see how the Germans are destroying everything as they retreat – churches are left nothing but one heap of bricks, and crucifixes which one finds at almost every corner out here are all broken. One place I saw our Lord upside down on the cross just as the Germans had left it. I am pleased to say that I am keeping quite well and happy but am looking forward to when we can all get back again to peaceful times. The weather is grand now after the wet week we had last week. Again, thanking you for the parcel."

W.J. Mills, the youngest son of the Stoneleigh game-keeper and second son to die in the war, was killed in October. His effects included "two religious books". An extract from the

Chapter Seven

Stoneleigh Parish Magazine (1st December, 1918) gives details of W.J. Mills' death.

There are three letters from the Rev. H.E. Cooke, the Vicar of Stoneleigh, describing some of his experiences on the Western Front in the early part of 1918. He was serving with the 1st Battalion King's Own (Royal Lancaster Regiment), although by the end of the year he had transferred to the 3rd Battalion of the West Yorkshire Regiment.

BEF February 26th 1918

"... it is a very welcome change to be out of reach, if not of sound, of Bosch shells and it adds enormously to one's peace at night. I cannot get used to sleeping through a barrage, as our last camp was literally surrounded with gun emplacements, they were hardly ever silent at night. Here I have had some splendid parades and other voluntary services and some of the most impressive Communion Services that it has ever been my happiness to take, though the atmosphere has been anything but helpful in one's surroundings for these services. In a raid some time ago, of 70 men all practically attended a service beforehand with Holy Communion. They went over the top next morning and had splendid success, losing only one man killed and one wounded and taking prisoners and killing many of the enemy. Everybody was surprised at the success, but we who had been with them knew why. You once were kind enough to say that if I wanted books I was to let you know. I am anxious to get a reading room fitted up for this battalion so that when the men come out of the line they shall have a hut with games, magazines and books to read. I am asking Mrs Cooke to send me some old magazines and any of the Nelson's editions of good works that she can find, and I thought that possibly you could spare some of this sort of thing. I think these pocket editions are best, because we have to be often on the move and a larger book takes too much packing. I am going to try and get these Lancashire boys their local paper sent out and the major of the battalion is getting games etc, so if you can help me in this I shall be grateful."

BEF March 17th 1918

" I have been waiting till that parcel of books arrived, to write and thank you for so kindly sending such a nice lot, also for the paper – Country Life – which is much appreciated – last but not least for your interesting letter. I was glad to hear that the confirmation was now fixed, I shall be with them in thought if not in presence. My four months will cease on April 23 and if I could get away a week before that I might manage to be present, which is what I should like. However I must not think too much about the possibility at present, for "leave" depends very largely on whether the Bosch does what the newspapers have foretold that he will do, before that date. We are much in the position of "waiting to see"! I have had rather an interesting Sunday after taking my own Battalion parade, I was given a Staff car to go a long way out to another regiment and after lunch to a Field Ambulance and give them a service – it was a lovely day and I passed through a good deal of country which was quite new to me. I was very interested to hear of the development of your weekly meeting and glad to know that it is growing, also to hear from Mrs Cooke today about the Women's Institute meeting of last week.

I liked that little book you kindly enclosed and feel it will be useful for men in the trenches as it has a few of their favourite hymns in as well. I shall get some for distribution when I visit them next in the line. At present we are in reserve and may go anywhere."

20th April 1918

Having thanked Cordelia for the 'Country Life', which had been given to the men coming out of the line, he continued:

> "We are up north now and the country is much more like England in many respects, and the people much more ready to welcome us than they were further south, where they appeared to be tired of having troops billeted upon them. The warfare is quite different, too – no trenches and heavily wired strongpoints, but quite open. I expect the nations feel more acutely here that we stand between them and the enemy more really at the present than they did when the warfare was more or less stationary. Quite the most pathetic thing to see is the number of peasants on the roads day and night, clearing out of their homes with their few goods packed on a cart or wheelbarrow. I fear many of them will have lost most of their stock, though they do generally like a cow also behind their cart, with them, but the greater part has been left behind. I have lost more than two thirds of my battalion these last few days – the majority ... but there has been no progress made here since we came in, though it has cost the enemy more still. These days I am busy at the Field Ambulance just behind the Front, but today things are quieter."

Some of the entries shed light on the more mundane duties of soldiers who were stationed in the United Kingdom. In February 1918, H. Mills, one of Cordelia's regular correspondents, wrote from Blyth, in Northumberland. After serving on the Western Front, he was now with the 7th (Reserve) Battalion of the Worcestershire Regiment, following a spell of sick leave at a convalescent camp at Ballyvoanare in Ireland.

Blyth, Northumberland 27 February 1918

> "It is a very nice place on the sea-coast, not far from Newcastle. ... I have been up to Whitley Bay Musketry Camp. .... I just managed to scrape first class shot – 93

Land girls Alice Chattaway and Nellie Collins, along with Miss Adcock, working for Mr Adcock at Leasowes Farm on the Stoneleigh Estate.

points. I have been on guard twice since being here. We have to keep guard on the coast. There are several observation posts along the coast, and some big naval guns. You have to report all vessels entering or leaving the harbour. I went for dental treatment the other week, but the dentist could do nothing for me as I could not open my mouth wide enough. So I am waiting for a TMB [? Temporary Medical Board] as my jaw seems to be fractured and I am unable to eat any hard food. I have been in the mess room since."

By May, Mills had returned to Ireland and was now stationed at Phoenix Park in Dublin with the "2/1st Q.O.W." [probably the Queen's Own Worcestershire Yeomanry].

"Things are still very quiet over here, we expected a bit of trouble over the arrests made in Dublin, and each regiment takes it in turns on Mobile Detachments in case anything should turn up. Phoenix Park is a very beautiful one. It has four or five entrances to it and there is a statue of General Gough, and one with a phoenix on top. There are also the zoological gardens, I have to go there sometimes. The Vice Regal Lodge is close to here, we have to find a guard for it. Every morning we have an hour cleaning our cycles and then we have a ride round, we enjoy it too, this weather. I have been put on a course of signalling now, and it looks like being very interesting. We are learning the Morse Code, we call A Ach and B is beer D is Dom, so as no mistakes can be made when reading the signals. Then we have the Buzzer for sending messages on. It is a bit hard to catch the Morse Code at first but it will come easier to us in time. We make notes of various things when we are on parade, but I have lost my wallet so shall have to start over again. We have a different method here for time, too. It is a bit of a nuisance to us when we get any rain, as it makes so much mud and you keep taking it into the tent."

In March 1919, Mills was still in Ireland and now serving with the 2/3rd Scottish Horse.

Ennis, County Clare. 13th March 1919

"...we are fairly comfortable when you think of the old times in France, it seems a palace. The people round here are very strong Roman Catholics. We went to a church on Sunday, we had to take rifles with us, it does not seem very nice to have to take arms into a church, but I suppose it is necessary as the people round here are very strong SFs [Sinn Feiners], and the troops who have been demobilised are worse. The YMCA here is run by church people and every Sunday night refreshments are given free. I was on railway guard the other day, we have coal, wood and rations to look after. It snowed very fast this morning but knocked off about eleven."

Cordelia's support for women's work on the land is reflected in a number of entries, including a recruiting leaflet for the Women's Land Army. Two land workers, Alice Clarke and Alice Chattaway, are mentioned in a letter dated 7th February, 1918, as having been working on the land for two years; another, Nellie Collins for nearly eight months. The girls were entitled to service stripes, a bit like soldiers, with one stripe being awarded, Cordelia thought, for each six months. Two of the girls, Alice Chattaway and Nellie Collins subsequently appeared in a photograph of girls working on Mr Adcock's farm, along with Miss Adcock. The girls were pictured in a haycart on 16th March, 1918. A letter from Catherine Margesson to Mrs Kay, dated 25th June, 1918, refers to the forthcoming procession of Women War Workers in London, for which nine girls had been chosen to represent Warwickshire. The hope was expressed that farmers would give the girls leave and enable them to assemble in Birmingham before journeying to London.

Some of Cordelia's other interests are shown in a booklet on the Kensington Square War Hospital Department, with an introduction by G.K. Chesterton, and a letter from Lady Baden Powell (22nd August, 1918) thanking Cordelia for having spoken to the Girl Guides Commission on the previous day. There is a lengthy account, by an unknown writer, addressed to Isobel Fitton of an air raid. The Zeebrugge Raid (23rd April, 1918) clearly captured Cordelia's attention and the Scrapbook contains a map and newspaper account. More bizarrely, a newspaper item on the Naval Pigeon Service was also thought worthy of inclusion.

A memorial card and order of service were retained for the funeral of Noel Rawstorne Wilkinson Kay RHA, 29th Division. Noel Kay was the son of Captain Kay, the Recruiting Officer for Coventry; he died of wounds in France on 5th July, 1918. The service was held at Holy Trinity Church in Coventry and is referred to in Cordelia's diary entry for 26th August, 1918. A letter from H.H. Metters (23rd May, 1918) mentions his award of the Military Cross, for "good work on March 24th" (see footnote to diary entry for 20th May, 1918) and a newspaper item records Winnie Mordaunt's Croix de Guerre, awarded for her hospital work in France (see footnote to diary entry for 8th November, 1914).

The telegram announcing: "Germany accepts armistice signed five o'clock this morning. The Times" was understandably retained and a letter from Major Rupert Leigh puts a slightly unusual slant on the Armistice celebrations in London:

November 11th 1918, Beaufort Gardens SW

> "I think you may like for your War book a copy of the Evening Standard which I bought about 11.30 a.m., the first edition published after the Armistice was officially declared. London was en fete today, inconveniently for I had to walk the whole way from the General Post Office, near St Paul's, home. I couldn't get on to the P.O. Station, Blackfriars, the Embankment trains, the Temple, Charing Cross, any buses nor get a taxi anywhere – and the crowd in Whitehall was stu-pend-ous. Armistices, though delightful in many ways, have their little faults. However, they don't come every day."

Cordelia forwarded Ernest Aris's letter about the surrender of the German fleet (see diary for 24th November, 1918) to "Country Life" and the reproduced letter was pasted into the Scrapbook. One or two news items relating to the peace celebrations in July 1919 are also included.

Finally, there is an undated account about a "new Joan of Arc". This was the story of Claire Ferchaud, a young French shepherdess, who came to fame in France at the height of the First World War with her belief that, if the image of the Sacred Heart was added to the French flag, then France would enjoy a rapid victory.

> "'A new Joan of Arc has arisen in France. Born of the same kind of parents as the original one, poor people from this part of France. This girl dreamed dreams and saw visions, and finally was brought to the notice of the Authorities and brought to Paris. Amongst other things she saw in visions was an ancient flag, buried at a certain spot in France which if found and carried into battle by a very devout a pious Roman Catholic would ensure victory to the Allied armies, but the only thing was, that the flag must not be carried by a Frenchman. They went to the place and found

> the flag exactly where she had told them to look for it and it has been given to the Colonel of one of the Irish Guards battalions, which is holding the line closest to the place. He is a most devout RC and the next time we attack he will carry the flag into battle. I was told his actual name but have forgotten it. The man who told me is a captain in the Coldstream Guards and had taken the trouble to find out the name of the Colonel who has the flag at this moment."
>
> The above is from a letter written by an English officer in France to his mother. What follows was told, I believe, to Mrs Little by Mrs Ponsonby-Fanes:
>
> "Another story told was that she had obtained an interview with Foch and she told him she must see Clemenceau, but was told it was impossible. But she insisted "for five minutes" and they say he kept her an hour and a half! She is said to have demanded the re-instatement of a general whose name, I think, was Gourmont and that he is the man who has been so successful lately."

Like a number of other items to be found in the scrapbooks, it is unclear as to why Cordelia chose to include this particular story. Was it an example of the power of faith and of what a determined woman could achieve – or was it simply an interesting story to be taken with a 'pinch of salt'?

Chapter 8: Epilogue

As Cordelia herself noted in her diary, the Peace celebrations at the Abbey in August 1919 were marred, for her and her family, by the death of her brother Rupert on August 14th. The celebrated "Captain of Hussars", Rupert had cut a dashing figure in his day. Cordelia's eldest sister Margaret had also suffered loss during the war years, with the death in 1915 of her husband the Earl of Jersey, which resulted in her losing not only her husband but her main home, Osterley Park, and retiring to Middleton Park in Oxfordshire as Dowager Duchess. Margaret did, however, survive to a grand old age, dying in 1945 in her 93rd year. In fact, with the exception of her eldest brother Gilbert, who met his death in Wyoming at the age of just 34, and the youngest, Harry, who died as a child of fifteen months, all of Cordelia's siblings survived into their eighties or beyond. Francis Dudley, the 3rd Lord Leigh, who had perhaps assuaged the loss of his first wife by busying himself during the war, became known as "the dancing peer" in London society of the 1920s before marrying again when in his sixties. Neither of his wives produced an heir, however, and the title and the Leigh estate passed, on Francis Dudley's death in 1938, to his nephew – the "Robin" of Cordelia's diary.

Those siblings perhaps closest to Cordelia – Agnes and Rowland – lived apparently quiet lives until their deaths in, respectively, 1942 and 1943. All three are remembered with great affection. Writing in his journal of reminiscences shortly before his death in 1979, Harry Edmunds, a Stoneleigh villager all his life, recalled how he had endured a particularly dreadful thunderstorm in order to convey Cordelia's Girls' Friendly Society girls from the village to Warwick and back. Despite shaking from the effects of the electricity and soaked to the bone, he recalled that "nothing was too much trouble for Miss Cordelia" and on another occasion remembered with simple pleasure the way that his father's sheepdog, after a hard day's work would be rewarded with bones saved for the purpose by "Miss Agnes and Miss Cordelia". When the dog died in suspicious circumstances, it was the two sisters who paid for an autopsy, discovering that he had been poisoned.

Cordelia's obituary picture, Leamington Spa Courier, 2nd March 1956.

Although Agnes was buried in the churchyard at Stoneleigh, Rowland was laid to rest in the churchyard at Ashow, and after his death Cordelia wrote to the PCC there, requesting that when her turn came, she be buried next to him. Her wish was duly granted upon her death in 1956.

At the close of the First World War Cordelia was 52; what activity occupied her for the next 37 years, until her death in her 89th year? Perhaps not surprisingly her main occupation was education: school logbooks at Ashow and Stoneleigh reveal weekly visits to each, and hers are the final remarks in the Ashow school logbook, when the school closed in 1924. She continued her Sunday School classes in both villages well into her old age.

There remains little documentary evidence of her activities during these years, however, and perhaps surprisingly, nothing about the years of the Second World War. Nevertheless she was far from inactive, as present-day villagers in Stoneleigh remember her still travelling by means of her trusty tricycle well into her eighties, even if she did, by then, need an encouraging push at the crossroads to send her on her way back to her beloved Abbey. Her close friendship with Alice Skipwith endured, and after Alice's death Cordelia inherited the flat in St Mark's Road, Leamington, although she returned to live at the Abbey, a fact which obviously gave her great pleasure as she recorded in her "Reminiscences" of 1954: "And now I have come back in my old age to end my days in the house where I was born, through the kind thought of Robin and Anne, the present good and much-loved owners of Stoneleigh Abbey." A charming letter of June 1955 survives, in which she congratulates one of her "old boys", a former member of the Stoneleigh & Ashow Naturalists' Club, on his Golden Wedding; clearly she was as fond of her former charges as ever, and hoped that he and his wife might call upon her in her flat at the Abbey, though they would find her "very old and deaf but very glad to see you both." Evidently they did so, as she presented them with a copy of her book of poems "A Sunday near Keswick", signing it "with the author's best wishes, June 21st 1955."

The *Leamington Courier's* obituary of Cordelia on March 2nd 1956 began by noting that with her death a link to the Victorian past had been broken. It went on to record that her lively mind had led to her continuing to write letters to that paper until a few weeks before her death; she had been particularly exercised by the increasingly poor observance of Easter, and wrote every year to condemn the modern practice of calling the Saturday before Easter Day "Easter Saturday". The article reporting her funeral cited the sermon given by her friend the Vicar of Stoneleigh, Canon Geoffrey Parks, who declared that despite failing eyesight and hearing she was continuing her study of Greek in her final months. For 69 years she had been engaged in Sunday School teaching, and for many years had worked as honorary secretary to various Sunday School Councils both in Warwickshire and further afield. Some of her teaching had been for a time in Camberwell, teaching a class of boys – presumably this explains the close ties she had formed with those young Londoners who became her godsons. Of course, she continued to write, producing books on the Bible and on Nature Study. In 1916 she had been elected to the Council of the Leamington High School for Girls (later known as The Kingsley School), becoming its vice-chairman in 1926 and chairman in 1935. In July 1945 she "felt the time had come" to resign from the School Council, as she was "approaching the age of eighty". Her resignation was received with "great regret at losing her", and members wished to express their "appreciation of the great debt owed to her" for nearly 30 years' service to the school. The Head Mistress wrote "I find it very difficult to express in any way adequately my personal gratitude to Miss Leigh for her unfailing interest and encouragement."

Mary Cordelia Emily Leigh died on 27th February 1956, leaving few effects of any monetary value, and in her Will leaving the majority of her estate to her dear nephew "Robin", the 4th Baron Leigh. Whilst other family members received bequests, she also bequeathed £100 each to the Universities Mission to Central Africa, and the Additional Curates Society. Her funeral was held in the tiny church of the Assumption of Our Lady at Ashow, and was attended by representatives of organisations to which she had belonged, and by members of Stoneleigh and Ashow families whom she had helped over so many years.

Cordelia's gravestone in Ashow churchyard reflects the simplicity with which she lived her life. There is no mention of her deeds; instead a simple statement of her name, "3rd daughter of the 2nd Baron Leigh", together with her dates of birth and death, is all that remains to record the existence of one who declared herself, in her letters and her actions "Always Your Friend".

Appendix

The following accounts, poems etc. were originally included at the end of Cordelia Leigh's War Diary:

Agnes Leigh:

Scenes Outside Buckingham Palace, 28th June 1919

On the day (June 28th) when we understood that Peace would be signed Dudley & I went in the motor to Buckingham Palace and found a crowd collected, mostly on foot but there were several carriages and motors. The police had orders apparently not to let carriages stand still, but they were not rigid about it. One man who told us to move allowed us to go round the statue of Q. Victoria & come back to the same place. I asked him in insinuating terms to let us remain – he looked at the front of the car, remarked "The horses do get tired, don't they?" & left us alone.

We waited patiently for over 2 hours, & during that time invited into our car a Naval officer & his wife – because the officer, rather a stout person, looked rather the worse for standing. He told us several things to the praise of British courage.

As time passed & still there was no sign that Peace was signed, we began to fear that there had been a hitch. There was also some uncertainty as to whether the King was in the Palace. The police had at first tried to make us think that he was not, probably hoping to prevent too big a crowd.

The first hopeful sign was a very domestic one. A servant came on to the balcony with a broom and spent some time in sweeping it. At last about 6 o'clock there was a move, everyone crowded to the front of the Palace gates. We got out of the car and stood in a splendid position facing the balcony of the Palace. The window opened and the King, the Queen, the Prince of Wales & Princess Mary appeared on the balcony. There was a roar of welcome and I could catch almost every word the King said:

"PEACE is signed. ... I join with you in thanking GOD."

The last two words were said very emphatically. The crowd struck up patriotic songs – there was a strange mixture. Without trying to name them in order I remember "Tipperary", "Land of Hope & Glory"; "He's a jolly good fellow", "GOD save the King"; "GOD save the Prince of Wales", &c. &c., together with Hymns "O GOD our Help &c." The Queen waved her hand at the crowd & looked very happy. At intervals interspersed with the singing were wild bursts of cheering. At last the Royal party retired & we went home. Besides the Prince of Wales two other young princes were on the balcony – but I am not very sure which they were.

In the evening Emily Ward joined us and we sallied forth after dinner. We started in the Motor but it was rather difficult to get on in it owing to the crowds and we found walking simpler. After trying one or two streets in the neighbourhood of the Haymarket we made our way back to Buckingham Palace.

There was a renewal of the singing we had heard in the afternoon. As we got near the Palace there were signs of the Royal people having just shown themselves on the balcony. After that there was a long interval during which everything seemed dark behind the balcony, & the weary monarch for aught we know was having supper or a cigarette.

The crowd became impatient, and a young man near us said half laughing, "We want our King".

Presently the crowd grew vociferous –

'We want our King! King! K-I-N-G.'

'We want King George, George. G-E-O-R-G-E!'

At last the light was turned on again in the room behind the balcony – and the Royal party once more appeared on the balcony. Never did I hear such cheers! It did one's heart good to know that the King was so popular. And he deserves applause for all the hard work that he and the Queen have done during the war.

I cannot pretend to have actually seen them this time. The crowd had grown so dense that to escape the pressure I had moved close to one of the pillars of the gates, and small boys climbing up the gates further obstructed the view. But to hear the cheering was a joy to my soul and we went home quite satisfied.

The crowd so far as we saw it on our way to the Palace was very orderly. There was a certain amount of good humoured gaiety but very little roughness. One woman solemnly tickled us under the chin with a long brush, but we were none the worse!

I ought to have mentioned that the Boy Scouts marched in front of the Palace while the crowd awaited the declaration of Peace and later a number of them were in Grosvenor Square where I saw an excited officer shake hands vehemently with various younger officers, probably congratulating them on the success of their demonstration.

Dudley and I got good places at the Thanksgiving Service at St Paul's when the King and Queen went to return thanks in state. Besides the Service in the Cathedral a short Service was held in which the vast crowds outside were able to take part. Before the Royal procession marched down the cathedral to take their places prayers were said and a Hymn was sung outside at the entrance."

Agnes Leigh:

The Peace Celebrations in London, 19th July 1919

"On the occasion of the great Celebration of Peace [19th July, 1919] we saw the march past from the Stand erected for Members of Parliament in Pall Mall. We were within view of Buckingham Palace, about 400 yards from it.

We could see Margaret Jersey & Mabel not far from us.

Emily Ward saw the same things from another vantage point, viz: near Albert Gate, and wrote a full account for an Irish Magazine.

I propose to copy her story with an occasional remark of my own, in addition and leaving out anything that only applies to what concerned her part of the route.

'It was a stroke of genius making the representatives of the Allied Forces march in Alphabetical order. There could be no reason for international resentment when

America led the procession. (America beginning with an A.)'

(Note by A.L.) We can appreciate this for at one time we were entertaining at Stoneleigh Overseas Officers and one night had at dinner officers who represented Canada, South Africa and Australia (or New Zealand I forget which). We discussed the question of precedence in the event of a march through London of Overseas troops and one at any rate of our guests became so vehement as to the claim of the part of the Dominions he came from (I do not clearly recollect which it was) that we could see what a burning question it might become in any procession.

To resume Miss Ward's account.

'There was a certain humour in the way the Alphabet ordered the precedence, like a kindly nurse whose word was law, and to whom it did not matter in the least which went first, so long as each was satisfied with the arrangement.

Belgium followed, and then China, and then Czecho-slovakia (who I thought got an unnecessary amount of cheering). The fifth in order of precedence was FRANCE with FOCH!, Greece coming sixth, Italy seventh, and Japan eighth, and so on through the Allies ending up with Siam.'

(N.B. I was particularly interested in seeing the martial figure of Foch, who was making great play as he went by with his Marshall's baton.) A.L.

'As each contingent passed through the gate, (Note Miss Ward was near Albert Gate) a stiff little pennon was carried, with the name of the corps clearly printed which throughout the procession added greatly to the interest, seeing that nearly all the soldiers were in khaki.

As Siam passed, with a band playing, the Navy prepared to start.

The huge Union Jack, which headed the procession, heralded Sir David Beatty, looking splendid, his cap slightly on one side, and walking with all the pride of the Navy in his step.

Cheers were ringing, and I heard gasps & 'Our Navy!' –

'Some Navy' – as the Admirals, their staffs, seamen, stokers, daymen, & marines went by, of the Battle cruisers, "the Queen Elizabeth", the 1st, 2nd & 3rd Battle Squadrons, representatives of each & all of the smaller crafts – destroyers, submarines, mine-sweepers, sea-scouts & all the rest.

It was a magnificent show, & there was great cheering, & not least when the 'ladies' of the Royal Navy went past – the Wrens & the Navy Nurses – very smart, very earnest & worthy of all the applause they received.

Bands of the different squadrons played gaily as they passed, and I think the Navy holds the deepest part in Britain's heart.

Now the representatives of the British Army moved forward.

Sir Douglas Haig looked the part, the very picture of a leader.[1]

(N.B. Sir Douglas Haig was ill at the time, but rose from a sick bed in order not to disappoint the spectators.)

Then after another his famous Generals passed by – Rawlinson, Birdwood, Byng, Horne, Cavan and all the others.[2]

Then came the Generals commanding the Canadians, Australians, New Zealand Corps, South Africans, Newfoundland Contingent – each with Staff Officer and standards of their particular corps.

When they passed to the music of the bands, & of the hearty cheering, a roar of applause arose as the "Contemptible" survivors of Mons, & of the Marne & of the Aisne went by – the remnant of the Expeditionary Force of 1914! The band of the 1st Life Guards, and of the Blues played them on their March. And after these had passed – the "Contemptible Little Army" – the most touching thing to my mind in the whole procession went by – the massed standards and colours.[3]

The glorious bit of colour amidst so much khaki arrested one. There was no wind, and the heavy folds of the colours drooped. Each was adorned with a laurel wreath surrounding the name of some famous battle. It seemed to represent the two sides of victory – the hour of glory and the price that was paid for it.

Now came the Horse Artillery, and the Cavalry, then the Field and Garrison Artillery and then the Engineers.

Bands were playing between each section.

And now came the band of the Royal Irish Rifles, playing in the whole of the British Infantry who were about to march past in small contingents of all the regiments. I think it must have been for their valour on the Somme and for their loyalty through good report and evil report that Ulster was thus honoured by the band of County Down heralding the advance of the representatives of the British Infantry.'

(N.B. The writer of the above hails from Co. Down and the account was written for a County Down Parish!)

Once more the little stiff pennons were of the greatest use, telling us the name of each regiment. The cheering for the Infantry was less even and continuous. The crowd were so much interested in spotting their own particular regiment, that the cheers sounded jerky, more like sudden shouts, as the looked for pennon came within reading distance.

(N.B. Duddy gave a special shout for the Warwicks.)

It was interest, not indifference that changed the quality of the applause. After the Infantry had all filed through the gate, all sorts of interesting varieties seemed to pass. Tanks, and lorries with searchlight apparatus, and anti-aircraft guns. But the thing that diverted me more than almost anything in the whole procession was the "Pigeon Loft" mounted on a lorry. It was like a little white house, and out of the windows gazed many mild white pigeons, entirely unconcerned at being part of the Victory Pageant – entirely unabashed at the crowds – and playing their part as doves of peace. When an hour and a half later they passed down the Mall they were pecking at their seeds! After these miscellaneous units went by, then came the 'Waacs', ending up with representatives of the entire Air Force, the 'Wrafs' being the last of all.'[4]

This closes Miss Ward's account.

(N.B. In one of the Women's Corps, I think the 'W.A.A.C.'s, was included a little girl with hair down her back. One wondered what part she played.)

The whole procession took about 2 hours to go by any given point.

Dudley & I had left Grosvenor Square, at an hour which enabled us to reach our places without having too long to wait before the procession passed and we had no difficulty in getting to our stand. But two ladies who sat near us had been there since a very early hour and were quite exhausted before the Show began – though they kept themselves refreshed with chocolate.

The sky had been overcast since early morning but no rain fell until the last of the procession had gone by our stand and the crowd were beginning to move. But, as we were hurrying homewards, it began to rain in good earnest and the greater part of the afternoon was wet. But this did not seem to affect the good humour of the crowd, though one felt sorry for the holiday-makers, more especially those who had come in from the country or more distant parts of the town in their best clothes.

During the days of Peace celebrations I was often amused by the sight of a little cart, drawn by some rather unkempt beast, with a particular little family out to divert itself – with probably a whip tied up with ribbons and a solemn child carrying a small Union Jack. I remember one such cart ornamented with a sort of banner.

In the afternoon Dudley went out to see the diversions in Hyde Park but as it was wet I did not do much more till the evening when we proposed to see the Fireworks. Meanwhile D. met Major Hussey who gave him tickets for a special Stand from which the Fireworks could be seen.

Emily Ward dined with me and we then went to Major Hussey's house that we may go with his party to the show where the stand was. Major & Mrs Hussey, two young girls & ourselves followed by a small procession of servants made our way through the crowd to where our places ought to have been. But! The crowd had rushed the stand and there remained. Nothing for it but to stand where we were and see what we could without being in a place of honour!

The Fireworks were the finest I ever saw – quite magnificent. Major Hussey, it turned out had had the arranging for them – and I think was pleased with their success. But there was to have been some special set piece – a Victory one – which did not come off owing to being spoilt by the damp. Happily it was not raining during the letting off of the Fireworks – but I suppose the rain in the afternoon had injured this piece during the preparations.

But otherwise we very much enjoyed the glorious showers of gold and silver, pink and mauve! – and the gasps from the crowd when anything unusually brilliant illumined the sky were worth hearing."

[1] Sir Douglas Haig ... the very picture of a leader: *Field Marshal Haig had been Commander-in-Chief of the British Armies in France and Flanders for most of the war.*

[2] Rawlinson, Birdwood etc: these were the Generals of the British Armies at the end of the war: *Sir Henry Rawlinson (4th Army), Sir William Birdwood (5th), Sir Julian Byng (3rd), Sir Henry Horne (1st); the Earl of Cavan had commanded the British Force in Italy. (Sir Herbert Plumer had commanded the 2nd Army.)*

[3] the "Contemptible Little Army" etc: *the survivors of the original British Expeditionary Force that had gone out to France in 1914, reputedly dismissed by the Kaiser as a "contemptible little army".*

[4] Waacs and Wrafs: *the Women's Auxiliary Army Corps, created in January 1917, and the Women's Royal Air Force, created in April 1918.*

Miss Ward:

Temporary War Memorials in London

"One afternoon, in London, I went to see two memorials to our Heroes. One was within Hyde Park at the Marble Arch – a temporary one – paltry as far as design went – hastily put together – poorly painted – and yet inexpressibly touching. The form was that of an enclosure in the shape of a cross – wooden palings – perhaps 3 feet high and an obelisk in the centre. The materials were perishable – and if one was cold-blooded enough to consider it – the proportions and decorations were common and out of taste.

But it met a deep and passionate want – as one knew, from the number of wreaths – one upon another within the cruciform enclosure. The pitiful inscriptions, and touching verse – all intensely personal – photographs, wreaths, crosses, fresh cut flowers, pots of growing plants – all laid in loving memory and sorrow on the Cross.

The other memorial was The Cenotaph at Whitehall – the National – the Imperial Memorial.[1]

Dignified – austere – impersonal, its simplicity of line – deeply suggestive of restrained feeling. A large wreath of laurel back and front – flags on either side but otherwise no ornament or symbolism – the words –

TO OUR GLORIOUS DEAD

in keeping with the severity of the Monument. London has approved of the Cenotaph – which dumbly expresses the inexpressible – and it is likely to remain permanently in Whitehall."

[1] The Cenotaph at Whitehall etc: *the temporary Cenotaph erected for the Peace Procession on 19th July, 1919. Designed by Sir Edward Lutyens, and made of wood and plaster, it was a symbolic tribute to the dead of the Great War. Such was the public response to the temporary Cenotaph that the decision was soon taken to replace it, on the same site, with a permanent monument, also designed by Lutyens. This was unveiled on 11th November, 1920.*

Agnes Leigh:

"The Water Pageant" 18th July, 1919

D. and I went to London for a night for the purpose of seeing the King go down the Thames in his barge, and we took with us Robin who had not so far seen much of any of the Peace Celebrations. I gave Robin luncheon at my Club and then we went into Bond Street that we might find some of the Picture Galleries open, but being a holiday all were shut. We returned to 31 Grosvenor Square, and then Duddy calling for us we made our way to the House of Lords.

We passed the Cenotaph that has been put up in memory of those who died in the War, before which many people were assembled.

After showing Robin something of the House of Lords we made our way to the Terrace which was already so full that we got seats with some little difficulty.

The scene was lively. Large flags were hung out of the windows above the Terrace and steamers were moored against the bank across the river, and the sound of music from a band on one of them floated across to us. Talking to our friends helped to while away the time, and there were plenty of small excitements to be watched on the river.

One of these was the frantic rush of two or three coastal motor boats, which went so fast that their keel was lifted out of the water. They tore up and down at a desperate pace, but whether with the kind intention of amusing the spectators or because they really had a purpose in view I do not know.

At length there was a murmur "They are coming" and all eyes turned towards the bridge underneath which the King was bound to come. A few larger craft came first and then the King and Queen were seen being rowed along in their barge, the Queen seated under an awning and the rowers clad in red. The Lord Mayor was in another and larger barge.

I cannot recollect, and the papers have given better than I can, a list of all the boats and ships we saw.

The general impression was that the procession was very interesting but would perhaps have been better had the ships followed on each other more closely and had there not been a long interval between each. The answer to this is I believe that space must be allowed to prevent collision.

The King and Queen were well cheered, except (I regret to say it) by the Terrace of the House of Lords which received them politely with the removal of hats but with a dignified want of "noise", which very much annoyed Robin. I am sure it was not from lack of loyalty but too much fear of letting themselves go!

Robin was kept busy almost from the moment of our arrival at the Terrace. He had found out a seller of programmes who could be approached through the railings dividing our Terrace from that of the House of Commons, and had bought Programmes for himself and me. Then some of our acquaintance began to find this out, and kept on asking him to get one for them. So he became quite a conspicuous figure on the Terrace before the afternoon was over.

When all the procession, merchant ships, training ships, police boats, about showing old and new patterns of guns &c. &c. had passed, and people began to leave – only Robin (and one or two besides) begged to remain and see the procession come back.

At first we were told they would not come back, but to satisfy Robin we did stay and that turned out to be perhaps the most amusing part of the show for some of the boats came back racing. Of course the Royal barge did not return but the Lord Mayor's barge passed us again and there was again the wild rush of the little coasting motors.

The weather was not bright but there was no rain. And we all enjoyed the Great Water Pageant."

Water Pageant 18th July, 1919.

Lord Leigh:

The Peace Celebrations at Paris and Destruction in Northern France

"I saw the Peace Celebrations at Paris and a very fine sight it was, with the great advantage Paris has over most places in the beautiful Champs Elysées, down which the procession of troops proceeded, after passing through the Arc de Triomphe. There was very great enthusiasm. The houses were crowded with spectators, many viewing the procession from the roofs. The English and American troops who took part in the march went remarkably well. The city was decorated with flags, and at night there were some fine fireworks to see. At the Arc de Triomphe there was a catafalque, consisting of an obelisk wider at the top than below. It was gilded and round it were figures of women. I went up to see it close at hand at night – the crowd was tremendous and the difficulty of reaching the obelisk great. Mounted soldiers were stationed there, and gendarmes were endeavouring to move the crowd away so that it might be photographed. I left them still struggling.

I motored from Paris to see the destruction wrought by the Germans at Château Thierry, at Rheims, and at Verdun.

At Château Thierry the destruction was very considerable, and at a village I passed through, not a very long time before arriving there, the devastation was complete. A bridge over the river at Château Thierry was practically destroyed, I think by the inhabitants themselves, to check the progress of the enemy.

At Rheims the façade of the Cathedral was, I was glad to find, not so much destroyed as one might have expected; some of the statues outside seemed to be not injured at all; the interior, however, showed a sad state of devastation. The painted glass windows had been removed, and will now be replaced. Much destruction had been done in the town by the terrible bombardment to which it had been subjected. But they are wonderful people, the French. Looking about for somewhere to have luncheon, though hardly expecting to get any, I entered a restaurant and found a nice man and his wife, who provided in a short time a really excellent meal, in a room that had been terribly battered about; they had been there, I gathered, all through the war, and the poor proprietor was in a state of anxiety as to how he was going to get along.

Mile after mile I now traversed where the whole country may be said to be completely desolate or under barbed wire, and mile after mile you travel without seeing a human being, but really such was the case as regards the population, even before the war. As to the wire the French are so industrious that perhaps, in the course of time, they can and will remove it, but what is perhaps more serious is that the whole country is seamed with unexploded shells. They are said to be everywhere – they are hidden from sight, and as the land is cultivated the plough by striking the shells causes them to explode. So frequently has this occurred that the peasants are becoming scared, and it is greatly to be feared that much of the land will remain permanently uncultivated. There is said to be an instrument by which the proximity of a shell can be detected, but even when a shell is detected it is a dangerous and difficult task for anyone to render it harmless, much more so for the unskilled peasant cultivator. The problem is acute and it is serious.

Verdun is a large and picturesque fort, with immense and beautifully constructed galleries, which could shelter a large army. They were of the greatest use as shelter for the troops against the shells of the Germans, as warehouses for their stores, as hospitals and so on. The galleries were constructed in the time of Louis XIV. I walked through some of the vast galleries, lighted as they were by electricity, and saw the comfortable quarters that they made for the troops, but what I saw was I believe but a fraction of the whole.

The Germans never entered Verdun, although they succeeded in penetrating extremely near to the fort.

It is much to be hoped and it seems more than probable that the French will be greatly helped by the money brought into the Country by the numbers who will wish to visit the battlefields and devastated regions, as soon as the means are provided for easily doing so."

Dorothy Hutton:

"Suspected Characters!"

"On Sunday, December 19th, Peggy and I arrived in London; very tired after a long journey from Aberdeen.

Peggy stayed in bed all day, but thought it would be refreshing to take a bath in the evening. I went into the Bathroom about 7 o'clock to prepare her bath; as the water was very hot, the room was soon full of steam, so I pulled up the blind and opened the window to let the steam out; about 3 minutes later I shut the window and pulled down the blind. As I came out of the bathroom the parlourmaid came running upstairs to ask if the blinds were pulled down in our rooms. Mr Leigh came upstairs, and said the Inspector had been to say, a bright light could be seen at the top of the house, and he would most probably be fined, as they were very strict about the lights after the last Air Raid. As Mr Leigh was going to Stoneleigh for a few days, he went to see a solicitor about it: in case he should be summoned.

Two days later the solicitor telephoned to ask if I would go and see him, as he would like to ask a few questions.

So Peggy and I went round to his Office and were shown into a dull little room. He asked me several questions (keeping his eyes on the toes of his boots).

"Were my Parents British?

Wasn't it rather unusual to have a bath at 7 o'clock in the evening?" etc., etc.

I explained we had been in Scotland for 3 months and I hadn't realised how strict the rules were about lights.

He said he hoped the police would overlook it, as it was the first offence, and the light was only showing for about 3 minutes.

I am very glad to say we have heard nothing more about it, but I shall be very careful in future about "lights" showing.

Dorothy Hutton"

Extract from a letter from Lt. F. Drake, Warwickshire Yeomanry:[1]

Palestine 14.11.17

Until today we have had hardly a minute's rest for three weeks, night nor day. I am well but tired and very dirty, no wash and the same clothes on night and day for a fortnight. The discomforts have been awful, but I have stuck it well, though we lost men and horses in numbers. The shortage of water all through the advance has been terrible and really without exaggeration we would have given 5/- a glass for cold water. You can't imagine what it is being parched with dust and heat and then having only a very small quantity of dirty water to drink and none to wash in, the same dirt on one for days and weeks. However I am very well so must not complain.

We were in action at the capture of Beersheba and bivouacked just outside the town that night. We were badly bombed on the way there by an aeroplane. One bomb dropped 10 yards from the Colonel and one killed his horse but missed us both. Then we were in action again further north, shelled and bombed well and did an attack in the evening, with plenty of shells and bullets coming our way.

A few days later, Nov. 8th, was the red letter day of the Regiment, and in fact one of the greatest feats that any Cavalry Regiment has ever performed.[2] The day began by a rapid advance against a retreating enemy in open country and we chased all the morning. About 1.30pm we came upon their strong position and a regular nest of guns and machine-guns. Suddenly our Colonel gave the order to charge the position with drawn swords. So our two squadrons and two squadrons of the Worcesters dashed into an absolute inferno of shells, machine-guns and rifle fire and it was marvellous how any of us came out alive. It lasted about 20 minutes and the result of it was that our two squadrons captured four small Camel guns, 4 field guns, 3 six-inch guns and the Worcesters 3 machine-guns.

Valentine was very badly wounded, Toby Albright killed, Alan Williams slightly wounded as also Gilman. It was a thrilling half hour but we don't want another like it. We captured about 60 prisoners and could have got lots more but we were such a small force just there. We live on nothing but tinned beef and biscuit and tea full of dust and dirt but I am still fit and well on it and have had some wonderful escapes. Our Colonel got a bar to his D.S.O. for this charge. I rode by his side all through it but Valentine's lot were in the hottest place of all. The guns fired at us from 20 yards' range, and the gunners were sabred at their posts. It was a day in history both for the Regiment and the army. You really should see us now – dirty, unshaven, torn clothes, and getting thin with shortage of food and water. At times during the advance our horses have been without water for 80 hours at a stretch and consequently have suffered very much. The arrangements as regards food and forage have been admirable throughout. Our casualties in the charge were heavy but considering what we captured in the way of guns and ammunition we must have been the cause of saving a large number of lives which otherwise these guns would have accounted for.

Nov. 16th, 1917

We are now miles up North – 2 miles from the sea and close to beautiful fresh water, so we have had a real good wash and many long drinks to wash down the bully beef and biscuits. Let me know what the English papers have to say about the charge of the Light Brigade.[3]

Valentine[4] seems to be going on all right but he was terribly wounded in that charge. He deserves the VC, his gallantry was quite wonderful.*

*Since that date he died of his wounds.

[1] Lt F. Drake, Warwickshire Yeomanry: *Captain Frederic Augustus Drake married Isabel Julia Adderley, a grand-daughter of Chandos, Lord Leigh. Cordelia was also a grand-daughter of Chandos and thus she and Isabel were second cousins. Captain Drake was to die by drowning six months later, on 27th May 1918, when the transport ship on which he was travelling, the Leasowe Castle, was struck by a torpedo fired from a German submarine, near Alexandria.*

[2] one of the greatest feats that any Cavalry Regiment has ever performed: *the cavalry charge at Huj – often referred to as 'The Affair of Huj' – took place on 8th November, 1917, during the British pursuit of Turkish armies retreating through Palestine after the 3rd Battle of Gaza, which had ended the previous day. The advance of the British 60th Division was held up by a well-placed Turkish rearguard on a ridgeline south of the village of Huj, in which Turkish troops were supported by Austrian artillery and machine-guns. A small force of 170 officers and men from the Worcestershire Yeomanry and Warwickshire Yeomanry were called upon to take the position. Their cavalry charge succeeded but at considerable cost, with 40% casualties, including all three Squadron Commanders killed – as well as 100 horses killed. Eleven artillery guns were captured. The action is regarded as the last classic, unsupported, cavalry charge made by the British Army.*

[3] the charge of the Light Brigade: *both at the time and subsequently, comparisons were made with the more famous Charge of the Light Brigade in the Crimean War. The Affair of Huj was, of course, only a small episode in a major war but it was one which, in the words of the Official Historian: "for sheer bravery ... remains unmatched".*

[4] Valentine: *Captain Rudolf Valentine M.C. is commemorated on the Snitterfield War Memorial.*

REFLECTIONS:

1.

When the LORD turned again
the captivity of Zion,
Then were we like unto them
that dream!
Then was our mouth filled
with laughter,
And our tongue with joy.
Then said they among the nations,
"The LORD hath done great
things for them."
Yea, the LORD hath done great things for us,
Whereof we are glad.

Psalm 126, King James Bible

2.

Mr VALIANT-FOR-TRUTH summoned:

"After this it was noised abroad that Mr Valiant-for-Truth was taken with a summons by the same Post as the other, and had this for a token that the summons was true, "That the pitcher was broken at the fountain." When he understood it, he called for his friends, and told them of it. Then said he, "I am going to my Father's, and though with great difficulty I have got hither, yet now I do not repent me of all the trouble I have been at to arrive where I am. My sword I give to him that shall succeed me in my pilgrimage and my courage and skill to him that can get it. My marks and scars I carry with me, to be a witness for me that I have fought His battles, who now will be my rewarder." When the day that he must go hence was come, many accompanied him to the Riverside; into which, as he went, he said:- "Death, where is thy sting?" And as he went down deeper, he said:-"Grave, where is thy victory?" So he passed over, and all the Trumpets sounded for him on the other side."

John Bunyan *The Pilgrim's Progress*

3.

THE DAY OF GOD

Cordelia wrote the following preface to her own poem, which was re-printed many years later in her collection *A Sunday near Keswick:*

"Years ago I took my Bible Class of boys for a ramble in the woods once a year in early Spring. One member of my Bible Class wrote to me from France that he could hear the birds singing when he was in the trenches, and in another letter spoke of the wild roses."

In the old happy day
We all rambled together,
In the freedom of May,
In the laughing Spring weather,
We strolled by the rushes,
The blue-bells a-ringing,
And the blackbirds and thrushes
Were singing and singing.
Did we think of the word
That the guileless in heart shall see God?

In this dread Day of God
Are you called to speed higher?
O'er the blood-sprinkled sod,
Through the storms and the fire.
Yet you tell of the beauty
Of wild roses upspringing,
And through your trench duty
You hear the birds singing.
Now I think of that word
That the faithful to death shall be crowned.

In the Day of His power,
When the heaven's new birth
Brings the Conqueror's hour,
And peace upon earth;
When the angels in brightness
Palm branches are bringing,
And the saints in their whiteness
Are singing and singing,
May we live in that day!
Yet not we, for He liveth in us.

1790 L H Shorley
26 Div Cyclist Coy.
3 Platoon
Sutton Veny

Dear Madam

Many thank for kindly sending The Rural World. It is very interesting to read what the Village people are doing & what they can do. I have Notice that the people down hear in Wilts are forward in hay making Some have got it cut and into the Barns. And the other night I was on Guard and could not help But Notice the Birds Singing, Such as the Black birds Sparrows Starlings & the Cuckoo. This was at Two. O clock in the Morning As I am a Scout we are learning about the Stars to lead us

right when we get out in France
which is very interesting But
we all are sorry. ata our Officer
is leaving us. He was in the
Navy, so he as to leave the Army
and go back in the Navy.
I am hoping to be at Stoneleigh
this week end or the next. But
I think it will be next week
The Weather is so very nice at
Nights that three parts of our
Boys are sleeping out. I think
we wake up more fit for our
work in the Morning than Sleeping
in doors. I am not sure But I
think we are moving very
Shortly, But cannot say where.

I remain
Yours Truly
G H Thorley

A letter from George Thorley.

Servicemen's letters found in the Scrapbooks were written by the following men:

- James Amos, Private 2344, Army Cyclist Corps, later 22889, 9th Bn West Riding Regiment
- Ernest Aris, 6660, HMS *Queen Elizabeth*; HMS *Impregnable*
- Victor Bonnard, Private 23820, 18th Bn Canadian Expeditionary Force
- Arthur Cadwallader, Private 19666, 3rd Worcestershire Regiment, later 124795 Machine Gun Company, 5th Bn Worcestershire Regiment
- F. G. Clifford, Private 29752, 14th Worcestershire Regiment (Severn Valley Pioneers)
- Herbert Cooke, Reverend, 1st Bn King's Own (Royal Lancaster Regiment)
- William Darlow, Private 24990, 8th Bn Dorsetshire Regiment
- Ernest Darlow, Private 289042, Special Brigade, Royal Engineers
- Fred Davis, Rifleman S/33158, 6th (Reserve) Bn Rifle Brigade
- George Henry Fardon, Private 498, Royal Marine Artillery Howitzer Brigade
- Tom Hewitt, Private 9304, 5th Bn King's Own Shropshire Light Infantry
- Harry (Henry) Jarvis, Corporal 9858, 2nd Bn Royal Warwickshire Regiment
- Harry King, Private 13571, 2nd Bn Oxfordshire and Buckinghamshire Light Infantry
- G.F. Lee, Private 3087, $2/4^{th}$ Bn Norfolk Regiment
- Henry Alan Leeke, Lieutenant, 9th Bn Royal Warwickshire Regiment
- Charles McReay, Private 11611, 2nd Bn Royal Berkshire Regiment
- Henry Hands Metters, M.C., Lieutenant, 8th Bn Leicestershire Regiment
- Harry Miles, HMS *Ajax*
- H. Mills, Private 263137, $2/8^{th}$ Worcestershire Regiment
- Joseph Mills, Private, Anti-Aircraft Brigade, Royal Marine Artillery
- Joseph Mills, Lance Corporal 2000, 4th Bn Royal Warwickshire Regiment
- Thomas Bant Mills, Private 16454/331199, 1st Bn Hampshire Regiment, later 2945 $1/8^{th}$ Bn Hampshire Regiment
- Tom Mills, Private 13570, 3rd Bn Oxfordshire and Buckinghamshire Light Infantry
- William James Mills, Sapper 203970, Royal Engineers
- Alfred John Morgan, Driver 118952, 7th Divisional Ammunition Column
- Arthur Albert George Morris, Private 13575, 9th Bn Oxfordshire and Buckinghamshire Light Infantry

- Walter E. Oldham, Private 211, Army Cyclist Corps
- George Paget, Private 03593, Army Ordnance Corps
- William Palmer, Lance Corporal 17671, Royal Warwickshire Regiment, attached Royal Field Artillery
- Sydney Rench, Private, 16th Bn Canadian Scottish Regiment
- George Rose, Private 8508, 10th Bn King's Royal Rifle Corps
- Fred Smith, Lance Corporal 13571, 7th Bn Oxfordshire and Buckinghamshire Light Infantry
- W. Smith, Private 4812, 7th Bn Royal Warwickshire Regiment
- Robert Stainton, Private, Royal Army Medical Corps, H.M. Hospital Ship *China*
- Thomas Steele, Corporal 3615, 9th Bn Royal Warwickshire Regiment, later 3rd Bn Royal Warwickshire Regiment
- Fred Stoney
- William Stoney, Private 66971, 140th Field Ambulance, Royal Army Medical Corps
- George Thorley, Private 13569, 7th Bn Oxfordshire and Buckinghamshire Light Infantry, 26th Divisional Cyclist Company, Army Cyclist Corps
- John W. Thorley, C Squadron Warwickshire Yeomanry
- Samuel Tuckwell, Private 65254, Machine Gun Company
- W. Tuckwell, Private, 3/20th Bn London Regiment
- John Walton, Sapper 60460, 96 Field Company, Royal Engineers
- F. Woodfield, Private 25163, Royal Berkshire Regiment
- Sam Wooding, Private 6026, Machine Gun Company
- Albert Worrall, Private 9211, 11th Bn Royal Warwickshire Regiment
- William Worrall, Private 19584, 1st Bn Royal Warwickshire Regiment

N.B. not all relevant service details are known.

Cordelia Leigh's published works:

Simple Lessons from Nature, James Nisbet, London 1889

Our Dayspring, a Short Course of Lessons for Bible Classes, SPCK, London 1893

Day Unto Day Uttereth Speech – A Year Book of the Bible and Nature, compiled by M. C. Leigh. Eyre and Spottiswoode, London c 1900

The Witness of Creation, Jarrold and Sons 1900

Nature's Story Book, Hutchinson London 1900

Nature's Playground, in Four Books, Collins, London and Glasgow 1900

Our School Out of Doors, A Nature Book for Young People, T. Fisher Unwin, London 1906

Prayers for Young People, 1913

Christmas in the Woods and Other Poems, Country Life, London 1919

A Syllabus for Church Junior and Senior Day Schools, 1932

The Pageant of Nature, Collins 1936

Stories from the Book of Books, Arthur H. Stockwell Ltd, Ilfracombe 1949

The Good Shepherd, 1950

Tommy's Catechism, 1952

A Sunday near Keswick and Other Poems, Arthur H. Stockwell Ltd, Ilfracombe 1952

A Day Book of the Church's Year

[Dates as found; some publishers unknown]

ROWLAND
LEIGH
Cordelia Leigh
The Name Tree

INDEX

Index of People

General Index